HANDBOOK
FOR
ACADEMIC
LITERACY

HANDBOOK FOR ACADEMIC LITERACY

Jill Lewis

Jersey City State College

D. C. HEATH AND COMPANY   Lexington, Massachusetts   Toronto

Address editorial correspondence to:

D. C. Heath and Company
125 Spring Street
Lexington, MA 02173

Acquisitions: *Paul A. Smith*
Development: *Linda M. Bieze*
Editorial Production: *Celena Sun*
Design: *Margaret Ong Tsao*
Photo Research: *Kathy Carcia*
Cover Photo Research: *Constance S. Gardner*
Art Editing: *Gary Crespo*
Production Coordination: *Richard Tonachel*
Permissions: *Margaret Roll*

Cover photo: *Steve Dunwell/The Image Bank*

International Standard Book Number: 0-669-33198-8

10 9 8 7 6 5 4 3 2 1

for Miles and Allison

To the Instructor

Handbook for Academic Literacy has evolved as the result of my twenty-plus years of experience teaching students enrolled in developmental reading courses at two- and four-year colleges and assisting high school teachers who are concerned about their students' academic readiness at the start of their college careers. During the past twenty years, our knowledge about the reading process and how students learn has grown considerably; the population we teach has changed; and the academic goals for and expectations of students have been reshaped to include a greater concern for critical thinking and personal response. Many of the readings, strategies, and activities in this text are based on these considerations. Those instructional strategies that have continued to serve students well over the years are also included. Many features of this text make it unique and give students ample opportunity to develop the reading and study strategies they need for academic success.

You will find that this text

■ **uses a process-oriented approach to instruction.** It takes students through the *thinking processes* used to achieve such reading/study goals as recognizing and creating main ideas, making inferences, determining meanings of words from context clues, drawing conclusions, notetaking, and reading visual aids. Students have opportunities to apply these strategies to other coursework and in other contexts throughout the text.

■ **develops metacognitive habits.** In each chapter students reflect on the approaches they use for comprehension and self-monitoring. This ongoing practice encourages students to develop the habit of thinking about *how* they are reading *while* they are reading. They develop reading flexibility, adapting their reading style to accommodate the demands of the readings tasks and their purposes. Self-assessment is continuous. Special *Thinking About Your Reading and Writing* activities identified by ▶ help students develop metacognitive habits.

■ **promotes critical and creative thinking.** In addition to an entire chapter devoted to aspects of critical thinking, throughout the book students are asked to justify selected answers or written responses, to evaluate and modify their responses after discussion and review, and to critique the responses of others.

■ **integrates reading and writing.** The processes of reading and writing are mutually supportive. This is demonstrated repeatedly in models throughout this text, and the activities included often engage students in both processes. Students learn to use writing as a complement to their reading and to clarify meaning for themselves.

■ **provides for partner and collaborative activities.** Within each chapter there are several stopping points at which students compare their responses to questions with those of a peer or a group. This offers additional opportunities to think about their reading processes and to understand their personal responses to what they have read, as well as to understand different perspectives. Such *Working Together* activities are identified by ↴.

■ **supports a variety of learning styles.** Questions and activities throughout this book are varied. Many visual models accompany explanations of concepts. The many built-in opportunities to discuss the concepts with peers provide another avenue for learning. As students use the language of the text, they gain confidence in the use of new discourse patterns, concepts, sentence structures, and vocabulary that are common in academic settings.

■ **includes challenging content.** The models and practice exercises are drawn primarily from sources that are commonly assigned to college students. High expectations encourage students and give them a reality-based context in which to practice reading strategies.

■ **gives students responsibility for their own learning.** This text puts students in control of their reading. Rather than reading author-determined chapter summaries, students create their own, based on ideas that will be useful to them. This process encourages students to take ownership of the ideas and to think about their wider application.

■ **provides alternative assessment opportunities for the instructor.** The *Extended Application* section at the end of each chapter invites students to apply developing strategies to whole texts. These, as well as other student responses throughout the text, will give instructors a fuller view of student progress than do traditional multiple-choice and standardized tests.

■ **lends itself to a variety of curriculum formats and teaching styles.** You might use this text in a number of ways: as the sole text for your course, as a supplement to a reader or textbook from an academic discipline, or as a supplement to materials students select to read. You may prefer to use this text in a straightforward way, progressing from one chapter to another, or you might wish to assign different chapters to different students based on their learning styles and self-assessments. Classroom activity may be largely independent, or you may want to convert independent assignments into group and peer ones in order to increase the number of those already available.

However you choose to use this text, I hope it will meet your needs and serve your students well.

Acknowledgments

I wish to thank the many reviewers whose advice at different stages of the development of this text assisted me: Ada Belton, Keystone Junior College; Ida W. Holmes, Florida A & M University; Karen Houck, Bellevue Community College; Cathy Leist, University of Louisville; Kathryn Esther Moore, St. Louis Community College at Meramec; Kay Lynn Moran, Houston Community College Systems-Northeast; Diane Scott, San Diego Mesa College; Meritt Stark, Henderson State University; and Sebastian J. Vasta, Camden County Community College.

Many individuals contributed to the efforts and encouragement necessary for completion of this book. In particular, at D. C. Heath my thanks go to Paul Smith, Senior Acquisitions Editor, who played a key role in helping to define the final shape of the text, and to Linda Bieze, Senior Developmental Editor, whose guidance through development was greatly valued. I am also indebted to Shira Goldberg, former Editorial Associate, to Leah Strauss, Editorial Assistant, to Margaret Roll, Permissions Editor, and to Celena Sun, Associate Production Editor, for their ongoing support, assistance, and attention to detail. At Jersey City State College, I owe much appreciation to the Separately Budgeted Research Committee and to Vice President Larry Carter and President Carlos Hernandez for periodically granting me release time. A special thank-you goes to Irene Wells, secretary of the Department of Literacy Education at Jersey City State College, for handling things so capably at the office while I was at home working on this project and for keeping in touch with me through e-mail. I would also like to express my continuing gratitude to my e-mail companions and my love to my friends Freda Wasserstein Robbins and Enid Friedman and my family, my husband Gray, and my children, Miles and Allison, for listening and—most especially—for waiting.

Jill Lewis

To the Student

Imagine that you are driving your car in an unfamiliar town, perhaps trying to get to a doctor's new office. You don't recognize street names. You don't know where to turn. You don't have any idea of the distance from one point to the next. And, even more distressing, since you are a stranger in this town, landmarks known to local residents are totally unfamiliar to you and you cannot use them as reference points. A map with clearly labeled street names and understood landmarks would certainly help you find your way around this unknown territory.

Reading unfamiliar text is similar, in a number of respects, to driving in such a situation. If you are unfamiliar with the subject matter, or if you are uncertain about which comprehension strategies will help you with interpreting the material, you are at a disadvantage compared to students who have prior knowledge and reading experience with that subject. Students who are equipped with a variety of strategies to use in different reading situations will find the reading assignments and related classroom lectures easier to understand.

This book can serve as your *road map* to reading and study strategies necessary for success in college. In this book you will learn and apply reading and study strategies needed to comprehend and retain academic material. You will participate in a number of activities that will serve as checkpoints for you in your travels through each strategy area.

The *Table of Contents* of this textbook identifies the "points of interest" on this map that you will encounter on your journey through this text. It also gives you the general picture of where you are. If you take a quick look at it now, you will notice that this text is divided into ten chapters, each of which has a different purpose.

Scan the entries to see what topics will be discussed. No doubt you are already familiar with much of the language in the chapter headings, such as *topic, main idea, details, inference.* These are critical elements of text that form the basis for reading comprehension. Your ability to take notes and listen to lectures are also important for success in college.

Numerous *Activities* in the *Handbook* give you the opportunity to apply the reading and study strategies that are discussed. The short reading passages used within the *Handbook* for most of this practice are primarily drawn from college textbooks and other material that is typical of college reading assignments. Further, the *Extended Application* section at the end of each chapter asks you to apply the strategies to longer articles that you or your instructor may choose. You will find many opportunities in the *Handbook* to work with your classmates to share and refine your understanding of the strategies and to evaluate your success with applying them. Such *Working Together* activities are identified by ⮯.

This *Handbook* is different from traditional skills development materials. It is based on the idea that it is more important for you to know *how* to do something than it is for you to get the right answer to every *Activity* question. You are frequently asked to think about the processes you are using to answer questions and to consider whether you need to make refinements in the strategies you use. This kind of practice will help you to transfer strategies you learn in the *Handbook* to your college reading assignments.

Another difference you will note is that in this book you are often asked to assess your ideas while you read and to write about what you notice in your reading process. In this way your reading and writing abilities are used to support each other. Such *Thinking About Your Reading and Writing* activities are identified by ▶. In many *Activities* in the *Handbook* you are also asked to justify, or to prove, your answers. To do this you must think about *why* your answer is adequate or correct. You will need to look for evidence in the material. Making this self-analysis when you read is similar to what you do when you drive. When you are driving, you have a goal—a destination. You must ask yourself where you are going. Then you understand why you are making a left turn or a right one, or why you have chosen to turn at the third traffic light, not the first one. You also have goals when you are reading and interpreting text. As you work with the *Activities,* it will not be sufficient to just select an answer. You will need reasons for your choices, and you will need to be able to explain them.

Many routes to learning these comprehension strategies are possible. Two people who are using the same map may start their journey from different places. If two people wanted to get to New York City, for instance, their routes could be different, even if they are using the same map of the United States; one person might be starting from California, another from Michigan. In the same way, your instructor may have different students start from different points in the *Handbook*. It is also possible that everyone in your class will make a similar journey, starting from the same place. Your instructor may choose to use only portions of the *Handbook* as a supplement to longer reading selections, or it may be the core of your course.

As you work with this text, your ultimate aim is to read with comprehension and to retain what you have read. You will be working toward this objective. Thus, you should not expect that you will be able to instantly apply everything you read in this text or to immediately understand all of your college reading assignments. Consider this text as a starting point. It is the map, or plan, to help you reach academic literacy. But you are the driver. Ultimately you will choose the path to take and will need to figure out how to handle the curves and bumps along the way.

It is my sincere hope that once you have worked with this text you will feel better prepared for academic reading assignments because you can better comprehend academic texts. You should then be able to experience success and enjoyment as you continue on your journey towards your college degree.

Jill Lewis
Jersey City State College

A room without books is as a body without a soul

—Cicero

Contents

Chapter 2   Strategic Reading for Topics in Academic Text   34

Chapter 3   Strategic Reading for Main Ideas   52

Chapter 7   Strategies for Critical Reading and Thinking   194

HANDBOOK FOR READING AND STUDY STRATEGIES

Chapter 1

Taking Control
of Your Reading

*W*hen a pilot first learns to fly, it is mandatory that the flight instructor sit alongside the pilot during flight time. After many hours of practice and a series of demanding tests, the pilot is set free from the instructor. At this point, the pilot becomes totally in charge of what happens in the skies. Occasionally, the pilot might encounter situations not practiced in flight school—perhaps tornadoes or engine trouble. But all the "pointers" taught in flight school ensure a safe flight.

In much the same way, you have spent many years in school, under the guidance of teachers, perfecting your literacy abilities. You have passed the test—been admitted to college—and are now ready to "fly on your own." This chapter will give you some pointers that will help you stay in command as you proceed through what may be some turbulent reading situations—situations that you may not have been prepared for but that you can handle if you have some basic strategies in hand for managing the unexpected.

How do you feel about your reading strengths right now? How confident are you about your ability to participate in an academic environment? At what level is your academic self-esteem? It is useful to assess honestly how you feel now about these issues so that you can immediately set your goals toward improving those areas where you have the least confidence. Through this self-assessment process, you will be able to identify your learning strengths. You also will be able to rely on these strengths while you develop other aspects of your academic self-esteem.

The survey that follows asks a series of questions that you should answer based on your experiences and your knowledge of yourself. Think for a few minutes about each question before you rate yourself. Be as truthful as possible. The information you obtain is to be used for your own benefit. It is not a test!

Survey of Academic Self-Esteem

Directions for Items 1 Through 23: For each item, circle the number that you feel best describes you as you are now. (1 = not true of me at all; 4 = very true of me)

1. I can successfully prepare to take exams.	1 2 3 4
2. I can figure out what will be asked on tests.	1 2 3 4
3. I have successful strategies for taking notes on lectures and reading assignments.	1 2 3 4
4. I know how to preview my textbooks.	1 2 3 4
5. I know how to come prepared for class.	1 2 3 4
6. I know how to mark and underline reading material for review purposes.	1 2 3 4
7. I know how to make predictions when I read.	1 2 3 4
8. I am able to answer questions in a college classroom.	1 2 3 4
9. I am able to read a college textbook with understanding.	1 2 3 4
10. I know when to slow down my reading rate for better comprehension.	1 2 3 4
11. I know how to use context to get the meaning of unknown words in college-level material.	1 2 3 4
12. I have good strategies for thinking critically about things I have read.	1 2 3 4
13. I am able to figure out the main ideas of college-type reading materials (for example, sociology, psychology, science).	1 2 3 4

14. I am able to set purposes for my reading.	1	2	3	4
15. I can read and interpret maps, graphs, and charts.	1	2	3	4
16. I know how to create summaries and visual aids to help me remember what I have read.	1	2	3	4
17. I know how to distinguish between important and unimportant details when I read.	1	2	3	4
18. I am able to participate successfully in a college classroom.	1	2	3	4
19. I am able to ask a professor for help when I have a question.	1	2	3	4
20. I believe I will be admitted to the major of my choice.	1	2	3	4
21. I believe I have a lot of knowledge to share with others.	1	2	3	4
22. I believe I will graduate from college.	1	2	3	4
23. I believe I will have a successful future.	1	2	3	4

Let's analyze the results of your survey. The following chart shows the category into which different items fall. Place your ratings on the chart. Then respond to the questions in Activity A.

SURVEY ANALYSIS

Category	Question Nos.
Study Skills	1　2　3　4　6　14　16
	Your ratings: ___ ___ ___ ___ ___ ___ ___
Reading Skills	7　9　10　11　12　13　15　17
	Your ratings: ___ ___ ___ ___ ___ ___ ___ ___
Participating in College Classrooms	5　8　18　19　21
	Your ratings: ___ ___ ___ ___ ___
Expecting a Successful Future	20　22　23
	Your ratings: ___ ___ ___

Questionnaire adapted from Lewis, Jill. "The Effects of a Precollege Reading Course on the Academic Self-Esteem of Underprepared College Students." *Inquiries in Literacy Learning and Instruction.* College Reading Association (Fall 1993).

ACTIVITY A. Assessing Your Academic Self-Esteem

1. Based on the information you've obtained from this survey, what area(s) could you improve? _____

    _____

2. In a few sentences, describe the academic self-esteem goals you would like to achieve this term. _____

_____

_____

WHAT DOES IT MEAN TO TAKE CONTROL?

Doing this self-analysis is the first step in taking control of your reading. You want to be in charge of what you read, how you read, and what to do when you do not understand something you are required to read. Taking control means that you know strategies that can enable you to comprehend what you read, strategies that you can call on when you have difficulty reading something. When you are in charge, you know, while you are reading, whether or not you understand the text. In addition, you know what to do whenever you read a passage you don't understand. In this chapter, you will learn some of these self-help tools. But because you are in charge, it will be your decision whether or not to use them. You are in command of your reading development from this point on.

BECOMING FAMILIAR WITH YOUR INSTRUCTOR

One of the first things beginning college students often notice about their college classes is that, unlike classes they took in high school, the instructors don't always "follow the book." In high school, your teachers may have gone through each textbook chapter, page by page, in systematic fashion. Homework was assigned on a particular chapter, and class time was spent reviewing the homework. High school teachers are usually bound by a set curriculum that must be followed by all teachers in that school system (sometimes in that state) who teach a certain subject to a particular grade. There is more flexibility in the college classroom where instructors have more leeway with curriculum.

The result may be that your college instructor will address the outside reading you have done only *peripherally*, that is, as a supplement to the other information given through a lecture. This means that class lectures may seem to have little relationship to the assigned reading. In such cases, you will need to look for points of overlap. Perhaps the reading and lecture carried the same theme, were about the same period, or were examples of the same principle. You will need to make such connections on your own. On the other hand, many instructors use class time to review outside readings and to clarify areas of confusion. They may do this by asking students to identify points of uncertainty from the reading or by questioning students directly about what they have read.

From the start of the term, you will want to know the relationship between the text and the instructor's lectures for each of your courses. This will help you prepare for each class and know how to use the information from the lecture when it is finished.

Another difference you may find between high school and college is that college instructors may have much higher expectations of their students. You are given much more independence in college—you make many decisions on your own about your personal life—and your instructors expect you to make decisions about your academic life as well. No one will check to see whether you have completed your assignments. You don't get a "detention" for coming to class unprepared. Instructors expect that assignments will be done, and done *well.* But it may not be until you take the final exam that you have an opportunity to show that you have been keeping up with the assignments and that you understood them.

It is critical, then, that you have some strategies for using your textbooks that will help you manage your academic reading on your own.

BECOMING FAMILIAR WITH YOUR TEXT

For practically every course you take at college, you will have at least one assigned text. If you are to get the most from your texts, you should immediately develop a working acquaintance with each of them. The following particular features of most texts can assist you with your reading.

Introduction to the Student.   You should thoroughly read this often-overlooked portion of a textbook. It will explain the purpose for which the text has been written, and it will probably tell you the author's point of view or perspective. By knowing the author's purpose and biases from the start, you are in a better position to evaluate an author's interpretation of events or situations. For example, a liberal-minded person who is writing a critique of the Reagan presidency will most likely offer an assessment very different from that of a conservative author.

Additionally, in the introduction or preface, you may find the author's suggestions for using the book. The preface may identify different sections of the text that can assist you, and it may give an overview of the text's contents and an explanation of how each part contributes to the whole text.

Table of Contents.   The table of contents provides a map of the entire book. Consider each chapter listed as a "point of interest" along the way. By scanning the table of contents, you will be able to determine the major areas that are covered in the text and the typical length of each chapter. By looking at chapter headings, you can learn the direction the text will take. For instance, information may be arranged topically or chronologically. In the table of contents for some books, you may also find a listing of the subsections within the chapters, which will give you an even better picture of the overall contents.

Chapter Introductions. An introduction to a chapter prepares you for what you will find in the pages ahead. The introduction may be separated from the rest of the contents and may even appear in a different type style, or it may be integrated with the rest of the contents at the beginning of the chapter. In the latter case, you can often tell that it is the introduction because it doesn't begin with a subheading. The types of information in introductions will vary. Some introductions will give you the major thesis or main points you will be learning about. You can use each main point like a peg on which to place the details as you proceed through the chapter. Other introductions may be anecdotes intended to spark your interest before you read the chapter. Assess the purpose served by the chapter introductions in each of your texts, and use them accordingly.

Chapter Summaries. The chapter summary is a review of the main points of the chapter. You will be making good use of the summary if you try to recall the details from the chapter that are related to each main point. As with the introduction, the summary might be separated from the rest of the text and may even appear in a different type style, or it may just be at the end of the chapter, integrated with the rest of the text. You should read the chapter introduction and summary before you proceed with more detailed reading. By doing so, you will see the total framework for the chapter. You will understand where the author is headed and will be more able to follow the route, through the details, along the way.

Chapter Titles and Subtitles. These two features of textbooks are *organizing aids* that will keep you focused while you read. From a quick scan of these before you read, you will know the scope of the topic within the chapter and how the author has organized the information. You will also be able to estimate how familiar you are with the subject and to use this information as a guide to the amount of time you should allow for your reading assignment.

Graphic Aids. Many books use graphic materials such as graphs, charts, diagrams, and photographs to clarify information or to serve as examples for material in the text. To be able to use a graphic aid effectively, you will need to analyze how the information on it is organized. Usually, there is a title that tells you what is depicted. *Graphs* usually depict quantitative data such as percentages. They often show comparisons and frequently there are comparisons of the data over time. *Charts* may be used to organize information and to show relationships among people, events, and ideas that might otherwise be difficult to explain, such as the variety of play activities of children in different countries from birth to age twelve, or forms of environmental pollution and the most common causes of them, as well as strategies for eliminating each. *Diagrams* that are clearly labeled can help you visualize information that is otherwise descriptive, such as a diagram showing cell division or one depicting how a television camera works. *Photographs* are subject to different interpretations. However, your textbook author may clarify for you, within the body of the text, what interpretation is preferred. Try to see it from the author's perspective, but don't be afraid to make interpretations of your own. In fact, with any graphic aid, you should try to draw your own conclusions in addition to those that are mentioned in the text.

Chapter Questions.   These are extremely useful for studying textbook material. They let you know what information the author believes students should have gained from their reading and what interpretations and conclusions could have resulted. It is a good idea to read these even before you begin the chapter. As with the titles and subtitles, prereading chapter questions will help keep you focused during your reading.

Glossary.   The glossary is your dictionary for the book. Technical terms, which may or may not have been defined in the chapter where they first occurred, are listed here. Refer to it as you come across terms you do not remember that are important to the subject you are reading.

Index.   The index appears at the end of a text and lists topics discussed in the text or references particular people or events, along with their page numbers. It will assist you in finding material quickly.

Textbook Assessment (1)

Complete the checklist for a textbook you are using this term. If your text does not have one of the features listed, note this.

Text: _

Course: _

How useful do you think each feature will be? Give reasons for your answer.

Introduction to the student _

_ _

Table of contents _

_ _

Chapter introductions _

_ _

Chapter summaries _____

_____

Chapter titles and subtitles _____

_____

Graphic aids _____

_____

Chapter questions _____

_____

Glossary _____

_____

Index _____

_____

Other features of this text: _____

Textbook Assessment (2)

Complete the chart for a textbook you are using this term. If your text does not have one of the features listed, note this.

Text: _____

Course: _____

How useful do you think this feature will be? Give reasons for your answer.

Introduction to the student _____

_____

Table of contents _____

_____

Chapter introductions _____

_____

Chapter summaries _____

_____

Chapter titles and subtitles _____

_____

Graphic aids _____

_____

Chapter questions _____

_____

Glossary _____

_____

Index _____

_____

Other features of this text: _____

PREPARING YOURSELF TO READ

Each time you begin a new text chapter, it is critical that you mentally prepare yourself to read. By doing so, you are again taking charge of your reading—putting yourself in control. Several strategies will help you do this.

Actively Preview the Chapter.   You will want to know what the chapter contents are before you begin reading the chapter. Does that sound odd? How can you know what it's about before you have read it? Actively previewing the chapter is the key. This occurs when you read chapter introductions, summaries, chapter titles and subtitles, questions at the end of the chapter, and graphic aids. Whenever you have to read a new chapter, or plan to review one already read, begin by skimming these essential parts. As you skim, think about how the chapter is organized, what the main topics are, what kinds of questions you are being asked, what the author's purpose for writing seems to be. Become as familiar as you can with what lies ahead in the chapter.

Determine the Prior Knowledge That You Can Use with Your Reading Assignment.   Ask yourself such questions as, How much do I already know about this subject? What have I read or heard about it? What about it is of interest to me? How might I be able to apply this information to my life? If you recognize your prior knowledge on a subject before you begin reading, you will have a memory bank of information to help you comprehend new material in the text. Your memory bank will assist you in recalling related concepts, similar situations or characters, and your emotional responses to the subject. This strategy will enable you to make connections between the new information and what you already know, which, in the end, will make the new material easier to learn and more meaningful for you.

Set Purposes for Your Reading.   This is another way to prepare for in-depth reading. Six common purposes for academic reading are to:

1. Preview a chapter to determine its contents.
2. Review major points from the previous night's reading before going to class.
3. Read with the intent to share the information with someone else in a study group.
4. Respond personally to what you are reading.
5. Learn everything in a chapter, including the minor details, in preparation for a test.
6. Assess the logic of an argument presented by an author.

Whatever your purpose, you should identify it at the outset.

Set an Appropriate Reading Speed.   Your reading speeds should vary, and they should be determined by your purpose for reading. Even if you are reading the same material several times, you may need to read it at a different rate each time.

Once you set your purpose, you can begin to assess whether you should skim the material quickly, as you would for purposes 1 and 2, or whether you need to read at a moderate speed, as you would for purposes 3 and 4. For purposes 5 and 6, you would need to use an even slower rate.

An additional factor that influences the speed at which you can read the text with comprehension is the *difficulty level of the material*. After you preread, assess your prior knowledge, and establish your purpose, you will be fairly familiar with any difficulties the material may pose for you. The level at which the text is written, your background and interest in the material, and your purpose for reading will all influence your reading rate. To achieve an appropriate pace, try the following:

- Make an initial guesstimate of how quickly you can read a certain number of pages in the text (for instance, ten pages in one-half hour).
- Read at your intended pace, but make sure you are comprehending the material.
- See whether you reached your target. (Did you read ten pages in one-half hour with comprehension? Did it take more or less time?)
- Adjust your target accordingly so that you stay at a comfortable speed, maintaining comprehension, while accomplishing your purpose.

Eliminate Distractions.   Finally, before you start your in-depth reading, identify those things that cause you to take your mind off your reading once you begin. This is sometimes the hardest step to take because it may require big changes in a few of your well-established study habits. Your determination to succeed, though, will get you past this hurdle. To eliminate distractions, you will first need to identify them. Distractions may include phones ringing, people talking, concerns about family or friends, poor lighting, music or television in the background, and other obligations. The list is practically endless. Once you've identified the negative influences on your studying, *develop a plan of attack*. For instance, if you are concerned about noise, music, people talking, or phones ringing, you will obviously need to find a more suitable place to study. Sometimes even libraries are noisy. If this is the case in your library, and noise disturbs you, you will need to look around campus or your neighborhood for a quieter place. You can take the phone off the hook during your study time to eliminate calls. Make a to-do list *before* you begin studying so that you will remember to call family or friends or to take care of other obligations afterward. By making the list before you open the text, you have eliminated the need to remember these things and will, thus, be more able to remember the text information.

▶ **Thinking About Your Reading and Writing**

ACTIVITY B. Strategies for Preparing Yourself to Read

Think about the strategies you have learned for preparing yourself to read. List the strategies you think will be most useful to you. Explain how you will apply each one.

STAYING MENTALLY ACTIVE WHILE YOU READ

Have you ever felt that after reading something, you have little idea of what the story, essay, or chapter was about? This is a common complaint among students. You can use a number of strategies to avoid detours in comprehension that you might otherwise make during the reading process. What you do during your in-depth reading is at least as important as your pre-reading activities.

Self-Monitor.   When you *self-monitor*, you ask yourself questions while you read in order to become more aware of how well you are comprehending the material. As you read and self-monitor, you should identify those parts of the text that you do or do not understand, note the ideas that seem particularly important to you, and determine whether you are able to see connections between ideas. Ask yourself, Does this make sense? What does this new information have to do with what I have read on previous pages? What can I predict or hypothesize based on this information? What conclusions can I draw? Your responses to these questions will be important indicators of whether you have comprehended the material.

Create Questions and Try to Answer Them.   Self-monitoring also involves using the subtitles of the chapters to ask questions *before* you read and then checking whether you can answer your questions *while* you read. For instance, you may read a chapter that includes the subheading, "Successful Television Advertising." The questions you create before you read this portion of the text might include: What are some characteristics of successful television advertising? What are some examples of successful television advertising? After reading this section of the chapter, you immediately verify your understanding of it by attempting to answer your questions. When you do this, you should try to use your own language and to paraphrase the key points. You will need to make sure your answers actually state the contents of what you've read. If you are able to do this, and if you can include most of the important information from that section, you have comprehended the material. If this does not occur, there are two possible explanations: (1) You may have had an unsuitable question, or (2) you may not have comprehended. You will need either to revise your question so that you can include the important information in your answer or to reread the material. At least, you will have realized your difficulty comprehending the material well before getting to the end of the chapter. Now you can give yourself another chance to understand the section.

▶ **Thinking About Your Reading and Writing**

ACTIVITY C. Self-Monitoring Strategies

Think about the strategies you have learned for self-monitoring. List those that you think will be most useful to you. Explain how you will apply each one.

ASSESSING YOUR LEARNING

The practice of checking your comprehension applies not only during reading, but also *after* you have completed the entire reading assignment. In the postreading assessment process, you will concentrate on tying together the main points of the material and connecting them to other knowledge you have. There are several steps to take in order to assess what you have learned.

Spend a Few Minutes Mentally Summarizing the Entire Chapter. What were the key points? What details for each key point can you recall? How does each main idea contribute to the whole of the information? Look again at headings, subheadings, and technical terms. Be sure you see the chapter as a whole, not just as bits and pieces of facts. The author has chosen to put all the details into a particular chapter because they have a relationship to one another. Focus on that relationship for a while.

If you still don't understand some part, it is critical that you reread that section for clarification. Again, try to connect the details and main points to see whether there are any remaining areas of uncertainty.

Think About How the New Information You Have Learned Compares to What You Knew at the Start of Your Reading.   To do this, you must recall the prior knowledge you had during the prereading phase. Ask yourself, What did I know then? What do I know now? You might also ask, What more would I like to know about this subject? These comparisons will show you how much you have gained from the reading; they also will enable you to connect your prior knowledge to new ideas and to adjust your thinking so that any misconceptions you had before reading will be modified.

Consider the Opinions and Attitudes of the Author and Compare Them to Your Own.   This step is especially important if your reading is about a controversial subject. It requires you to make distinctions between facts and the author's opinions, to assess the logic of the author's ideas, to reconsider your opinions, and to identify support for either the author's ideas or your own.

Think About How Your New Knowledge Affects You Personally.   Once you have assessed your knowledge and are clear about the information, you can ask yourself, How can I apply this knowledge to my life? You may be reading about social issues, environmental issues, the economy, philosophical issues and points of view, or business matters. This process will make what you have learned more meaningful for you and will help you remember the material.

▶ **Thinking About Your Reading and Writing**

ACTIVITY D. Postreading Assessment Strategies

Think about the strategies you have learned for postreading assessment. List those that you think will be most useful to you. Explain how you will apply each one.

TAKING OWNERSHIP OF IDEAS IN TEXTS

A key to improving your comprehension of academic material is to be able to put the author's ideas into your own language. Your goal is to restate the text language well enough so that you can create a sentence that conveys the author's ideas. By restating the author's ideas in your own language, you verify that you have understood the main points. If you do not understand, you will not be able to do this. Furthermore, by restating the ideas in language that is more comfortable for you, you take ownership of those ideas, and you will remember them longer. In a sense, you are rehearsing those ideas for a later, final performance in a class discussion or on an exam. When you restate ideas, you need to:

1. Identify the essential ideas in each sentence.
2. Look for important *embedded* ideas within long sentences.
3. Rewrite the ideas so that the main points are clear.

We next describe strategies to help you with each of these three steps.

Identifying Essential Ideas in Sentences

You are no doubt aware that most textbook authors write sentences that are quite different from everyday conversation. Text language is more formal, and ideas are sometimes complicated. A key to understanding academic text is to apply some of the same language knowledge to reading text that you use when you are having a conversation.

When you listen to someone speak, you are trying to get to the essential meaning of what is being said. The same goal is true for reading. There are things you already know about sentence structure, and you use this knowledge automatically when you listen to someone speak. When you read academic text, you may need to deliberately apply this knowledge. A brief review of some elements of grammar will help you recall how sentences are structured—knowing this is critical for comprehending text.

To find the essential meaning of a sentence, you will need to determine (1) who or what is being discussed and (2) what is being said about the "who" or "what."

These two parts of the sentence are sometimes referred to as the *subject* and *predicate* of the sentence. They provide the fundamental meaning, the basic thought, of the sentence. You may now start to recall some grammatical features of sentences that you have learned in English classes. You should remember that:

1. Some sentences may have more than one subject or verb, and the two subjects or verbs are usually joined by *coordinating conjunctions* such as *or, but, and, for, yet.* Both subjects or both verbs are important.

   ### Example:

   John Dewey *and* Henry Rousseau had some worthwhile ideas about how children learn.

2. Some sentences have two or more important complete thoughts in them. Each thought has its own subject and verb. Each thought is critical to the meaning of the entire sentence. These two thoughts are also often joined by coordinating conjunctions, and they are separated by a comma. They may also be joined by a semicolon and no coordinating conjunction.

   ### Example:

   We do not know exactly how many regular gamblers are unable to control their gambling, *but* some experienced gamblers estimate that it is as high as 50 percent.

   We do not know exactly how many regular gamblers are unable to control their gambling; some experienced gamblers estimate that it is as high as 50 percent.

3. Some sentences will contain two ideas, but they are not equally important. In these cases, one part of the sentence, the most important part, is called the *independent clause.* It makes sense by itself and does not depend on the rest of the sentence for its meaning. The part of the sentence that also has a subject and verb, but which cannot stand alone as a sentence, is called the *dependent clause.* It depends on the rest of the sentence for its meaning. The two clauses are usually separated by a comma. Dependent clauses are often introduced by clause markers such as *because, when, as, since, that, so, although, where, if, unless, who, after, while, even though, which.*

   ### Example:

   If the union officials could not agree with management on a settlement, there would undoubtedly be a strike by the railroad workers.

ACTIVITY E. Identifying Essential Ideas in Sentences

Decide whether each sentence is an example of sentence structure 1, 2, or 3. Write your answer in the space provided.

1. Energy can exist in several forms and can be converted from one form to another. _____
2. Insurance companies accumulate large amounts of idle funds that must be invested to generate income to pay off claims. _____
3. General Electric and other large companies have found robots to be more effective in some work than human workers. _____
4. Jury panels are selected from voter registration or tax lists, and such panels are supposed to be generally representative of the community. _____
5. Some small business managers guard their positions jealously, and they may deliberately hire ineffective subordinates. _____
6. No one was quite certain if the spread of the disease would be halted, although every precaution had been taken. _____
7. It was Muller who helped convince biologists that it was possible to think of the gene as a molecule. _____
8. In 1900, House representatives had no personal staff, and senators averaged fewer than one staff member each. _____

Working Together

With a partner, create one example of each of the three types of sentences. Identify each type.

Most sentences have simple as well as complete predicates. The *simple predicate* is the "what" or the verb itself. It tells what is being said about the subject in the simplest terms. The *complete predicate* consists of the simple predicate plus words that add information necessary for the complete meaning of the sentence. In these cases, the important thought includes the complete predicate, not just the verb. In the following example, the simple predicate is underlined; the complete predicate is the underlined word plus the italicized words. Note the importance of the information in the complete predicate.

Example:

Bill Clinton tried *to get a health care reform bill passed in 1994.*

Clause markers serve specific purposes. They can indicate a number of relationships between the dependent clause and the independent clause of the sentence. If you know the purpose the clause marker generally serves, it will be easier for you to determine the relationship between the dependent and independent clauses. Knowing these relationships is critical for sentence comprehension. One way to identify the purpose of the clause marker is to determine what question the dependent clause answers. Here are some common questions clause markers answer. The dependent clause is underlined, but the clause marker is italicized.

1. Which one (ones)?

   Examples:

   > The businesses *whose* offices were in the building next to the playground closed for the month of August.

   > The plants *that* had not been treated with the chemical showed greater leaf loss over a shorter period of time.

2. When?

   Examples:

   > The interest rates on home mortgages were expected to rise *after* the Federal Reserve Bank raised the prime rate.

   > *When* the twentieth century began, America was already an industrialized nation.

3. Who?

   Examples:

   > The candidates *who* had presented their views at the open meeting had a good chance of being elected.

   > The runner *who* came in last was cheered into the home stretch by the crowd.

4. How?

   Examples:

   > The new recruits looked *as if* they were ready to furnish the needed strength.

   > The social worker spoke *as though* the family would soon be reunited.

5. Why?

   Examples:

   > You will need to take a course in keyboarding *so that* you can type more easily and more accurately.

   > It was nearly impossible to identify the origin of the skeleton *because* it was so badly deteriorated.

6. Under what conditions or circumstances?

   Examples:

   > *If* she touched the clay models, the blind girl was able to describe the clothes worn by the Victorians.

The community resolved to establish its own nightwatch *unless* the police could do a better job keeping the gangs and drug dealers away.

Several questions may be answered by several clauses within a single sentence, as in the examples that follow. The clause markers have been italicized.

Examples:

1. Children usually make greater progress in their schoolwork *if* the number of hours of TV they watch is reduced *so that* they have more time for their homework.

2. The scientists *who* investigated global warming found *that* temperatures of the earth's surface had risen only slightly during the past ten years.

3. The countries *that* were near the North Korean border were feeling more threatened recently *because* the United Nations' investigators had not been able to determine North Korea's nuclear power.

4. *After* she had investigated for two months, the anthropologist concluded *that* the shaman was well respected in the village.

Working Together

With a partner, decide what questions are answered by each underlined clause in examples 1 through 4.

Finding Embedded Ideas in Text

Textbook sentences are often lengthy. This poses a major problem when students attempt to restate main points because several ideas are often stated within, or embedded in, a single sentence. The complex sentence structure often results from an author's use of multiple clauses and phrases in a single sentence. To unravel sentences such as these, it will help to remember that even very long sentences have at least one subject and verb, even when these two critical parts of the sentence are separated by clauses or phrases. The following two example sentences illustrate this point. In them, the main clause, consisting of the subject and predicate, have been underlined, the clause markers have been circled, and those phrases that only modify either the main clause or a dependent clause have been italicized.

Examples:

1. A number of small businesses, (which) are businesses (that) are usually started *by people* (who) have developed a product or service (that) can be produced and sold only *in a new business*

(which) is set up *for that purpose,* often evolve into large corporations.

2. Cognitive psychologists, (who) developed theories *about* (how) people learn and remember and (who) were also studying the thinking processes individuals use (when) they read and write, made important contributions *to the field of reading.*

Dependent clauses and modifying phrases may also appear at the beginning of the sentence, and in such cases you need to look further on in the sentence to find the main clause.

In other long sentences, the subject and a verb are very close to each other, but the sentence length prompts us to look toward the end of the sentence for the main verb. If you do this, you may feel as though you have lost your place in the sentence. This type of sentence is illustrated next. The main clause is underlined.

Example:

The sugars and other organic materials formed by green plants constitute the basic fuels for all of us, for when we walk, pound on a keyboard, or sing a lullaby, we are using the energy released by the combustion of sugars in our body.

Once you have identified the main subject and verb, you can separate out all the key ideas that are embedded in the rest of the sentence, as in the two examples that follow.

Example 1:

So enormous and dazzling was the progress made in the course of the seventeenth century toward scientific understanding of the human body, the earth, and the heavens, that it is not too much to say that by 1700 a radical change was taking place in the attitude of Europeans toward the interrelationship between humans, God, and nature.

In this sentence, the main idea is that *a radical change was taking place.* The following ideas all give important information about this *radical change* and are embedded in the remainder of the sentence.

Some embedded ideas:

1. Scientific research of the seventeenth century revealed much new information about the human body.
2. Astronomy was becoming more scientific in the seventeenth century.
3. Prior to the seventeenth century, Europeans had a less scientific view of the interrelationships between humans, God, and nature.
4. By the seventeenth century, Europeans were willing to consider scientific explanations for aspects of human life and nature.

In the next example, the main subject and verb are near the beginning of the sentence, and they are followed by a series of descriptors that would be important to know if you were studying this material.

Example 2:

After developing and evaluating objectives, *the manager selects the overall policies* that will fulfill the company objective and still satisfy market, industry, and company criteria.

Some embedded ideas:

1. Managers develop objectives.
2. Managers evaluate objectives.
3. Managers select policies that are designed to meet the company objective.
4. Managers also have to consider the market when they set policy.
5. Managers also have to consider the industry when they set policy.

Determining which of the embedded ideas are important is usually a matter of finding those ideas that answer questions about the main subject and verb of the sentence. In Example 1, the question "What is the radical change?" is answered by the embedded ideas that are listed. In Example 2, the main subject and verb phrases generate the question "How does the manager select the policies?" The embedded ideas listed provide answers to these.

ACTIVITY F. Finding Embedded Ideas in Text

For each sentence, list as many important embedded ideas as you can.

1. People who have trouble motivating themselves under normal work conditions may react to stress by producing at a lower capacity or by frequent absences from the job.

   ### Embedded ideas:

   a. _____

   b. _____

   c. _____

   d. _____

2. At every Democratic National Convention since 1972, the newer delegates have had views on a variety of important issues that were vastly different from those of rank-and-file Democrats.

Embedded ideas:

a. _____

b. _____

c. _____

d. _____

3. Companies make use of general-purpose software such as word processors and database systems, as well as more specialized software to manage records, prepare payroll, produce accounting reports, and analyze business finances.

Embedded ideas:

a. _____

b. _____

c. _____

d. _____

Rewriting Sentences

Once you have identified the embedded ideas in a sentence and have restated them in your own words, you are ready to create a new, less complicated sentence that restates the author's idea. You will need to determine which of the embedded ideas are more important. You already know that important ideas will answer questions about the main subject and verb. In addition, you should consider the major focus of the paragraph, chapter, or article. This process is outlined in the following example, in which a key sentence has been italicized and then restated.

Example:

When Nelson Mandela speaks to black audiences, he often reminds them that democracy and majority rule in South Africa will not change the material circumstances of their lives overnight. *He rarely practices the modern politician's art of telling his listeners what he thinks they want to hear.* His message to white audiences is also sometimes not typical of an elected official who would like to be reelected. He tells the white citizens of South Africa that they must take responsibility for the past and that they will have to accept that their nation will now have majority rule.

Restatement   (based on focus of paragraph and important information preceding and following sentence):

Nelson Mandela is not like most politicians because he does not speak to his audiences in ways that will especially please his listeners.

ACTIVITY G. Rewriting Key Sentences from Text

Each of the following paragraphs contains an underlined key sentence. Rewrite this sentence, keeping its main idea, but simplifying the language. You should refer to the rest of the information in the paragraph.

1. Politics is not necessarily always violent and clear-cut. There is politics in the board room, in the inter-departmental conference, in the school staff meeting, and in the annual conference of the dog-lovers' association. If these meetings consist of anything more than just reading of the minutes and the adjournment for tea, they are political situations. If the bodies concerned consist of people who know each other well and do not differ over fundamentals, the politics of the situation may be confined to polite inquiry. If there is a lack of confidence amongst those concerned, or if there have been arguments over policy or the way in which a policy has been carried out or if the body in question has been subjected to pressure from outside, the strictly political element will be more obvious.

Miller, John Donald Bruce. "Politics and Diversity." *The Nature of Politics*. London: Duckworth, 1962. 15.

Your restatement: _____

_____

_____

2. Although school attendance is not compulsory, it is urged by many of the village leaders, and most Hopi boys and girls go to school for a period of from six to ten years. Regularity of attendance differs among Hopi families and Hopi villages, and children in the more acculturated, or educated, groups have the highest attendance records. When school interferes too greatly with ceremonial or economic activities, however, the children are likely to drop out for two or three days. To overcome this difficulty, last year the principal of the Polacca Day School persuaded the First Mesa leaders to hold some of the ceremonials on weekends, rather than during the week, and since this time, he reports, regularity of attendance has increased.

Adapted from Thomas, L., and A. Joseph. "Youth." *The Hopi Way*. Chicago: University of Chicago Press, 1944. 58.

Your restatement: _____

_____

_____

3. The sense of taste conveys information mainly about the general chemical nature of potential food substances. Insects such as flies and moths taste with their legs and mouth parts, the receptors being in bristles on these appendages. In mammals, the taste receptors are taste buds, clusters of elongated ciliated cells set into depressions in the tongue. Some chemicals stimulate buds in different regions of the tongue, and different taste sensations are then perceived. The four primary tastes are sweet, sour, salty, and bitter. Stimulation of buds near the tip of the tongue produces sweet tastes, those at the back, bitter tastes, and those along the tongue edges, sour and salty tastes.

Adapted from Weisz, Paul B., and Richard N. Keogh. *Elements of Biology.* 4th ed. New York: McGraw-Hill, 1977. 290.

Your restatement: _____

_____

_____

4. The peer group is not an agent of deliberate socialization. Its major purpose for its members is recreational. It exists because its members enjoy peer group interaction for its own sake. Nevertheless, cliques and gangs unintentionally exert a great amount of pressure on their members to acquire the values, orientations, and outlooks of the group. Thus, the individual member usually internalizes strongly the codes and expectations of his peer group so that his position in this highly valued group will not be endangered.

Adapted from DeFleur, M., W. D'Antonio, and L. DeFleur. *Sociology: Man in Society.* Brief Edition. Glenview, Ill.: Scott, Foresman, and Co., 1972. 160.

Your restatement: _____

_____

_____

5. Effective violence and endurance are the measure of "roughness" of the pro game, rougher today than ever before. To ask why is to go to the heart of the matter. Most likely, every pro at some time in his life as a football player has experienced a precise moment of understanding, a point in time after which he knows the game in a way that releases his body from domination by the mind and enables him to respond creatively to his function. If it hadn't happened, regardless of his native strength or speed, he would be in some other line of work. Once it happens (the result of talent, practice, and luck), he plays at a new level of awareness.

Morgan, Thomas B. "The American War Game." *Mastering Reading Skills.* Eds. S. J. Rauch and A. B. Weinstein. New York: American Book, 1968. 55.

Your restatement: _____

_____

_____

Working Together

Compare your restatements from Activity G with those of a partner. Did your sentences for each paragraph convey the same idea? What were some differences? Make any revisions to your sentences that you now think would improve them. Make sure that you are comfortable with the language and that the restatements keep the original idea.

When you compared your answers as directed, you had an opportunity to share what you know with someone else's knowledge. This is another effective strategy for taking ownership of ideas in texts. By talking with classmates about them, you are using the language you need to learn, and you are able to think through the ideas and restate them in a way that someone else will understand them. If you cannot discuss them with someone else, then you still do not understand them. At this point, you should reread the material you were unable to explain in order to feel more confident of your knowledge.

Writing out what you know, making a permanent record of your text summaries and restatements, is also a good comprehension strategy. Again, you are working with the text language and trying to reconstruct its meaning so that you will understand and remember it. If you copy the information from the text word for word, you have not learned it. You are merely copying. Rewriting, restating, and rewording are critical to remembering what you read.

USING OUTSIDE SOURCES TO GAIN BACKGROUND KNOWLEDGE

Textbook authors, you must remember, have often spent many years learning about a subject before they write their books. You do not have that privilege. You need to learn the information today, this week, or this term. Since the authors are so familiar with their subject, they often assume students have enough background knowledge to assist them with the text. This is not always so. When you are confused or feel you can't understand some portion of your assigned reading, you can do many things to get outside assistance. The most obvious is to find a tutor on campus. Your college probably has many students majoring in the subject that gives you difficulty. Some of these students are likely connected to a tutoring service. The only drawback to using the college tutoring service may be the lack of teaching experience student-tutors have.

Another way to improve your background knowledge of a subject or to understand at a higher level the new material you've been assigned to read, is to locate other books on the subject that may make fewer assumptions about what you already know. Such books may be available at your college library. Another source for them is the public library where, in addition to the adult section, the young adults' section may have books on the subject. In the past decade, there has been an explosion in informational books for young readers, some of which are quite remarkable in their depth and quality. (If you feel embarrassed checking these out, you can always claim it is for a younger relative.) A third source for additional material is the federal government, which publishes many informational brochures. You can obtain a listing of them from the Government Printing Office in Washington, D.C.

Also consider people that you know who could be sources for information and assistance on particular subjects. A relative who works in an auto factory may have considerable knowledge about air pollution. A friend working at a local restaurant or pharmacy can possibly explain, in simplified terms, some principles of economics to you. If you know a teacher, he or she may be able to shed some light on issues raised in sociology or psychology texts. Try to explore every possible avenue for sources.

Once you have gathered all the outside information you need to help you understand the text material, you should sort through it and decide which ideas are more important or worthwhile. Reread the text material, which should now have more meaning for you, and synthesize your new information with the knowledge you already have from outside sources. You are now ready to record the vital information, in your own language, for later use.

The following chart gives you an opportunity to reflect on the outside sources that are available to you for courses you are taking this term.

Outside Source Action List

Course: _____

Outside Sources Available to You: _____

_____

_____

Course: _____

Outside Sources Available to You: _____

_____

Students who have taken charge of their reading also know that tests are a fact of academic life. Examinations are the primary way in which many instructors are able to assess whether you have learned course content. Different instructors may give tests once or twice a term, weekly, or every few weeks. If you have used the strategies described in this chapter, you will be well on your way to success with tests. You will have used all available resources to check and expand your understanding, and you will have recorded what you know in language that is your own so that you have a usable set of study notes. There are, however, still a few remaining things to do as you prepare to take tests. You should use some of these strategies several weeks before the exam. Others you will want to do shortly before the exam. And some are strategies to use during the exam.

Several weeks before the exam:

1. Practice distributed review. This means to review your notes at regular intervals throughout the term. Don't wait until just before the exam to begin studying.
2. Find a study partner. Study partners can help each other tremendously if they really focus on their task. They can prepare questions for each other to answer, and they can listen to responses to see whether the information is adequate. They can keep each other focused and provide encouragement.

Shortly before the exam:

1. Make a final review of your notes the evening before the exam. Don't do anything afterward that will interfere with what you have reviewed, such as going to a party.
2. Get up a little earlier than usual the next morning to review your notes once more.
3. Take all materials you will need during the exam. This includes a watch, as well as any paper and pencils or pens you might need.
4. Be on time for the exam. If you arrive late, you are setting yourself up to do poorly. If you arrive too early, others may distract you.

During the exam:

1. Sit in a quiet spot away from talkative and noisy people.
2. Read over all the directions on the exam before you begin. Spend a few minutes thinking about what is required before you begin.
3. If you come to a question you can't answer, remind yourself that you don't need to get *every* answer right in order to pass.
4. Work from your strengths. If there are questions you definitely know,

answer these first so that you can feel self-assured before tackling the more difficult questions.

5. Budget your time. Don't spend too much time on any one question.

6. Use all the time allotted to you. There is no need to be the first one finished. If you finish early, use the remaining time to review your answers and to spot and correct careless errors.

▶ **Thinking About Your Reading and Writing**

ACTIVITY H. Test-Taking Tips

1. Which of the tips about taking tests will benefit you?

----

2. What else do you think you can do to improve your test-taking strategies?

Congratulations! If you have been working with the strategies mentioned in this chapter, you have taken control of your reading. You now understand what is necessary for successfully reading academic text, and you have accepted responsibility for monitoring your own comprehension. You can congratulate yourself on a job well done!

CHAPTER SUMMARY

Based on your reading of this chapter, list at least five points that were made that you believe will help you with future reading assignments.

1. _____

_____

_____

_____

2. _____

_____

_____

_____

3. _____

_____

_____

_____

4. _____

_____

_____

_____

5. _____

_____

_____

_____

Now that you have worked with the strategies necessary for taking control of your reading, you can practice applying them to full-length reading selections. Choose (or your instructor may choose) a reading selection that is typical of what you will be expected to read for your other college courses, such as an essay or a textbook chapter. Use this selection to practice:

- Preparing yourself to read
- Staying mentally active while you read
- Taking ownership of ideas in text

Decide the practice strategies you will use. Apply them to your selection. Then in a few paragraphs, write a description of what you did and how the strategies you used worked for you.

Name of material used: _____

Page numbers: _____

Your description:

Chapter 2

Strategic Reading
for Topics
in Academic Text

What's the first thing you do when you turn on your television? Do you start your viewing by switching channels? If you do, you are not alone. You probably want to know the different possibilities on TV and how much they interest you before you make your final choice. Most of us channel-surf our TVs to find the "topic" that is appealing to us. A channel that has few viewers will probably go off the air. Authors, like television producers, must find ways to appeal to their audience. When authors choose topics that are interesting to their readers, their readers "stay tuned" to the text a little longer. Sometimes, though, it is difficult for readers to figure out what the topic is. When this occurs, how can you know if the text will interest you? This chapter will show you some strategies for identifying topics in any type of reading material. You will then be able to make more informed choices about your reading.

WHAT IS THE TOPIC OF A READING SELECTION?

The topic is, essentially, the subject matter the author has chosen to write about. It can be a situation, a feeling, an event, a person, a hobby, a scientific principle, a belief, a particular country, a design element of a piece of art, an exercise routine, a type of plant. Anything. The list is endless. Anything you think about, feel, touch, read about, experience, or hear about can be the topic of a reading selection.

Some topics that college students often read and write about include:

drug abuse

peace

civil rights

abortion

football games

the national debt

relations with foreign countries

AIDS

peer pressure

homelessness

drunk driving

the environment

the death penalty

love

UFOs

race relations

music

What are some topics you might like to read or write about that aren't listed

here? _____

_____

_____

_____

HOW CAN KNOWLEDGE OF THE TOPIC
HELP READERS COMPREHEND?

If you know the topic of something you are preparing to read, it will help you in a number of ways. First, it will help you stay focused. If you remind yourself periodically of the topic while you are reading, you will have little difficulty staying focused; even if your mind wanders, it will be easy for you to get back on track. Second, if you know the topic, you will be better able to see how several ideas in a reading selection are connected. All the important ideas will be saying something about the same topic. This will make it easier for you to pick out important ideas from less important ones. Those ideas that have little relationship to the topic may have been included to add interest to the material or to serve as examples, but they are of less importance than those ideas that have a clear relationship to the topic. When you know the topic, you are also in a better position to make predictions about the content. You may be able to anticipate some of the subtopics, the smaller but related parts of the topic, that will be discussed. Then you can mentally prepare yourself for your reading. Each of these advantages of knowing the topic is explained more fully in the remainder of this chapter.

DISTINGUISHING BETWEEN BROAD TOPICS
AND NARROW TOPICS

Topics can be very broad. To write all there is to write about a single topic might take many pages, even volumes. In such cases, writers not only decide the general topic to discuss, but they also must choose what aspect of the topic to focus on. That is, they must decide how to narrow the topic. For instance, instead of writing a book about myths from all over the world, one might be written that concentrated only on *Native American Myths*. The author writing this book could then further divide this topic into smaller units, or chapters, such as these:

Tales of Human Creation

Tales of World Creation

Tales of the Sun, Moon, and Stars

Monsters and Monster-Slayers

War and the Warrior Code

Tales of Love and Lust

Stories of Animals and People

Ghosts and the Spirit World

As another example, instead of writing a text on all facets of photography, an author might choose to narrow the topic of the book to unique photography tricks. The author might divide this text, titled *Creative Photography,* into the following chapters:

Viewpoints: Wide Angles, Telephotos, and Composition

Color, Grain, and Contrast

Color Effects

Filter Effects

Mixing Images

Adding Color

Photographic Tricks

In the preceding examples, each chapter focuses on a smaller part of the larger topic, but the topic itself has already been narrowed considerably before the writing was begun. The divisions within books are usually called *chapters.* Groups of chapters in textbooks may be clustered into *units* or *parts,* as in Unit 1 or Part 1 of the book. Each unit or part would have a name that shows how the several chapters included within it are related to one another. Divisions within the chapter itself, or within a single article, are usually called *subtopics.*

Even when the topic of a book title sounds very broad, the author narrows the topic by dividing the contents so that there is a particular focus to the book. Not everything about the topic is discussed in the single text. A book titled *American Government,* for instance, is divided into the following chapters. Despite the broad title, the author discusses primarily the *structure* of American government; there is, for example, no chapter with the title "Corruption in American Government," "Women in American Government," or "Government Controls on American Businesses."

Book title:

American Government

Chapters:

1. What Should We Know About American Government?
2. The Constitution
3. Federalism
4. Civil Liberties and Civil Rights
5. Public Opinion and the Media
6. Political Parties and Interest Groups
7. Campaigns and Elections
8. Congress
9. The Presidency
10. The Bureaucracy
11. The Judiciary
12. American Government: Continuity and Change

STRATEGIES TO HELP YOU IDENTIFY TOPICS

Some strategies you can use to help you identify the topic of a reading selection include:

1. Preview the material.
2. Use titles and subtitles to help you determine the scope of the topic.
3. Use your prior knowledge to anticipate topics.
4. Look for repetition.
5. Notice how the major points refer to the topic.
6. Make a mental map that shows the relationship of the sentences to the topic.

We next discuss the process involved for using each of these steps.

Previewing the Material

Recall our discussion of previewing in Chapter 1. Previewing is a particularly useful strategy when you begin a new reading assignment. There are many clues to a topic of a selection that you can look for while you preview, including the title, subtitles, introductory and concluding paragraphs, chapter questions, and visual aids. Previewing a chapter or article for the purpose of identifying the topic should be done at a rapid reading rate. You are not trying to learn the details or even the main idea. Your goal at this point is to be able to answer the question "What is this about?"

Using Titles and Subtitles to Help You Determine the Scope of the Topic

If you are working with a textbook chapter, essay, or magazine article, the title usually indicates the topic. Any subtitles in the text usually indicate the subtopics that are discussed throughout the chapter. If you examine these subtitles, you will be able to identify the more narrow focus of the author's topic. For example, one chapter title from a text on American government might be called "Civil Liberties and Civil Rights." This title is quite broad. Based on it, the chapter could discuss such things as what these terms mean, what the civil rights and liberties of individuals are, how the civil rights and liberties of individuals have changed over time, and landmark cases that have given people civil rights and liberties. The subtitles, listed next, show the specific parts of the topic that will actually be discussed in this chapter. Once you know the title and subtitles, or topic and subtopics, you can identify their connection to each other. Then you are better prepared to do an in-depth reading. This preparation for reading should also be done quickly. Your goal is to be able to answer the question "What about this topic is going to be discussed in this material?" Following the outline is an explanation of the specific relationship between the title and subtitles in this example chapter. The explanation illustrates how you can use your knowledge of the relationship between title and subtitles, or topics and subtopics, to help you predict the contents of the material.

Chapter title:

Civil Liberties and Civil Rights

Subtitles:

Freedom of Expression

Church and State

Crime and Due Process

Equal Protection of the Laws

Explanation of Topic–Subtopic Relationship. Each subtitle mentions one area or aspect of civil liberties or civil rights. We can safely assume that in the "Freedom of Expression" section the author will discuss the connections between civil liberties and civil rights and freely communicating your ideas to others. Most probably the "Church and State" section will discuss such rights as the freedom of religion. The title and subtitle work together and enable us to predict the nature of the contents we will be reading.

This next example is from a magazine article. Here, too, the topic is fairly broad. We know, generally, that the topic is nutrition. Consider, though, how the subtitles help you better understand and prepare for the contents of the article because they direct your attention to particular parts of the topic. The explanation following the outline again describes the relationship between the topic and subtopics, which is what you will want to think about each time you look at a chapter outline.

Article title:

Treat Yourself to Nutrition

Subtitles:

From Scarcity to Plenty

The Food We Eat

Nutrition and Disease

Nutrition at Every Age

Everyday Nutrition

Explanation of Topic–Subtopic Relationship. Since the article is about how you can enjoy nutrition, you can expect that each topic will focus primarily on that. You may not be certain what the first section is about, but the others are pretty clear. The section titled "The Food We Eat" will probably discuss the typical diets we have and may mention their nutritional value (or absence of it). The section on "Nutrition and Disease" will obviously give information about the role good eating plays in staying healthy. By looking for these connections, even before you begin reading in depth, you can have a good idea of the direction the text will take, and you can prepare mentally for the rest of it.

ACTIVITY A. Identifying Topic and Subtopic Relationships

For each list, identify the topic (T) and the subtopics (S). Then, in your own words, explain the relationship between them. These headings are typical of what might appear in a textbook chapter or in an article a professor might assign to you.

List 1

___ Social Strata in Iran   ___ Early Political Parties
___ Ethnic Groups in Iran   ___ Islam in Modern Iran
___ Iran
___ The Problems of Economic
      Development

In your own words, explain the relationship between the topic and subtopics in this list.

List 2

___ Jawless Fishes   ___ Amphibians
___ Vertebrate Evolution   ___ Reptiles
___ Cartilage Fishes   ___ Birds
___ Bony Fishes   ___ Mammals

In your own words, explain the relationship between the topic and subtopics in this list.

List 3

___ The Importance of Memory   ___ Uncommon Memory
___ Aging and Memory   Conditions
___ Memory   ___ Improving Memory
___ Why People Forget

In your own words, explain the relationship between the topic and subtopics in this list.

▶ **Thinking About Your Reading and Writing**

ACTIVITY B. Chapter Subtopics

You have already seen how the chapter on civil liberties was divided for a political science book. What are some subtopics the author might use for the chapter titled "Campaigns and Elections"?

The source from which this chapter is taken actually divides the chapter into the following sections: Political Participation, Historical Voting Patterns, Explaining—and Improving—Turnout, Political Campaigns, The Effects of Campaigns, Opinion and Voting, Election Outcomes, Modern Technology and Political Campaigns, Elections and Money, The Effects of Elections on Policy. Were you able to predict any sections similar to these?

Using Your Prior Knowledge to Anticipate Topics

If you use your prior knowledge to think about a broad topic, it may help you predict ways in which the author might have narrowed it. For instance, if your instructor had told you that you were assigned to read an article on homelessness, you could use your prior knowledge about this topic before you begin your reading to anticipate several ways in which the author might have narrowed the topic. The chart that follows illustrates the thinking process that might have occurred. On the left are things you might already know about homelessness. You might have spent some time using your prior knowledge to consider how each of these ideas could have been developed into a narrower topic. On the right are some narrowed topics that might have occurred to you. Any one of these topics, or any several of them, might actually be the topic of the assigned reading. Once you begin to read, you would be able to verify your predictions.

Topic: Homelessness

What you already know	***Narrowed topics***
It is a big problem. It occurs in most major cities.	Seriousness of the problem

There is not enough low-income
  housing.
There are not enough places for
  the mentally ill to live.
	Causes of the problem

Some of the homeless are drug
  abusers.
Many homeless people have left
  their families.
	Effects of the problem

More cities are building shelters for the homeless.	Solutions to the problem

Thinking about all these issues related to homelessness before you read gives you momentum, or intellectual energy, for reading. Once your mind is charged with information, you are ready to go.

This process is analogous to starting your car on a cold morning. You can press on the gas pedal immediately, in which case you'd probably experience the sluggishness of your car's cold start. You might even have a number of false starts. Or you can leave your car in park and let the engine idle for a while until it warms up. Then, after a few minutes, you can press on the gas and take off to a smooth start. If you warm up to your reading assignments by tapping in to your prior knowledge first, your in-depth reading will go more smoothly.

Looking for Repetition

Even in short reading selections, or those without subtitles or other aids, identifying the topic is fairly easy because the author keeps repeating the idea, person, place, or feeling being discussed. For instance, in the paragraph that follows, notice how many times the author refers to "myotonic dystrophy."

> Myotonic dystrophy, the most common form of muscular dystrophy affecting adults, strikes roughly 1 in every 8,000 persons worldwide. Symptoms of myotonic dystrophy include muscle spasms and wasting, particularly in the head and neck. Whereas mildly affected people may simply have difficulty unclenching a fist, those with more severe forms of myotonic dystrophy cannot walk and have difficulty swallowing. The disorder's other symptoms include cataracts, premature balding, shrunken ovaries or testicles, and mental retardation.

Adapted from *Science News*, Vol. 141, No. 7, p. 103. February 15, 1992.

The same principle of repetition applies to longer selections, too.

Noticing How the Major Points Refer to the Topic

Readers sometimes assume that the first piece of information available to them when they read is, in fact, the topic. They fixate on this one point and ignore the rest of the paragraph or selection. A better approach is to read through the entire selection and then decide on the topic. Think about all the text that you have read. When you do this, you will see that several sentences elaborate on one topic—a single person, place, event, feeling, belief. A number of sentences make reference to it or give more information about it. When you are reading material that is several pages long, you should be able to recognize that the same topic is referred to throughout most paragraphs within the essay.

Making a Mental Map That Shows the Relationship of the Sentences to the Topic

You can make a mental note of the topic you believe is being discussed. Then, as you read, mentally check off each idea to see that it is, in fact, related to the topic you had in mind. The picture in your mind for the paragraph about myotonic dystrophy might look a little like the mental map shown here.

By organizing the information you read in this way, you will see relationships between the topic, subtopics, and other material. Notice that the information on the map is not precisely in the author's words. As you learned in Chapter 1, when you express ideas in your own words, you are

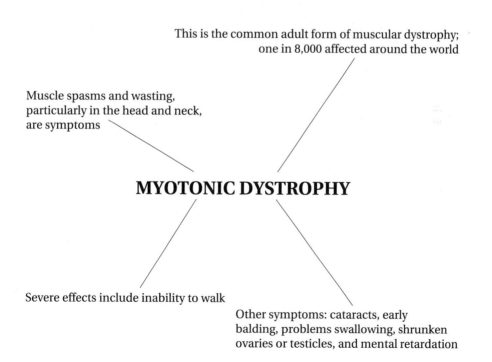

This is the common adult form of muscular dystrophy; one in 8,000 affected around the world

Muscle spasms and wasting, particularly in the head and neck, are symptoms

MYOTONIC DYSTROPHY

Severe effects include inability to walk

Other symptoms: cataracts, early balding, problems swallowing, shrunken ovaries or testicles, and mental retardation

more involved with the text. You are required to think about it a little more and to verify that you understand it. Restating it in your own words and actually creating a map will also help you retain the information longer.

ACTIVITY C. Identifying Topics and Major Points About Topics

Create a map for each of the following paragraphs. Use your own words for your major points.

1. The inability to recognize faces seems to result from damage to the back of the brain. At first, it was thought this was a disability of the right cerebral hemisphere, the right side of the "thinking brain." This made sense because in most people the right hemisphere is particularly good at spatial organization, putting together objects like noses and ears into a recognizable whole. On the other hand, the left hemisphere, which is best at assembling sequential information like language, might be content with a simple list of facial features. However, it now seems that in most cases of *prospagnosia* there are problems on both sides of the brain and that each hemisphere plays a role in face recognition. The right may be good at long-distance identification—knowing that the object on top of that torso forty meters away is a face—with the left taking over when fine close-up detailed analysis is necessary.

Adapted from Ingram, Jay. *The Science of Everyday Life*. New York: Viking, 1989. 121.

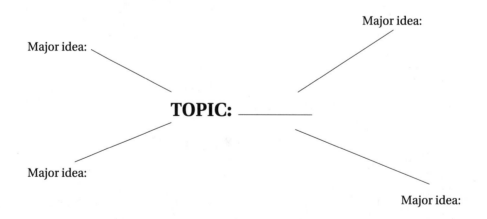

How is your map similar to others' maps? How is it different? Make any changes on your map that you feel would improve it.

2. Creative thinking can result in the discovery of a new or improved solution to a problem. It leads to the birth of new ideas. Another type of thinking, critical thinking, is the examination and testing of suggested solutions to see whether they will work. It tests ideas for flaws and defects. Both types of thinking, critical and creative, are necessary for effective problem solving. But sometimes they are incompatible. Creative thinking can interfere with critical thinking, and vice versa. Their demands on our thought processes are nearly the opposite of each other. To think creatively, we must let our thoughts run free. The more spontaneous the process, the more ideas will be born, and the greater the probability that effective solutions to problems will be found. Critical judgment then selects and refines the best ideas, picking the most effective solution from the available possibilities. Although we must engage in the two types of thinking separately, we need both for efficient problem solving.

Adapted from Lindzey, Gardner, Calvin S. Hall, and Richard F. Thompson. "Creative Thinking and Critical Thinking." *Psychology.* 2nd ed. New York: Worth, 1978.

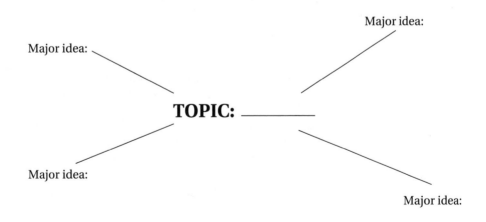

Working Together

How is your map similar to others' maps? How is it different? Make any changes on your map that you feel would improve it.

ACTIVITY D. Recognizing Topics in Paragraphs

Read each of the following paragraphs and identify the topics. Use the strategies suggested so far in this chapter.

1. The relationship between population trends and social change defies any simple analysis. In the Western world, the Industrial Revolution combined with accompanying improvements in agriculture, sanitation, and medicine to lower death rates and thus to increase population growth during the eighteenth and nineteenth centuries. But population growth then combined with other variables to promote new patterns.

    DeFleur, M., W. D'Antonio, and L. DeFleur. *Sociology: Man in Society.* Brief Edition. Glenview, Ill.: Scott, Foresman, and Co., 1972. 180.

    Topic: _____

2. If the government tries to entrap a person into committing a crime, even if the person commits it, he or she will be found not guilty of the crime. Such was the case of John DeLorean, a wealthy car manufacturer. In 1982, DeLorean was arrested on charges of trying to smuggle cocaine. Videotapes were even made showing DeLorean participating in a criminal act. But in DeLorean's case, government agents had set him up; they devised a plan and then got DeLorean to participate in it. Because the government had deliberately tried to get DeLorean on these charges, he became a victim of entrapment. DeLorean was found not guilty.

    Topic: _____

3. According to the stereotype, a typical welfare family consists of a black woman and five or six children. This woman spends her time watching Phil Donahue while awaiting the arrival of her fat check. This picture could not be further from the truth. The average family receiving welfare consists of a thirty-two-year-old white woman and two children. Nationwide, says Levin-Epstein, 13 million individuals (or 5 percent of the U.S. population) receive benefits through the Aid to Families with Dependent Children (AFDC) program, the country's principal welfare system. Nine million of the beneficiaries are children, and at least 3.8 million are women.

    Topic: _____

4. There is an inescapable and persistent element of excitement in the search for the origins of humanity. It affects everyone, professionals and nonprofessionals alike, because there appears to be a universal curiosity about our past, about how a thinking, feeling, cultural being

emerged from a primitive apelike stock. What evolutionary circumstances molded that ancient ape into a tall, upright, highly intelligent
creature who, through technology and determination, has come to
dominate the world? This is the question we ask about ourselves. And
it is not mere idle curiosity because, without doubt, the key to our
future lies in a true understanding of what sort of animal we are.

Adapted from Leakey, R., and R. Lewin. *Origins.* New York: E. P. Dutton, 1977. 8 and 11–12.

Topic: _____

5. In 1968, Arthur Mitchell was at the peak of a successful career as leading dancer with the New York City Ballet. Conscious of the fact that he
was still the company's "token" black dancer and that opportunities for
others of his race in American ballet were limited, Mitchell decided to
devote himself to teaching ballet in Harlem, where he was born, and to
create those opportunities by forming a company of his own. This became the Dance Theatre of Harlem. For Mitchell, the Dance Theatre
came first; its earliest premises were in a garage whose doors were left
open so that passersby could watch and, if they liked, enter and join
in. Starting with thirty students, by the end of the first summer, the
school had 400.

Adapted from Clarke, Mary, and David Vaughan, eds. *The Encyclopedia of Dance and Ballet.*
New York: G. P. Putnam, 1977. 105.

Topic: _____

USING KNOWLEDGE OF TOPICS AND SUBTOPICS
WHILE YOU READ

The way in which an author designs the discussion of a topic might be
referred to as the *plan* or *organization.* The plan, of course, is primarily the
set of decisions the author has made about the overall topic, the subtopics
to include, and the order in which to discuss the subtopics.

If you recognize the author's plan *before reading,* and if you try to keep
this plan in mind *while reading,* you have several advantages over less
skilled readers:

■ You can progress more easily through the selection because you know
what is coming next and how this new information fits into the total
plan. It's like having a map of where you are going in your mind (or in
your hand) before you head in that direction. Imagine how difficult it
would be to drive to your college or home if each time you went there
you had to relearn the route. Your familiarization with it eases your
travel. In the same way, knowledge of the passage you will be taking
with your text can make reading less stressful for you.

- Knowing the author's plan is also advantageous because you are better able to establish your reading rate as soon as you start. You will have some idea of the breadth of information you will be reading, as well as how much information about the topic you bring to the reading task. This, as well as your purpose for reading, will guide your reading rate.

- A knowledge of topics and subtopics at the start of your reading will also enable you to create good questions to use to direct your attention throughout the chapter or article.

- Finally, the skilled reader who knows the author's plan is able to make distinctions between subtopics that are important to remember and those that are not. The subtopics that have a clear relationship to the topic are the most important ones. On occasion, an author will give a separate subtopic heading to an example or illustration of a point being made. This illustration is only to help you understand the major points discussed either before or after the example. You can reduce the amount of material you must try to remember by focusing on those sections, or subtopics, that provide more information than that provided by just an example or illustration.

ACTIVITY E. Composing Questions to Check Comprehension Before and During Reading

Based on what you now know about topics, narrowed topics, and subtopics, what are some questions you could ask yourself before reading and during reading? You should ask questions that you believe would be beneficial; in other words, the answers to your questions should provide enough information to let you know whether you are comprehending what you are reading.

Before reading I could ask:

During reading I could ask:

CHAPTER SUMMARY

Based on your reading of this chapter, list at least five points that were made that you believe will help you with future reading assignments.

1. _____

2. _____

3. _____

4. _____

5. _____

Now that you have worked with the strategies necessary for strategic reading for topics in academic text, you can practice applying them to full-length reading selections. Choose (or your instructor may choose) a reading selection that is typical of what you will be expected to read for your other college courses, such as an essay or a textbook chapter. Use this selection to practice:

■ Composing questions before reading

■ Identifying topics and subtopics

■ Composing questions during reading

Decide the practice strategies you will use. Apply them to your selection. Then in a few paragraphs, write a description of what you did and how the strategies you used worked for you.

Name of material used: _____

Page numbers: _____

Your description:

Chapter 3

Strategic Reading
for Main Ideas

*B*eing able to identify the topic of what you are reading is a good starting point for effective comprehension, but anything you read is *more* than just a topic. For example, you are probably familiar with the play *Romeo and Juliet*. If you were asked what it was about and you replied "the deaths of two young lovers," you would be naming the topic, but think about how much you would be leaving out! Authors have major points they want to make about topics. These major points are often called *main ideas*. In this chapter, you will learn how to identify and restate main ideas in text and how to infer them and create your own main idea sentences when the author doesn't directly state them for you.

Perhaps the most important thing to remember about the main idea is that it is an *idea,* not a single word. It is *at least one sentence that contains a particular point of view or theory.* Most ideas cannot be stated in a single word. Notice, in the list that follows, the difference between the single words (topics) and the statements (main ideas) about the topics.

Single word (topic)	*Statement (main idea)*
Poetry	a. Some English Romantic poetry has remained popular for a long time.
	b. Many different poetic forms can be used to express an idea.
	c. Good poetry is difficult to write.
Washington, D.C.	a. There are some wonderful places to visit in Washington, D.C.
	b. Washington, D.C. has undergone major demographic changes in the last twenty years.
	c. Some residents of Washington, D.C. would like their city to have full status as the fifty-first state.
Holiday shopping	a. People who wait to do their holiday shopping until the last minute can have a difficult time.
	b. For some, shopping during the holidays is depressing.
	c. The kinds of shopping people do during the holidays can be an indication of the state of the economy.
Photography	a. Steiglitz is considered one of the best photographers who ever lived.
	b. Photography can be an expensive hobby.
	c. Doing fashion photography is quite different from taking photos on a trip.

▶ **Thinking About Your Reading and Writing**

ACTIVITY A. Distinguishing Between Topics and Main Ideas

1. What are some differences that you notice between topics and main

   ideas? _____

   _____

2. What does an author have to think about in order to get from the topic to the main idea? _____

_____

_____

_____

PROGRESSING FROM TOPICS TO MAIN IDEAS

If your answer to question 2 in Activity A suggested that an author's thinking has to progress from a broad topic, to a narrowed topic, to the main idea, you are correct. You learned in Chapter 2 that a broad topic is narrowed when the author selects the part of the topic to discuss. Once that choice is made, the author needs to determine the major or key point to make about that narrowed topic. The result is the main idea.

If you are able to identify the narrowed topic, you have the starting point for figuring out the author's main idea. This holds no matter what type of material you are reading. To further clarify the relationship between broad topic, narrowed topic, and main idea, let's look at this process from the reader's rather than the author's perspective.

Suppose you read an article whose main idea was Roseanne Barr's childhood was a difficult one. If someone asked you what you had read about and you said, "Roseanne Barr," you would have stated only the *topic.* If you said "Roseanne Barr's childhood," you would have stated the *narrowed topic* and given more information.

But if you went a step further and said you had read about "some of the difficulties Roseanne Barr had when she was growing up," your listener would have a much more accurate picture. You would have been very close to stating the *main idea* of the selection.

Here are two more examples of how broad topics are narrowed, followed by a particular statement about the narrowed topic—that is, the main idea.

Broad topic: Sports

Narrowed topic: Championship sports events

Author's statement about the narrowed topic (main idea): Cable television companies benefit considerably from pay-per-view championship sports events.

Broad topic: Commuting to work

Narrowed topic: Car pools and commuting to work

Author's statement about the narrowed topic (main idea): Companies that arrange car pools for their employees have made it easier for people to commute to work.

ACTIVITY B. Identifying Topics of Main Idea Sentences

A number of sentences that represent main ideas from academic text follow. For each, indicate the broad topic and narrowed topic for the sentence. Then suggest another narrowed topic related to the broad topic that you think would be interesting to read or write about.

Example:

Main idea: Most economists agree that it will take a long time for the recession to end.

Broad topic: the recession

Narrowed topic: when the recession will end

Your suggested narrowed topic: hardships the recession has caused

1. **Main idea:** *Some experts agree that drinking one glass of red wine each day can be beneficial to your health.*

   Broad topic: _____

   Narrowed topic: _____

   Your suggested narrowed topic: _____

2. **Main idea:** *There are many useful strategies for building one's everyday vocabulary.*

   Broad topic: _____

   Narrowed topic: _____

   Your suggested narrowed topic: _____

3. **Main idea:** *Much of the fear of leprosy results from greatly exaggerated accounts handed down years ago, and authentic modern cases are few.*

   Broad topic: _____

   Narrowed topic: _____

Your suggested narrowed topic: _____

4. ***Main idea:*** *The gap between the presidential candidates appeared to widen just before the election.*

   Broad topic: _____

   Narrowed topic: _____

   Your suggested narrowed topic: _____

5. ***Main idea:*** *Violent crime in American cities has increased significantly in the past decade.*

   Broad topic: _____

   Narrowed topic: _____

   Your suggested narrowed topic: _____

6. ***Main idea:*** *Genes are located in particular positions on chromosomes.*

   Broad topic: _____

   Narrowed topic: _____

   Your suggested narrowed topic: _____

7. ***Main idea:*** *Once the chronology of the start of the Vietnam War was made known, many thought there could have been a way, besides war, to resolve the internal political struggles of the country.*

   Broad topic: _____

   Narrowed topic: _____

   Your suggested narrowed topic: _____

8. ***Main idea:*** *Recent investigations into domestic violence have increased the willingness of husbands and wives to file charges against each other.*

   Broad topic: _____

   Narrowed topic: _____

   Your suggested narrowed topic: _____

Working Together

With a partner, create main idea sentences for two of the narrowed topics you have suggested in Activity B. Verify that your sentences state your idea or viewpoint about your narrowed topic.

ACTIVITY C. Summing It Up

In a sentence or two, explain what you have learned about the relationship between narrowed topics and main ideas.

PURPOSES FOR CREATING MAIN IDEA SENTENCES

In Chapters 1 and 2, you learned about the importance of putting the author's complicated sentences into your own language. This strategy also applies to main ideas. Main ideas that are directly stated in the material you are reading are sometimes worded in ways that are quite formal. This can make remembering the ideas difficult. By restating the main ideas in your own words, you are more likely to retain the information, partly because the language is your own and partly because creating a new sentence requires that you think about the meaning of the original statement of the main idea. The following example shows how a main idea can be simplified:

Original main idea:

Many young adolescents would like to quickly bypass their teen years in order to gain entry into adulthood and many of its benefits.

Student's reworded version:

Many teens are in a great hurry to grow up and to gain the benefits of adult life.

Creating your own main idea sentences will be important in other academic reading situations, including:

■ *Reading situations where the main idea is not stated.* Writers frequently state their main ideas in a sentence, sometimes referred to as a *topic sentence.* These often appear as the first or second sentence of a paragraph, but they may be located elsewhere. Sometimes, however, the main idea is not stated at all. When there is no main idea sentence, you will need to create one to be sure you are able to explain how the details in the selection are related to one another. The process you use to create a main idea sentence gives you a chance to verify that you understand what you are reading.

- *Reading situations in which several paragraphs relate to a single main idea.* In these cases, even if the main idea is stated, it will probably appear in only one of the related paragraphs. The other paragraphs may provide illustrations or descriptions to support the main idea. In this situation, you should first try to create a main idea sentence on your own. Then reread the material to see whether a sentence in the text actually states the main idea. If there is such a sentence, and if it has the same meaning as your own sentence, you have verified your comprehension.

- *Reading situations where your goal is to comprehend a lengthy essay or article.* In this type of situation, the author may have several main ideas, all of which are tied together by a single *thesis*, or controlling idea. The *thesis statement*, like the main idea, consists of a particular slant, angle, or point of view about the narrowed topic. In fact, thesis statements sound much like main ideas. But the author may discuss the thesis over a number of pages, and it may be developed through a discussion of several main ideas with supporting details for each. In such cases, you will need to look at the entire array of main ideas in the article to see how they are related to one another; then you will need to create your own thesis statement if the author hasn't directly stated one.

THE PROCESS FOR CREATING MAIN IDEA SENTENCES

The process for creating main idea sentences is not complicated. To create a main idea sentence:

1. Identify the narrowed topic.
2. Decide what is the most important thing the author wants to tell you about that narrowed topic.
3. Create a sentence that describes the most important thing the author wants to tell you about that narrowed topic.

You've already practiced the first step in several of the previous exercises. Just keep in mind that identifying the narrowed topic is a critical part of creating main ideas.

How do you figure out what is most important? Think back to the paragraph maps you created in Chapter 2, in which you had to pull out all the key ideas that related to a single topic. You may have noticed that these key ideas shared a common relationship to the topic. The paragraph that follows also contains several important ideas, all related to a single topic.

A paragraph map then illustrates the relationship. Study the map, and then read the explanation beneath it, which describes the connection between the ideas.

> A unique advantage of small businesses is that they develop people as well as goods and services. Their freer, less specialized environment enables employees to strive for more balanced, well-rounded development than they could hope for in larger firms. People in small firms have to be more versatile, and they have a greater variety of work activities than they would if they were working in specialized jobs in larger companies. Instead of just being cogs in the corporate machine, employees have greater freedom to learn by making decisions and living with the results. This freedom, in turn, lends zest and interest to work, trains people to become better leaders, and encourages more effective use of individual talents and energies.
>
> —Adapted from Megginson, L. C. *Business*. Lexington, Mass.: D. C. Heath, 1984. 97.

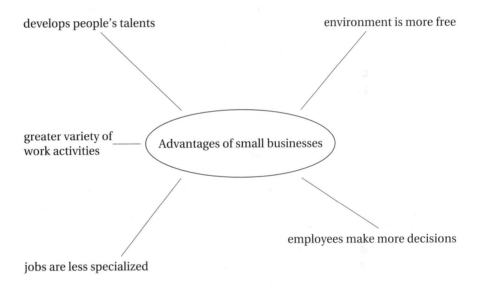

Look at the map and ask yourself, How are these ideas connected? What do they have in common? They obviously have the topic advantages of small businesses in common, but the author could have gone in several different directions with this topic. For instance, the author could have discussed the economic aspect of this topic by describing some of the profit benefits that small businesses have; the author could have focused on the interpersonal relationship advantages that result for people who work in small businesses; or the author could have emphasized the advantages to consumers when they patronize small businesses. Instead, the author has chosen to discuss the advantages of small businesses to the employees. The first sentence of the paragraph states this main idea, along with some additional information. The sentence reads, "A unique advantage of small businesses is that they develop people as well as goods and services." The latter part of this sentence is not necessary to the main idea. "Goods and services" are not discussed in the paragraph, only the development of people. For this reason, then, you might slightly alter the sentence to create your own main idea sentence.

You are now ready to create a main idea sentence. We will use a "main idea starter" to help you with this. Notice that the starter is a partial sentence that you will complete.

Main idea starter:

What the author really wants me to understand about the narrowed topic is that _____.

For our example paragraph, your main idea starter might read this way: *What the author really wants me to understand about the narrowed topic is that* small businesses offer many advantages to their employees. This sentence works as the main idea. In fact, if you put this sentence, instead of the topic that is now there, at the center of the map, you would see that it connects to all the other sentences; it ties them together, as this map illustrates.

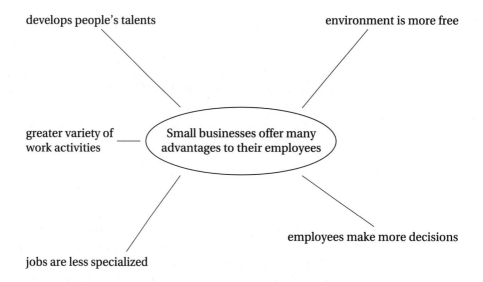

OTHER CONSIDERATIONS FOR CREATING MAIN IDEA SENTENCES

■ Your main idea sentence must contain both the topic and the statement the author is making about the topic. This requires that you keep an open mind when you read. If the author's main idea is unusual, or if it differs significantly from your own views, keeping an open mind might be difficult. Your prior knowledge should be used to help you understand the material. And your viewpoints, whether they agree or disagree with the author's, can help you evaluate the author's ideas. But a major goal for readers of academic text is to learn the information, ideas, and viewpoints presented by the author. At least initially, you will need to set aside your own attitudes and concentrate on determining those of the author.

■ Since a main idea is an *idea* about the narrowed topic, and since ideas are complete thoughts, your main idea sentence must be a *complete* sentence. Your main idea sentence, including the starter portion, should read as a complete sentence. A complete sentence should result when you fill in the space that follows the main idea starter: What the author really wants me to understand about the narrowed topic is that:

-- .

This will work only if what you write following the main idea starter fits grammatically with the starter. When you read the entire sentence aloud, including the starter, it must flow naturally, as though you were speaking it. It must sound grammatical. If you begin your completion with a question word (how, what, why, and the like), you will not have a complete sentence.

Example:

The author wants me to understand that *growing numbers of wealthy Americans are choosing to put their money into foreign investments.*

(Not: The author wants me to understand that *how growing numbers of wealthy Americans are choosing to put their money into foreign investments.*)

Remember that whatever you write on the line should be able to serve as a sentence by itself. Using the starter will help you avoid fragments and incomplete sentences.

In summary, to identify main ideas and create main idea sentences:

1. Identify the broad topic being discussed.
2. Identify the narrowed topic being discussed.
3. Decide what is the most important thing the author wants to tell you about that narrowed topic.
4. Complete the main idea starter: What the author really wants me to understand about the selected aspect of the topic is that:

-- .

ACTIVITY D. Main Ideas in Longer Selections

Finding main ideas is more complicated in longer reading selections than shorter ones. Why do you think this is so?

_____

_____

_____

_____

_____

In your answer, you may have correctly noted that longer reading material often has several main ideas. Or you may have said that sometimes the main idea is not stated, so it must be inferred. (Remember, the main idea might not be stated in shorter essays, either.) Finally, you may have suggested that in the longer essays there could be several main ideas, all or most of which are related to a single thesis. For all these reasons, it is sometimes more difficult to identify main ideas in longer selections. On the other hand, readers are given more information in longer selections than in shorter ones, and this extra information gives you more material to use to verify your thinking about the main ideas.

ACTIVITY E. Creating Main Idea Sentences

For each of the following paragraphs, identify the broad topic and the narrowed topic. Then create a main idea sentence for each paragraph.

1. For some time now, the federal government has tried to reduce the federal deficit. The effect of this on state and local governments has been tremendous. Monies previously provided to the states and cities were reduced, yet most of these governments were legally required to balance their budgets. The result was that many people lost their jobs because of budget cuts, services in the states and cities were reduced, and, in many cases, taxes went up.

   Broad topic: _____

   Narrowed topic: _____

   Main idea sentence: _____

   _____

   _____

2. Chinese immigration began in the midnineteenth century, following the news of a California gold rush. Chinese men also came as miners and were imported as cheap labor for building the transcontinental railroad. Initially unable to bring their wives, they formed an almost exclusively male society; many took advantage of this situation to establish such small businesses as laundries and restaurants. The Chinese soon became the object of prejudice and discrimination. It was felt that by accepting low wages they were competing unfairly with white laborers; their success as small businessmen was also resented. Following several incidents of lynchings and other violence directed against them, the government passed legislation in 1882 to restrict their immigration. These restrictions were not lifted until 1952 and 1965.

Broad topic: _____

Narrowed topic: _____

Main idea sentence: _____

_____

_____

3. Harry Harlow (1971) studied rhesus monkeys to test the effect of lack of normal mothering. Infant monkeys were reared in an apparatus where a "wire" mother (a wire mesh arrangement with a simulated head on top) *provided food* (in a bottle in the mesh), and a warm, terrycloth mother *provided nothing* except "her" presence. The infant monkeys spent the great bulk of their time with the terrycloth mother, going only to the wire mother to eat. They would venture away from the terrycloth mother, but would scamper back when startled. Harlow concluded that contact comfort was more important to the infants more of the time than was feeding. Stimuli associated with feeding (the wire mother) were less attractive than the comforting contact stimulation from the terrycloth mother. This runs contrary to theories that stress that infants become attached to those who satisfy their hunger–thirst–pain needs.

Adapted from Beck, Robert C. *Applying Psychology: Understanding People.* 2nd ed. Englewood Cliffs, N.J.: Prentice-Hall, 1986. 123.

Broad topic: _____

Narrowed topic: _____

Main idea sentence: _____

_____

_____

4. We might say that a person is *in* the market for an automobile or a stereo, which is *on* the market. Or a person might invest *in* the stock market. In some parts of the country, one goes to the market for groceries. In general, though, a market is people (including governments and institutions) who have the necessary authority, purchasing power, and willingness to buy a good or service. For instance, fifteen-year-olds may have the wherewithal and willingness to buy alcohol but not the authority to buy it. Many people may have the authority and funds to buy elephants but aren't willing to. In neither of these cases is the group a real market.

Adapted from Megginson, L. C., et al. *Business.* Lexington, Mass.: D. C. Heath, 1984. 323.

Broad topic: _____

Narrowed topic: _____

Main idea sentence: _____

_____

_____

5. An increasing number of economists have suggested that all necessities should be exempted from excise and general retail sales taxes. In their view, the loss resulting from this exemption can be regained by substantially raising taxes on luxuries. Following this suggestion would allow excise and general retail sales taxes to conform to the ability-to-pay principle. The difficulty with such a procedure lies in determining what constitutes necessities and what constitutes luxuries. People with low incomes spend a greater percentage of their income on tobacco, for instance, than people in the upper levels of income do. What would be the problem with exempting clothing? Although there may be some items that everyone considers luxuries, such as expensive jewelry, furs, and limousines, the amount of revenue yielded by a tax on these items would be too small to meet the needs of government.

Adapted from Gordon, Sanford D., and George G. Dawson. *Introductory Economics.* 7th ed. Lexington, Mass.: D. C. Heath, 1991. 260.

Broad topic: _____

Narrowed topic: --

Main idea sentence: --

----

6. Have you ever examined your paper money closely? See if you can locate a $5, $10, or $20 bill printed before 1964 and marked "Federal Reserve Note" over the portrait. In the upper-left portion above the seal, a statement written in fine print says that the note is "legal tender" and that it "is redeemable in lawful money at the United States Treasury, or at any Federal Reserve Bank." Does this mean that the bill is *not* lawful? At the bottom center, the same bill says "Will pay to the bearer on demand X dollars." Does this mean that the dollar bill amount designated on the bill is *not* X dollars?

Gordon, Sanford D., and George G. Dawson. *Introductory Economics.* 7th ed. Lexington, Mass.: D. C. Heath, 1991. 354.

Broad topic: --

Narrowed topic: --

Main idea sentence: --

----

7. In 1843, James Nesmith traded guns twice in one day. A horse he had purchased en route from a Snake Indian he subsequently exchanged with a Chinook brave for a canoe. William Chamberlain's 1849 trading activity was considerably more energetic. After beginning by exchanging tents with a Fort Kearny soldier and trading his lantern for butter with some Mormon travelers, he got down to serious swapping at Fort Laramie by exchanging his mules with a Cincinnati emigrant. Three days later, he traded his new mule for a pony; two weeks later at the Green River, he swapped the pony for a mule with a French trader (paying $10 extra); four days later, "Peg-leg" Smith, another trader, got the mule and $20 in exchange for an Indian pony. A month later, Chamberlain was once again riding a mule.

Broad topic: --

Narrowed topic: --

Main idea sentence: _____

_____

_____

8. The art of the West is usually divided into "fine" and "applied" arts. In the first category are painting, sculpture, and architecture—the arts usually studied in the humanities. The second category includes more utilitarian objects such as furniture, ceramics, textiles, and clothing. These divisions do not, however, exist in African art. For the African artists, the objects of everyday life may express beauty, harmony, and philosophical concepts as much as or more than something to hang on a wall. The museum or the gallery does not exist in traditional Africa. Although some Western and African arts are "useful" in the same way—a place for kings, temples, objects for religious ceremonies—it must be kept in mind that all African art is in some way integrated into the life of the community. At the same time, even the most humble object may manifest a complex relationship between people and society and their experiences and understanding of the world.

From Witt, Mary Ann Frese, et al. *The Humanities.* Vol. 1, 3rd ed. Lexington, Mass.: D. C. Heath, 1985. 468.

Broad topic: _____

Narrowed topic: _____

Main idea sentence: _____

_____

_____

9. Once you stop thinking about the energy your refrigerator uses, think about its impact on the ozone layer. Chlorofluorocarbons (CFCs), the compounds that eat away the earth's protective ozone shield (and cause about 20 percent of the greenhouse effect) make up the refrigerant that cools both your refrigerator and freezer. CFCs are also used to manufacture the foam insulation in the refrigerator. Unfortunately, all refrigerators on the market today contain CFCs, so for the moment, the best you can do to control their release into the atmosphere is to keep your unit in top working order until CFC-free models become available (which should be within the next five years). If your refrigerator does wear out, try to find a salvager (identified through your local utility or telephone book) who can both cart the appliance out of your house and recover and recycle the CFCs prior to dismantling the refrigerator.

Broad topic: _____

Narrowed topic: _____

Main idea sentence: _____

_____

_____

10. There was no record of eruptive activity on Tristan da Cunha during historic time, so it was not on the list of active volcanoes. Then in the summer of 1961, some mild earthquakes began shaking in the village. By mid-September they had become more severe. The people began keeping track of them. In one five-day period, they counted eighty-nine shocks. They also found that the shocks seemed to be localized near the settlement. At the same time, they began to notice other effects. Doors jammed tight and then were released. Walls cracked, then closed. Cracks appeared in the ground, grew bigger, and then closed. Some of the ground cracks were within 600 feet of the nearest house. One crack was rather startling: on one side the ground remained stationary while on the other, it lifted more than ten feet, creating a cliff. The villagers thought some enormous pressure must be forcing up the ground. They were right.

Leet, L. Dan, and Florence Leet. *Earthquake: Discoveries in Seismology.* New York: Dell, 1964. 111.

Broad topic: _____

Narrowed topic: _____

Main idea sentence: _____

_____

_____

ACTIVITY F. Creating Main Idea Maps for Paragraphs

Either on your own or with a small group, select two paragraphs from those in Activity E, and create a map that shows the relationship between the main idea and several other sentences in the paragraph. To recall how this is done, refer to earlier models in this chapter. If you work with a group, you will first need to reach agreement on the main idea sentence for each of the two paragraphs you choose. You may also see that you need to revise your Broad and Narrow topics.

1. Paragraph no. _____

Map

2. Paragraph no. _____

Map

With a partner, discuss the following chart. What do you think it shows?
Write your response in the space beneath the chart.   ●

Broad topic	*Narrowed topic*	*Main idea*
1. AIDS	1. Prevention	1. People are not practicing safe sex.
2. AIDS	2. Research	2. The money being spent on AIDS research is inadequate.
3. AIDS	3. Epidemic	3. AIDS has become an international problem.

TESTING YOUR MAIN IDEA SENTENCES

At this point, it is useful to know how to verify that the main idea sentence
you created is, in fact, really the main idea of the selection. Making maps,
either written or mental, such as you did in Activity F, is a good starting
point. But there is even more you can do to make sure your sentence is
*a statement of the most important thing the author wants to tell you about
the narrowed topic.* You can test your sentence in this way:

1. Determine what questions are raised by your main idea sentence.
2. Determine whether most of the reading selection's details provide answers to those questions.

A main idea sentence must be fairly general for it to cause the reader
to ask questions. A sentence such as "It is 93 million miles to the moon"
does not generate many questions. It is too specific. On the other hand, a
sentence such as "Scientists have learned much about the relationship of
the moon to earth" is much broader. It generates questions in the reader's
mind such as "What is the relationship?" and "What have scientists
learned?" Your ability to distinguish between general and specific statements obviously plays a major role in the quality of the main idea sentences
you create.

ACTIVITY G. Distinguishing Between General and Specific Sentences

For each pair of sentences, indicate which is general (G), because it raises
questions, and which is specific (S), because it provides at least a partial
answer to a question raised by the other sentence.

1. A reduction in the military budget was one of the items that was under serious consideration. _____
At a meeting in the White House, the president's top national security advisers considered alternative options for reducing the deficit. _____

2. The report said there was substantial evidence that peer pressure can cause students to do better in school than they would do without such pressure. _____
Friends can influence us both negatively and positively. _____

3. The college was trying to find a remedy for the shortage in student housing. _____
A twelve-story student housing complex was being built in the downtown area. _____

4. Just as there are cycles in style, there are cycles in literature. _____
During the last few decades, the exposé story has been popular. _____

5. Most of the advances in electronics, including the ever-smaller chips and faster computers, have been made possible by a process called *photolithography*. _____
The intricate electronic circuit designs on microchips are etched by light passing through a stencil-like mask cut into the shape of the circuit. _____

6. Having been abandoned by his mate shortly after the laying of their egg, the male emperor chick sits on the egg for two beak-chilling months, huddled together with other forlorn males against the shrieking Antarctic winds. _____
Nature is not kind to the male emperor penguin. _____

7. How are the young to learn what work is like in offices, factories, or hospitals? _____
The separation of the young from the adult world, though necessary to a degree in industrial societies, does limit our children to some extent. _____

8. There are many factors that will influence the direction of cancer research in the future. _____
Presently, there is criticism that preferential funding consideration is given to research that addresses cancers most common in males and particular ethnic groups. _____

9. Japanese economists were voicing pessimism about their country's prospects for economic recovery this year. _____
Fifty-one percent of the heads of Japan's one hundred largest corporations predict that land prices, already down 30 percent in some areas from the previous year, will continue to fall. _____

10. The act of writing helps people understand things better. _____
If you are a student of history, and you write about historical theories,

data, issues, and problems, you will begin to sort out those theories, data, issues, and problems more clearly. _____

The second step for testing your main idea sentences is to determine whether most of the details of the reading selection provide answers to the questions raised by your sentence. In the next paragraph, the main idea has been underlined. See what questions it brings to mind.

> Like condominiums and cooperatives, mobile homes have become more popular as single family homes have risen in price. However, <u>there are certain drawbacks to mobile home ownership</u>. First, mobile homes are financed more like cars than houses. Mobile home loans are typically for a shorter period than are home mortgages, and buyers are usually charged a higher rate of interest. Second, after buying a mobile home, the owner must find someplace to put it. This is sometimes a problem because many cities restrict the areas where mobile homes may be located. Finally, because some mobile homes are poorly constructed, buyers should carefully check out the dealer's reputation for service and the warranty that accompanies the mobile home.

This main idea sentence raises several questions, including "What are mobile homes?" and "What are the drawbacks to mobile homes?" In the main idea map for this paragraph, note that the phrases connected directly to the main idea answer the second question. They are major details that support the main idea. This map verifies that the main idea has been correctly identified. Also included on the map are some minor details that elaborate on the major details. In Chapter 5, you will learn more about details as well as some other mapping formats.

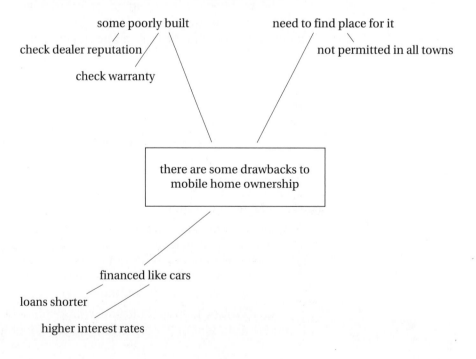

The same process for verifying stated main ideas can be applied to main idea sentences you infer or create. In the following paragraph, there is no main idea sentence. One that has been inferred and then created by the reader has been written beneath the paragraph. In the space provided, write the questions that this main idea sentence brings to your mind. Then look at the supporting sentences in the paragraph. Ask yourself whether they answer most of the questions generated by the main idea sentence.

Many retailers use hand-held tag readers that enter sales information into the register automatically. Some firms are using newer systems that can use the data entered to update inventory and automatically print out purchase orders when new merchandise is needed. Large supermarkets use laser scanners to read the universal product codes printed on almost all grocery items. The sales tape prints out for the customer the items that were actually bought. Simultaneously, the data entered in the computer system help management analyze which products are selling well. Some of the latest systems are even saying "Thank you for shopping with us."

Main idea sentence:

Many retailers are using computer-based sales registers.

Questions (based on main idea sentence): _

_ _

_ _

_ _

Answers to your questions provided by this paragraph: _ _ _ _ _ _ _ _ _ _

_ _

_ _

Working Together

Compare your questions with those of a partner. Are they similar? Refer to the paragraph to see whether each of your questions was answered. ●

What about the main idea sentences you created in Activity E? Do they raise questions? Are the questions answered by the details in the passage? To test some of your own main idea sentences, complete Activity H.

ACTIVITY H. Testing Your Main Idea Sentences

Return to Activity E, in which you created some original main idea sentences. Select four of your main idea sentences. Then, in the spaces provided, (1) indicate the paragraph you are using; (2) write the main idea sentence you created for that paragraph; (3) write the questions raised by your sentence; (4) write at least two details from the passage that provide answers to your sentence; and (5) if your main idea sentence does not meet the test, revise your sentence, repeating steps (1), (2), and (3).

1. Paragraph being used _____
   Your original main idea sentence for that paragraph.

   Questions raised by your main idea sentence.

   Answers to your questions provided by the paragraph.

   Do you need to revise your main idea sentence? Yes _____ No _____
   (If you answered yes, return to the paragraph and create a new one. Then repeat the preceding steps.)

2. Paragraph being used _____
   Your original main idea sentence for that paragraph.

   Questions raised by your main idea sentence.

   Answers to your questions provided by the paragraph.

_____

_____

_____

Do you need to revise your main idea sentence? Yes _____ No _____
(If you answered yes, return to the paragraph and create a new one.
Then repeat the preceding steps.)

3. Paragraph being used _____
   Your original main idea sentence for that paragraph.

_____

_____

Questions raised by your main idea sentence.

_____

_____

Answers to your questions provided by the paragraph.

_____

_____

_____

Do you need to revise your main idea sentence? Yes _____ No _____
(If you answered yes, return to the paragraph and create a new one.
Then repeat the preceding steps.)

4. Paragraph being used _____
   Your original main idea sentence for that paragraph.

_____

_____

Questions raised by your main idea sentence.

_____

_____

Answers to your questions provided by the paragraph.

Do you need to revise your main idea sentence? Yes _____ No _____
(If you answered yes, return to the paragraph and create a new one.
Then repeat the preceding steps.)

▶ **Thinking About Your Reading and Writing**

ACTIVITY I. Main Ideas to Raise Questions

In your own words, explain the reasons your main idea sentence should be
one that raises questions.

Based on your reading of this chapter, list at least five points that were made that you believe will help you with future reading assignments.

1. _____

_____

_____

_____

2. _____

_____

_____

_____

3. _____

_____

_____

_____

4. _____

_____

_____

_____

5. _____

_____

_____

_____

Now that you have worked with the strategies necessary for strategic reading for main ideas, you can practice applying them to full-length reading selections. Choose (or your instructor may choose) a reading selection that is typical of what you will be expected to read for your other college courses, such as an essay or a textbook chapter. Use this selection to practice:

■ Identifying main ideas
■ Creating main ideas
■ Mapping main ideas

Decide the practice strategies you will use. Apply them to your selection. Then in a few paragraphs, write a description of what you did and how the strategies you used worked for you.

Name of material used: _____

Page numbers: _____

Your description:

Chapter 4

Understanding Organizational Patterns in Academic Text

*H*ow would a song sound if it had no structure? Would there be a recognizable beginning, middle, or end? What would hold the piece together? How would the rhythm of one part connect to the next? As they write music, composers consider each section of their musical composition and how it contributes to the total effect desired. Certain patterns for organizing music are associated with classical music, others with jazz, rap, and so on. These patterns give the musical score cohesiveness, or unity. The parts fit together to create a well-coordinated whole. Writers of prose also need organizational patterns so that the various sections of their text fit together in a way that makes sense or so that there is cohesiveness. Such a plan is often referred to as the *writer's organization*. In this chapter, you will learn how writers achieve organization and how this contributes to their overall success in conveying a message.

HOW DO WRITERS USE ORGANIZATIONAL PATTERNS?

Organizational patterns are extremely beneficial to writers. They provide the framework for connecting the main idea and details of an essay. They help writers assist readers in understanding the development of ideas, stay on target and avoid digressions from the main point, and provide variety in their writing and maintain audience interest. Writers can choose from a number of ways to organize their ideas. There are six common organizational patterns:

1. Simple listing
2. Definition and explanation
3. Comparison and contrast
4. Thesis and proof or opinion and reason
5. Cause and effect
6. Problem and solution

ACTIVITY A. Recognizing What You Already Know About Patterns

In this exercise list the pattern(s) with which you are familiar. For each one you list, indicate what you know about it or in what kinds of writing situations it might be useful. Also note any signal words you can recall that are associated with the particular pattern. Don't worry if you can't do too much with this activity. We will explain each pattern in this chapter.

1. Pattern I know: _____

   What I know about it: _____

   _____

   Signal words I know for this pattern: _____

   _____

2. Pattern I know: _____

   What I know about it: _____

   _____

   Signal words I know for this pattern: _____

   _____

3. Pattern I know: _____

   What I know about it: _____

   _____

   Signal words I know for this pattern: _____

   _____

Knowledge of patterns of organization also offers benefits to readers. If *before* and *during* your reading, you search for the organizational structure, you may be able to:

- Follow the development of an author's ideas
- Stay focused on the main ideas
- Make predictions about what might be the next topic of discussion or next set of details
- See relationships between details
- Remember information (using the pattern as the organizing structure for memory)

▶ **Thinking About Your Reading and Writing**

ACTIVITY B. Recognizing the Benefits of Patterns

Which of the benefits listed do you think will be particularly useful to you?

_____

_____

_____

_____

_____

HOW MANY PATTERNS CAN BE USED IN A SINGLE ESSAY?

A single essay may be structured around a single pattern, such as thesis and proof or comparison and contrast. But within such an essay, individual paragraphs may have their own patterns or arrangements of details. Sometimes a single paragraph may contain several patterns. As you will learn later in this chapter, the author's purpose for writing, along with the main idea or thesis to be developed through the essay, plays a key role in determining what patterns, and how many patterns, he or she will use.

The patterns discussed in this chapter are used more frequently in expository writing (such as essays or informative writing like textbooks) than in narrative writing (such as plays, novels, short stories, and poems). Narrative writing most often uses other mechanisms, such as dialogue and plot, for creating cohesiveness.

HOW CAN PATTERNS BE IDENTIFIED?

In the following sections, we offer a more detailed explanation of each pattern, including discussion of the *signal words* that are often associated with each pattern, sample sentences that suggest the pattern the author will probably use, and example paragraphs. A signal word does not need to be used every time a new pattern begins. However, you should be alert to these words because they will enable you to predict the way the material will be organized and to follow the author's thinking while you read.

Simple Listing

In this pattern, a number of details are given in list order. The list may be written in order of importance, chronologically, spatially, or enumerated in no particular order.

Signal Words for Simple Listing

Order of importance: Most important, less important, least important

Chronological: First, second, and so on; next, then, today, yesterday, finally; 1991, 1992, and so on; after, before, previously, once, meanwhile

Spatial: To the right, to the left, on top, inside

Enumeration: Also, in addition, further, another, furthermore, moreover, besides, a number of, several

Examples of Sentences That Suggest a Simple Listing Pattern

1. You should follow some major safety rules when you ride a bike in the street. *You would expect a listing of the rules, perhaps in order of importance.*

2. Over the last five years, New Jersey taxpayers have expressed increasing dissatisfaction with the state government. *You would expect a listing of the dissatisfactions, perhaps in chronological order.*

3. You should take several steps when you are planning to apply for a job in a new field. *You would expect a listing of the steps, perhaps in order of importance or chronological order.*

With a partner, write one sentence that you believe could suggest a simple listing paragraph. ●

Sample paragraph: simple listing pattern (chronological) (with signal words underlined)

Several days before every press conference, members of the president's staff compile a list of every conceivable question that might be asked. They then formulate a well-worded response to each one. The president studies the answers carefully, committing the content and sometimes the exact language to memory. This enables him to appear informed and concerned about all issues. When he finally meets the press, he is well-armed for even the most hostile reporter.

Sample paragraph: simple listing pattern (order of importance) (with signal words underlined)

Since the 1970s, some interesting studies have been done on the treatment of girls in the classroom. Perhaps the most important finding is that stereotypes about girls influenced teacher expectations with regard to acceptable classroom behavior and academic performance. Girls were expected to be "ladylike" and to "control themselves." Aggressive behavior by girls was discouraged. Also significant were the findings concerning specific subject areas. Teachers have had the general attitude that girls are likely to "love" reading and to "hate" mathematics and science. Girls were not expected to think logically or to understand scientific principles. It was also noted in many studies that if there were student-organized activities, boys were typically in charge, with girls assisting, perhaps in the stereotyped role of secretary. Today's educators have worked hard to eliminate these sex biases in the classroom.

Definition and Explanation

This pattern is used to define a new term or concept, or to explain or describe a topic, idea, or process that the author thinks may be unclear to the reader. An entire paragraph may be written in this pattern. The definition may be straightforward and may sound almost like a dictionary entry. Or the definition may include *classification* of the unknown term or concept. For instance, an author might define the musical style of a new group by defining the type of music it plays, such as *rap* or *alternative*. Or an animal may be defined by such classifications as its *phylum, genus,* and *species.* Readers are often able to understand a new term or concept by associating it with one they already know when the classification is given.

This pattern also refers to paragraphs of elaborate explanation, such as an explanation of how personal computers work or how to use a high-speed drill.

Signal Words for Definition and Explanation. This is, for example, in other words, such as, for instance, which means.

Examples of Sentences That Suggest a Definition and Explanation Pattern

1. Someday the VTOL may be seen as commonly in the average American's driveway as the automobile is today. *You would expect a definition of VTOL. Then you would expect to learn why it might become so common.*

2. Before the breakup of the Soviet Union, *perestroika* was thought to be the answer to that nation's economic problems. *You would expect a definition of* perestroika. *Then you would expect to learn why this was thought to be the answer to the economic problems.*

3. It is not difficult to use a single-lens reflex camera. *You would expect a definition of single-lens reflex camera. Then you would hope for an explanation of how to use it, perhaps in a chronological, spatial, or order-of-importance listing pattern.*

Working Together

With a partner, write one sentence that you believe could suggest a definition and explanation paragraph.

Sample paragraph: definition and explanation pattern (with signal words underlined)

The control unit is the computer's internal police officer. This CPU component maintains order and controls all the internal activities of the machine. The control unit sends out electronic signals directing the computer to perform specific tasks such as moving data between memory and the CPU, activating the ALU, receiving data and sending information. The control unit manages the flow of data throughout the machine based on the instructions it receives from programs. No instructions are processed by the control unit. Rather, it directs other parts of the computer to perform their functions in a specific order, at a specific time.

Kershner, Helene G. *Computer Literacy.* 2nd ed. Lexington: D. C. Heath, 1992. 77.

What term in this paragraph did the author think needed to be defined for readers? _____

Explain what the author did to help the reader understand this term.

_____

_____

_____

Comparison and Contrast

This pattern is used to show similarities (comparisons) or to show differences (contrasts). Writers use this pattern when they want to show how something or someone is similar to or different from something or someone else. Often, both similarities and differences are included within a single comparison and contrast paragraph. Signal words associated with this pattern are then used to let the reader know a shift in focus is occurring.

Signal Words for Comparison and Contrast

Comparison: In the same way, similarly, likewise, both, in comparison

Contrast: Although, on the other hand, however, but, nevertheless, on the contrary, instead, yet, unlike, conversely, in contrast

Examples of Sentences That Suggest a Comparison and Contrast Pattern

1. The Mets fans behaved better than those who were rooting for the Yankees. *You would expect a contrast to be made between the two groups of fans.*

2. The garden my neighbor had cultivated was as beautiful as those I had seen in the New York Botanical Gardens. *You would expect a comparison to be made between the two gardens.*

3. Moderate exercise for a few minutes every day is more beneficial than doing a whole day of strenuous physical exercise once a week. *You would expect a contrast between the two exercise regimens to be made in order to show why one is better than the other.*

Working Together

With a partner, write one sentence that you believe could suggest a comparison or contrast paragraph. Indicate what type of paragraph will result from your sentence.

Sample paragraph: comparison pattern (with signal words underlined)

Roberto Corelli, the main character in the story "Rise Up and Fall Down," reminds me of my maternal grandfather in several respects. Roberto came to America in 1900, a penniless nine-year-old orphan, and was apprenticed to a brutal uncle in Chicago who kept him out of school and put him to work in a blacksmith's shop. My grandfather sailed to America in steerage just a few years after 1900. Like Roberto, he had little chance for formal education. As soon as he had learned to read, write, and add, he was taken out of his second-grade class by his impoverished parents and made to sell newspapers on the Boston streets. Roberto ran away, joined a circus, and at the age of twenty-one became the Strong Man in a sideshow set. My grandfather started to practice boxing at the YMCA and by the age of eighteen was a promising light heavyweight. Both Roberto and my grandfather eventually fell in love with immigrant girls, married, and settled down as local shopkeepers—Roberto as a butcher and my grandfather as a newsdealer. Similarities such as these continued to occur to me as I read "Rise Up and Fall Down," making it easy for me to give Roberto the understanding and compassion that his life's story was intended to evoke.

From Ezor, Ed, and Jill Lewis. *From Paragraph to Essay: A Process Approach for Beginning College Writing.* New York: McGraw-Hill, 1984. 255.

Sample paragraph: contrast pattern (with signal words underlined)

The new Surveillance and Destiny cars have surprisingly little in common. They're comparable in size—inside and out—but the Surveillance is a front-driver with a strut-type suspension whereas the Destiny uses rear-wheeled propulsion and control-arm front-and-rear suspension. Inside, the Surveillance relies on leather and wood-paneled elegance. The Destiny, on the other hand, gives more attention to functional details. Bucket seats in the Destiny slide forward automatically for rear entry. Its center console is artfully twisted toward the driver for a handier reach to sound-system and climate-control switches. During the test drive, the Surveillance demonstrated a tighter grip on the road during steady cornering, unlike the Destiny, which occasionally wagged its tail at the time of adhesion. Both on and off the test track, there's a significant difference in the sensations delivered to the driver through the steering wheel.

Sample paragraph: comparison and contrast pattern (with signal words underlined)

Shamika's college adviser told her that she possessed many of the traits similar to those reported in accounts of successful business-women, and he suggested that she should consider majoring in business. Shamika had excellent rapport with other people. She was a good public speaker and had shown leadership skills when she served as one of the key organizers for the college's first Environmental Awareness conference. On the other hand, she had some traits that her adviser thought might hinder her chances for success. For instance, she was often late with her assignments, and she was impatient with herself when things took longer to do than expected. She also needed to improve her math skills. Her adviser suggested that Shamika consider all that he had said before she selected a major.

Thesis and Proof or Opinion and Reason

This pattern is used to persuade readers to accept an idea. The idea may be one that is factual or well-researched, supported by substantial evidence, or supported by information drawn from authoritative sources. The author may have conducted a research study and have cited evidence or findings from this study to support the thesis. Or the material may be a statement of opinion, supported by unresearched reasons, personal beliefs, or information from unauthoritative sources. The sentence that states the opinion or the thesis serves as the main idea for the paragraph or essay. The author offers proof for the thesis and reasons for the opinion. The proof or reasons are intended to convince the reader that the author's view is correct. These arguments may be enumerated and may be listed in ascending or descending order.

Signal Words for Thesis and Proof or Opinion and Reason.   It is widely known, one must consider, the reasons for this, in my opinion, there is evidence, evidently, it should be accepted, as proof, it is believed.

Examples of Sentences That Suggest a Thesis and Proof or Opinion and Reason Pattern

1. The "greenhouse effect" theory is supported by much scientific evidence. *You would expect several sentences to give the scientific evidence.*

2. The city council argued that the town pool should be built immediately. *You would expect several sentences to give the reasons that the council argued this way.*

3. It has been established that dinosaurs were both herbivores and carnivores. *You would expect sentences to show how this has been "established."*

Working Together

With a partner, write one sentence that you believe could suggest a thesis and proof or opinion and reason paragraph. Indicate which type of paragraph your sentence suggests.

Sample paragraph: opinion and reason pattern (with signal words underlined)

Dog owners ought to accept more responsibility for their animals. They should not let their dogs run wild because dogs can be very destructive to other people's property. Further, dogs sometimes carry rabies, and if they bite another dog, or worse, a human, the dog or human can develop rabies and die. Dog owners also have responsibility for their pets' own welfare. If dogs are allowed to run loose, they can get killed by cars or hurt by wild animals such as raccoons and squirrels.

Sample paragraph: thesis and proof pattern (with signal words underlined)

Although we used to believe that "folk" medical remedies were merely forms of superstition, now we know otherwise. Biomedical research has shown that the active ingredient in many folk remedies is the same as in the medicines doctors prescribe. There is also new evidence that supports the view that many prohibited foods in folk medicine were based on sound biological principles.

Cause and Effect

Text may be written that describes only the *causes* of something: what made something happen. Or text may be written that describes only the *effects*, or *results*, of some action. These two terms are often confused. It may help you remember the distinction between them if you bear in mind that the *cause* results in the *effect*. The *cause* may show what led up to the event or idea—that is, what caused it to become what it is now. The consequences of the event or idea are the *effects* of it. *Cause* or *effect* paragraphs are sometimes written separately; in this case, one paragraph will state the causes, and the other will give the effects. Often, though, both the *cause* and the *effect* are combined into a single paragraph.

Signal Words for Cause and Effect

Cause: Because, since, as, the reason for this, a cause

Effect: As a result, thus, consequently, so, hence, therefore, one outcome, an effect

Combined: If (cause), then (effect); (cause) resulted in (effect); because of (cause), (effect) happened

Examples of Sentences That Suggest a Cause and Effect Pattern

1. The sudden rise to fame and fortune for some professional athletes may result in financial and personal problems for them. *You would expect a discussion of the effects of sudden fame and fortune on the finances and personal lives of athletes.*

2. Computer technology has caused some major changes in the way industries operate today. *You would expect a discussion of the results (changes) of computer technology on industry.*

3. The changes in the transportation-to-work possibilities for Myrna made her reconsider her best alternatives. *You would expect a discussion of the changes in Myrna's transportation possibilities (causes) and a discussion of her new possibilities (effects).*

Working Together

With a partner, write one sentence that you believe could suggest a cause and effect paragraph. Indicate whether it will result in a cause, effect, or a combined cause and effect paragraph.

Sample paragraph: cause pattern (with signal words underlined)

Farming has become a much easier occupation in recent years. One reason for this is that cows are now milked by automatic pumps rather than by hand. Eggs are hatched in incubators instead of by the hens themselves, which <u>also results</u> in less work for the farmers, who no longer have to keep nesting hens warm or watch over them to make sure they don't damage the eggs. The temperature and humidity in the hen houses are controlled by thermostats, not by nature's whim; and the amount of feed chickens get each day is determined by a computer rather than by a farmhand's estimates. <u>Another factor</u> that <u>makes</u> farming easier is that the farmhouse itself probably features an electronic range in place of the old coal kitchen stove. Unlike farmers of olden days, today's farmer can actually take a vacation and leave all the work to the brain of a computer, which will sense when each chore must be done and will signal the technological innovation that will accomplish it.

Adapted from Ezor and Lewis, 1984. 219.

This paragraph gives causes of:

Two causes mentioned are:

1. ---

----

2. ---

Sample paragraph: effect pattern (with signal words underlined)

The recent flood of immigrants into the schools in New York City has <u>resulted in</u> a new set of problems for educators. At some schools, <u>more than</u> twenty-six different languages are spoken by children, <u>which means that</u> parents who do not speak English are often unable to talk to school personnel about their children's progress. <u>Another consequence</u> is that parents feel intimidated and do not understand notes that come home to explain school events or school policies. <u>As a result</u>, children feel isolated, and teachers feel frustrated by their <u>inability</u> to communicate with the children or to understand aspects of the child's culture, which may affect what happens in the classroom.

This paragraph gives effects of:

Two effects mentioned are:

1. _____

_____

2. _____

_____

Sample paragraph: cause and effect pattern (with signal words underlined)

Until World War I, the United States had always been a debtor nation. The value of the goods and services we imported often exceeded the value of the goods we sold to foreigners, and foreigners were investing far more in the United States than Americans were investing in other countries. Thus we had to pay interest and dividends to investors abroad. During World War I, the situation was reversed. The war-torn nations of Europe needed U.S. goods, so our exports more than doubled, while the value of the goods we imported declined. By 1919 we had become a creditor nation—foreign nations owed more to the United States than the United States owed to them. This net credit position continued until 1985, at which time the United States once again became a net debtor nation. The value of our imports greatly exceeded the value of our exports, and foreigners were investing heavily in U.S. securities, largely because of the relatively high interest rates here. [*Note:* A chronological listing is also evident in this paragraph, but the cause and effect relationship of the events is the major emphasis.]

Gordon, S. D., and George G. Dawson. *Introductory Economics.* 7th ed. Lexington: D. C. Heath, 1991. 433.

This paragraph gives causes of:

_____

_____

Two causes mentioned are:

1. _____

_____

2. _____

_____

This paragraph gives effects of:

Two effects mentioned are:

1. --

----

2. --

Problem and Solution

This pattern is used to explain a problem and to offer recommendations. Most often the causes and effects of the problem are also stated, which means this pattern may not be clear until you have read several paragraphs. The statement of the problem is usually at or near the beginning of the paragraph or essay, and this should alert you to look for this pattern in the text that follows.

Signal Words for Problem and Solution

Problem: Unfortunately, the problem, a difficulty

Solution: Clearly, consequently, obviously, to solve, one solution

Examples of Sentences That Suggest a Problem and Solution Pattern

1. Although there are major obstacles for women who seek entry into top management positions, these can be overcome. *You would expect an explanation of the obstacles (problems) and how these can be overcome (solutions).*

2. Those who rent apartments must find ways to deal with landlords who are often unresponsive to tenants' needs. *You would expect an explanation of the solutions to the problem already stated.*

3. Multinational corporations have found ways to refute accusations that they are exploiting the labor force in third-world countries. *You would expect some solutions to be offered and, probably, an explanation of the accusations.*

Working Together

With a partner, write one sentence that you believe could suggest a problem and solution paragraph.

Parents often have difficulty determining how much allowance to give their children. One reason for this is that they are torn between believing their children should have an opportunity to budget their money and the feeling that their children will not use their allowance wisely and will continue to ask for additional money. Parents also have trouble deciding what to include in the child's list of items that the allowance must pay for. The result of such dilemmas is that children are often given too little or too much allowance, with little clear guidance about how it is to be spent. The rules keep changing. One way to solve this problem is for parents and children to confer regularly about how allowance is being spent and to establish clear guidelines, with revisions being made every so often as the child's needs and interests change.

The problem that is stated is: _____

_____

The cause(s) given for the problem is (are): _____

_____

The effect(s) of the problem is (are): _____

_____

The solution(s) offered is (are): _____

_____

RELATIONSHIPS BETWEEN MAIN IDEAS AND PATTERNS

As you know, each example sentence in the preceding section indicated the pattern that would probably be used by the author. These sentences could have been main idea sentences for paragraphs or entire essays. The main idea often suggests how the material will be organized—what pattern, or patterns, will be used. Recall from Chapter 3 that main idea statements raise questions in the mind of the reader. The writer's choice of organizational patterns is often based on a decision about which questions raised by the main idea, or thesis statement, will be answered. The example main idea sentence that follows illustrates this point.

Example:

> There are at least three good reasons people should participate in community service activities.

The author of this sentence will certainly need to give at least three reasons for this belief about community service activities. The sentence lends itself immediately to two patterns: (1) *opinion and reason* and (2) *simple listing*. The next example suggests a different pattern of organization even though the sentence is about the same topic as the previous example.

Example:

> Teenagers who participate in community service activities have greater self-esteem than those who don't.

Although the author will probably be giving opinions again, the comparison and contrast introduced in the main idea sentence needs elaboration. This sentence lends itself to a *comparison and contrast* essay, which may easily incorporate a simple listing format. In the next example, also on the same topic, the author will probably use a different pattern of organization to develop the idea.

Example:

> *Community service* means different things to different people.

Very likely, this author will use a *definition* pattern to explain the different meanings.

To some extent, then, the main idea controls the form the essay will take. This is similar to the way in which a movie theme, such as love or suspense, suggests a particular type of background music. After you identify a stated main idea or thesis, you should be able to predict the pattern that will be used. You can use your knowledge of these patterns to help you follow the development of the main idea or thesis while you read; you will know to look for certain kinds of information, such as definitions, reasons, and comparisons. If you need to create a main idea or thesis statement, you will be able to create one that suits the organization of the reading material. Your knowledge of patterns will also help you remember the information and comprehend how the different details are related to each other and to the main idea.

RECOGNIZING PATTERNS OF ORGANIZATION

Four steps will help you recognize what pattern is being used, whether it provides the organizing structure for an entire essay or is the basis for a single paragraph.

1. Identify the stated main idea or thesis, or create one.
2. Make a prediction about the pattern that might be used as the author elaborates on this main point.

3. Locate key words within the supporting sentences that suggest a pattern.

4. Verify your prediction. For example, if you had predicted an *opinion and reason* pattern, you should be able to find opinions or reasons in the content. If you had predicted a problem and solution pattern, you should find each of these as well as, perhaps, some causes and effects of each.

Keep each of these steps in mind as you complete Activity C and D.

ACTIVITY C. Predicting Patterns

Read each main idea sentence. Make a prediction about the pattern or patterns that the author will most likely use in elaborating on this main idea. Be prepared to explain your predictions. Your choices of patterns are listed below. Be as specific as possible in your identification.

Simple listing (chronological, order of importance, spatial, enumeration)

Definition and explanation

Comparison and contrast

Thesis and proof or opinion and reason

Cause and effect (or one of these)

Problem and solution

1. Psychologists have found that people who visit an aquarium experience a sense of peace and security.

   Pattern(s) the author will probably use: _____

   Reasons for your prediction: _____

   _____

   _____

2. Using HyperCard can be an enjoyable experience for computer buffs if they know how the program works.

   Pattern(s) the author will probably use: _____

   Reasons for your prediction: _____

   _____

   _____

3. The federal government's long debate over the new budget produced several positive outcomes.

   Pattern(s) the author will probably use: _____

Reasons for your prediction: _____

_____

_____

4. The best way to begin a research paper is to have an organized plan of attack.

   Pattern(s) the author will probably use: _____

   Reasons for your prediction: _____

   _____

   _____

5. *Neoteny* can change an animal's evolutionary course.

   Pattern(s) the author will probably use: _____

   Reasons for your prediction: _____

   _____

   _____

6. Although rare, negative reactions to new packaging designs do occur.

   Pattern(s) the author will probably use: _____

   Reasons for your prediction: _____

   _____

   _____

7. It has been proved that color plays a key role in a consumer's response to how food tastes.

   Pattern(s) the author will probably use: _____

   Reasons for your prediction: _____

   _____

   _____

8. When you use a computer, it is important to have a *surge protector.*

Chapter 4 Understanding Organizational Patterns in Academic Text

Pattern(s) the author will probably use: _ _ _ _ _ _ _ _ _ _ _ _ _ _ _ _ _ _ _

Reasons for your prediction: _

_ _

_ _

9. Gun control laws must be strengthened.

Pattern(s) the author will probably use: _ _ _ _ _ _ _ _ _ _ _ _ _ _ _ _ _ _ _

Reasons for your prediction: _

_ _

_ _

10. Madonna's sudden rise to fame can be easily understood.

Pattern(s) the author will probably use: _ _ _ _ _ _ _ _ _ _ _ _ _ _ _ _ _ _ _

Reasons for your prediction: _

_ _

_ _

Working Together

Compare your answers to Activity C with those of a partner. Make any changes to your answers that you believe are justified as a result of your comparisons.

ACTIVITY D. Identifying Patterns in Text

For each paragraph, decide the pattern(s) of organization being used. Consider the main idea of the paragraph as well as the details when making your decision. Circle any signal words within the paragraph that are associated with the pattern(s) you select. Then write a sentence below each paragraph in which you explain the reasons for your selection.

Pattern choices:

a. Simple listing

b. Definition and explanation

c. Comparison and contrast

d. Thesis and proof

e. Opinion and reason

f. Cause and effect

g. Problem and solution

h. Combination (list each pattern name)

1. The Arab dream is for lots of space in the home, which unfortunately many Arabs cannot afford. Yet when he has space, it is very different from what one finds in most American homes. Arab spaces inside their upper middle-class homes are tremendous by our standards. They avoid partitions because Arabs *do not like to be alone.* The form of the home is such as to hold the family together inside a single protective shell, because Arabs are deeply involved with each other. Their personalities are intermingled and take nourishment from each other like the roots and soil. If one is not with people and actively involved in some way, one is deprived of life. An old Arab saying reflects this value: "Paradise without people should not be entered because it is Hell." Therefore, Arabs in the United States often feel socially and sensorially deprived and long to be back where there is human warmth and contact.

Hall, Edward T. "Proxemics in the Arab World." *The Hidden Dimension.* New York: Doubleday, 1966. Reprinted in Rivers, William E. *Issues and Images.* New York: Harcourt Brace Jovanovich, 1992. 586.

Pattern(s): --

Your explanation: --------------------------------------

----

2. The formation of primary groups begins early in life when children find playmates whose company they particularly enjoy. As the years go by, they continue to seek close association with others who are like them in age and interests. Primary groups of this type are usually termed "peer groups" by sociologists. Common examples are cliques in school, boys' gangs, dating couples, and close friends at work. Our need to associate with others in intimate, face-to-face interaction is so strong that we continue our interest in peer group activity until we die. The old man's cronies are just as important to him as were his special friends at any other age.

DeFleur, M., W. D'Antonio, and L. DeFleur. Brief edition. *Sociology: Man in Society.* Glenview, Ill.: Scott, Foresman, 1972. 64.

Pattern(s): --

Your explanation: --------------------------------------

----

3. Winston Churchill once said, "We build our buildings and then they build us." A society's success is ultimately based on its culture. A society whose culture builds productivity, hard work, education, and scientific research will build wealth. A culture that encourages hedonism, sloppy work, poor worker motivation, and illiteracy will be eclipsed. A nation whose culture easily obtains from its citizens cooperation, discipline, and self-sacrifice has a cultural foundation much firmer than those countries whose work ethic has been eroded, whose sense of mission is undercut, and whose destiny is less manifest.

Pattern(s): _____

Your explanation: _____

_____

_____

4. I was following the crest of a ridge along one of the many old elephant trails that crisscrossed the bamboo. Soon the tracks became fresh. The toenails were still clearly defined, and swarms of tiny black flies hovered about the heaps of dung. I pushed my fingers into some dung. It was still warm. Clouds drifted in and grey fog crept from stem to stem, reducing my visibility to about fifty feet. I continued on silently and carefully, straining my senses, trying to see the bulky grey forms of the elephants in this shadowless dusky world, trying to smell their musky odor. But the only sound was the pounding of my heart.

Schaller, G. B. *The Year of the Gorilla.* Chicago: University of Chicago Press, 1964. 78.

Pattern(s): _____

Your explanation: _____

_____

_____

5. In May of 1779, the First Company of Philadelphia Artillery petitioned the Assembly about the troubles of the "midling and poor" and threatened violence against "those who are avariciously intent upon amassing wealth by the destruction of the more virtuous part of the community." That same month, there was a mass meeting, an extralegal gathering which called for price reductions and initiated an investigation of Robert Morris, a rich Philadelphian who was accused of holding food from the market. In October came the "Fort Wilson riot," in which a militia group marched into the city and to the house of

James Wilson, a wealthy lawyer and Revolutionary official who had opposed price controls and the democratic constitution adopted in Pennsylvania in 1776. The militia were driven away by a "silk stocking brigade" of well-off Philadelphia citizens.

Zinn, H. *A People's History of the United States.* New York: Harper and Row, 1980. 79.

Pattern(s): --

Your explanation: ---

----

6. One of my problems was to determine the approximate age of each gorilla so that I might have some ideas about how long infants remain with their mothers and at what age the apes begin to breed. Fortunately, I had visited gorillas in several zoos in the United States and in Europe before coming to Africa. By comparing the weight and the size of captive gorillas of approximately known age to that of free-living ones, I derived a very crude aging scale. At one year of age a youngster weighs fifteen to twenty pounds, at two years about thirty-five pounds, at three years about sixty pounds, at four years about eighty pounds, and at five years about one hundred and twenty pounds. Older animals show a great disparity in weight, due both to sexual and individual differences.

Schaller, G. B. *The Year of the Gorilla.* Chicago: University of Chicago Press, 1964. 123.

Pattern(s): --

Your explanation: ---

----

7. In early 1936, at the Firestone rubber plant in Akron, makers of truck tires, their wages already too low to pay for food and rent, were faced with a wage cut. When several union men were fired, others began to stop work, to sit down on the job. In one day the whole of plant #1 was sitting down on the job. In two days, plant #2 was sitting down, and management gave in. In the next ten days there was a sit-down at Goodyear. A court issued an injunction against mass picketing. It was ignored, and 150 deputies were sworn in. But they soon faced ten thousand workers from all over Akron. In a month the strike was won.

Zinn, H. *A People's History of the United States.* New York: Harper and Row, 1980. 390.

Pattern(s): _____

Your explanation: _____

_____

_____

8. Before the dawn of the computer age, manufacturing companies had to devote considerable time and expense to ordering and scheduling the shipments of new parts. For example, a large company might inventory 10,000 or more individual parts. Manufacturers typically used what is called an order point system. In this system, an order would be placed when the number of each part fell to a designated level in an effort to keep adequate stocks on hand. Although this method may seem logical, it has two important drawbacks. First, it does not take into consideration when a part is actually going to be used. Consequently, a particular part may actually remain in a warehouse bin unused for many months occupying space and tying up a company's money. A second and a related problem is that the system does not indicate whether a particular item has to be matched with another item to make a finished product. Even if the manufacturing plant has 99 percent of the components for a given product on hand, if it lacks one component, the product cannot be completed and sold.

Golob, R., and E. Brus. *The Almanac of Science and Technology.* New York: Harcourt Brace Jovanovich, 1990. 259.

Pattern(s): _____

Your explanation: _____

_____

_____

9. Clarence Birdseye was in Labrador on a hunting trip in the early 1920s. He was hunting for bears. During his trip, he noticed how fish that were kept outside in the subzero temperature froze immediately and tasted delicious months later. When he returned to the United States, Birdseye experimented with ways of freezing fish as quickly as possible to preserve their flavor. People thought he was crazy for spending so much time and energy on this. But he continued to experiment over the next several years. Eventually, he worked out methods of freezing food so fast that it went through the zone of maximum crystallization in a few minutes instead of taking the usual several hours. This way, the large dangerous crystals had no time to form. Birdseye developed his own

machinery to do this quick freezing, and by the end of the 1920s, the first packages of frozen food were available at the grocery store.

Pattern(s): _____

Your explanation: _____

_____

_____

10. Most people begin and end their working years willing, even anxious, to compromise their career goals with what they assume to be the harsh realities of the marketplace. Just think of the many people you know who wanted to be something really special when they reached adulthood, and seemed to have the ability to achieve this goal, who are now in seemingly dead-end jobs. Often this shift in career goals results from an attitude developed during childhood. Sometimes it is the result of an unpleasant interview during their twenties. Parental pressure, financial strain, or lack of patience can all contribute to this unnecessary tragedy. But it is never too early or too late to correct this situation and to find yourself the job that you desperately want and deserve.

Pattern(s): _____

Your explanation: _____

_____

_____

11. The term *personal computer,* or *PC,* was originally coined by IBM to describe its microcomputer. It has come to refer to a flexible and memory-rich microcomputer, not necessarily an IBM. Other words that originated as brand names have taken on more general definitions, such as Kleenex for tissue and Xerox for photocopy. Personal computers are relatively inexpensive, single-user machines most often found in business settings. Increasingly, they are used in the home. Some businesses even supply their employees with computers to take home so that their work can be continued out of the office. This probably benefits the business quite a bit. Personal computers can solve very sophisticated problems. They can process between 1,000 and 6,000 instructions per second, depending on processor design and layout. Newer processors will increase these speeds. Personal computers frequently have color monitors and a laser printer attached.

Adapted from Kershner, H. G. *Computer Literacy.* 2nd ed. Lexington, Mass.: D. C. Heath, 1992. 15.

12. Up from the deep dusk of a cleared spot on the edge of the forest a mellow glow arose and spread fan-wise into the low-hanging heavens. And all around the air was heavy with the scent of boiling cane. A large pile of cane-stalks lay like ribboned shadows upon the ground. A mule, harnessed to a pole, trudged lazily round and round the pivot of the grinder. Beneath a swaying oil lamp, a Negro alternately whipped out at the mule, and fed cane-stalks to the grinder. A fat boy waddled pails of fresh ground juice between the grinder and the boiling stove. Steam came from the copper boiling pan. The scent of cane came from the copper pan and drenched the forest and the hill sloped to factory town, beneath its fragrance. It drenched the men in circle seated around the stove. Some of them chewed at the white pulp of stalks, but there was no need for them to, if all they wanted was to taste the cane. One tasted it in factory town. And from factory town one could see the soft haze thrown by the glowing stove upon the low-hanging heavens.

Toomer, Jean. "Blood-Burning Moon." Ed. P. Lauter et al. *The Heath Anthology of American Literature.* Vol. 2. Lexington: D. C. Heath, 1990. 1,473.

Pattern(s): _____

Your explanation: _____

_____

_____

13. In the last few decades, several styles of leadership have been identified. The authoritarian leader holds all authority and responsibility. Communication usually moves from top to bottom within the organization. At the other extreme is the laissez-faire leader, who does not accept any responsibility and allows subordinates to work as they choose with a minimum of interference.

Pattern(s): _____

Your explanation: _____

_____

_____

14. Opponents of capital punishment have many reasons for opposing the death penalty. They say that anyone who values life cannot approve this form of punishment. They argue that it is morally wrong and that it is not constitutional. Another point they make is that it does not deter crime, as some who favor it would have you believe. Minority members are more likely to be executed which, opponents argue, means this penalty is applied unfairly.

Pattern(s): _____

Your explanation: _____

_____

_____

15. The main structural units of nervous systems are nerve cells, or *neurons*. Each typically consists of a nucleus-containing *cell body* and of one or more filamentous processes, or *fibers,* extending away from the cell body. Nerve fibers that carry impulses toward the cell body are *dendrites,* and those carrying impulses away are *axons.*

From Weisz, Paul B., and Richard N. Keogh. *Elements of Biology.* 4th ed. New York: McGraw-Hill, 1977. 278.

Pattern(s): _____

Your explanation: _____

_____

_____

16. There are many choices of colleges in the United States, and they vary in size, academic program, and quality of life offered to students. At one college, the fine arts program may be very strong. It may also have wonderful athletic programs and lots of options in the humanities. But the science facilities may not be as good, and the business programs may be weaker than those found at other colleges. Unless students know what they want, they may have difficulty choosing which college to attend. Students today have so many options—what music to listen to, what movies to see, what books to read—they can end up feeling overwhelmed and unable to make a decision. Some colleges provide a small, closely knit community, in which students live in the dorms and know practically everyone on campus. At other institutions, the campus is so big that buses transport students from one class in one building to another. Tuition also varies quite a bit from college to college. The cost of tuition is not always a reflection of the quality of the academic program, either. Every year, one popular magazine lists those campuses that give students a lot for their money.

Pattern(s): -

Your explanation: -

- -

- -

17. The sight of the dog put a wild idea into his head. He remembered the tale of the man, caught in a blizzard, who killed a steer and crawled inside the carcass, and so was saved. He would kill the dog and bury his hands in the warm body until the numbness went out of them. Then he could build another fire. He spoke to the dog, calling it to him; but in his voice was a strange note of fear that frightened the animal, who had never known the man to speak in such a way before. Something was the matter, and its suspicious nature sensed danger—it knew not what danger, but somewhere, somehow, in its brain arose an apprehension of the man. It flattened its ears down at the sound of the man's voice, and its restless, hunching movements and the liftings and shiftings of its forefeet became more pronounced; but it would not come to the man. He got on his hands and knees and crawled toward the dog. This unusual posture again excited suspicion, and the animal sidled mincingly away.

London, J. "To Build a Fire." Ed. P. Lauter et al. *The Heath Anthology of American Literature.* Vol. 2. Lexington: D. C. Heath, 1990. 735.

Pattern(s): -

Your explanation: -

- -

- -

18. The basic reason for failure of the Edsel was the curiously unscientific approach of Ford's management. For instance, the car was designed in group sessions with too many fingers leaving their marks in its identity. Also, it was ordered into production without research to determine whether or not there was a need for it. To compound the error even further, it was pushed through production so rapidly that there were more than the usual number of flaws and defects. And once produced, the Edsel was undermined by Ford executives, who almost immediately wrote it off after a disappointing introduction to the market. Perhaps no product could have survived with all these handicaps, and certainly not one called Edsel, the name of the deceased son of Henry Ford, the founder of Ford Motor Company.

Megginson, L., L. Trueblood, and G. Ross. *Business.* Lexington: D. C. Heath, 1985. 333. Adapted.

Pattern(s): _____

Your explanation: _____

_____

_____

ACTIVITY E. Patterns in Multiparagraph Essays

Essays often use a variety of patterns. This adds interest to the writing and enables the writer to accomplish a number of purposes within a single essay. For instance, in a single essay, an author may wish to present a problem, along with solutions; give a number of examples; compare one aspect of the problem with some other aspect; and describe in chronological order how the problem developed. Multiparagraph essays usually have an introductory paragraph that introduces the topic and, perhaps, states the main idea to be developed. They often also have a concluding paragraph that restates the main idea and summarizes major points.

Read the following multiparagraph essay to see how many different patterns within it you can find. Look for signal words. See also whether there is an introductory or concluding paragraph.

1   What makes you see red? For most people, it's light with a wavelength just a shade over 550 nanometers (billionths of a meter). But what you call red and what I call red may be horses (or apples) of a different hue. The color you perceive, researchers have discovered, may differ subtly, but significantly, from the color someone else sees. What's more, they've traced the mechanism for this color mismatch right down to a single amino acid sequence in our genes.

2   Color perception begins when light strikes specialized cone-shaped receptor cells in the retina. The cones are called red, blue, and green because proteins embedded in them respond selectively to different wavelengths of light. But the terms are misleading; in fact, each protein responds to a wide range of colors. "Color perception is a comparative system," explains molecular biologist Jeremy Nathans of Johns Hopkins. "A red apple illuminated by the afternoon sunlight is giving off all wavelengths of light. But it mostly reflects red wavelengths while absorbing blue and green and, to a lesser extent, yellow wavelengths. That distribution of light will excite the eye's red pigment most, the green somewhat less, and the blue least of all. That distribution is what your brain gets, and it says, 'That ratio means red.'"

3   But figuring out just how colors appear to people has always been a problem. "We couldn't get inside people's heads," says Nathans. "All we could do is design a test and ask, 'Do these two colors look identical or do they look different?'" Along with colleague Shannath Merbs, Nathans

figured out a way to determine at least which colors a person was capable of perceiving. Nathans first analyzed DNA from a number of people and then genetically engineered the proteins found in their red, green, and blue cone cells. Using a spectrometer, he measured the precise wavelengths of light absorbed by the so-called pigment proteins. He then plotted the results and came up with a bell curve representing the absorption spectrum—or range of responses—for each pigment. In effect, he found a way of seeing the same colors other people saw, using their own color receptors.

4   It was in the course of sequencing the DNA that Nathans found a surprising natural variation. The string of amino acids on the chromosome that codes for the red pigment protein came in two slightly different forms. "It happened to be position number 180," says Nathans. "Some people have an alanine there, some people have a serine." Color receptors with the amino acid serine at site 180, he found, respond most strongly to light with a wavelength of 557 nanometers; those with alanine prefer a wavelength of 552.

5   To determine the effect of this difference in the actual eyes of beholders, Samir Deeb and colleagues at the University of Washington put people from both the serine and alanine groups through standard color-matching tests. "Those with serine would be more sensitive to red light," says Nathans. "When asked to mix ingredients to form a standard color, they would require less red." Further studies then determined how frequently each variation appeared in a population of normally sighted men: approximately 60 percent had serine at site 180, and 40 percent had alanine.

6   It may come as no surprise that we each color our world somewhat differently, that even normally sighted people don't always see eye to eye. What is remarkable, however, is the ability to trace this difference right down to a single amino acid, making a direct link between gene and brain.

Meehan, B. A. "Seeing Red: It's Written in Your Genes." *Discover.* June 1993: 66.

What patterns did you find? List the patterns and the paragraphs in which you found them. Circle the signal words that support your findings.

Working Together

Compare your answers with those of a partner. Make any revisions to your answers that you believe are needed.

Based on your reading of this chapter, list at least five points that were made that you believe will help you with future reading assignments.

1. _____

_____

_____

_____

2. _____

_____

_____

_____

3. _____

_____

_____

_____

4. _____

_____

_____

_____

5. _____

_____

_____

_____

Now that you have worked with the strategies necessary for understanding paragraph patterns, you can practice applying them to full-length reading selections. Choose (or your instructor may choose) a reading selection that is typical of what you will be expected to read for your other college courses, such as an essay or a textbook chapter. Use this selection to practice:

- Identifying paragraph patterns
- Predicting paragraph patterns

Decide the practice strategies you will use. Apply them to your selection. Then in a few paragraphs, write a description of what you did and how the strategies you used worked for you.

Name of material used: _____

Page numbers: _____

Your description:

Chapter 5

Understanding Details

*Y*our first response to an attractive person might be based on an overall impression. That is, the person may seem well-groomed or appear to have a good personality. After a while, you might notice *particular* features of the person, such as an interesting way of dressing, a hairstyle that is particularly suited to the person, or a laugh that has some special sparkle. Readers may experience main ideas and details in much the same way. At first, the reader gets the big picture, the main idea. Then, the details might be examined for how they contribute to the total effect of the text. In this chapter, we explore connections between main ideas and details.

You have already learned that a relationship exists between the main idea and the remainder of the text you are reading. You now know that the main idea or thesis provides the focus of the reading material and that it often directs the pattern, or patterns, that will be used for development of the ideas. As you also know, the pattern provides the framework for the essay or paragraph. Within this framework, the *details* give the information and answer the questions about the main idea.

The design of an essay or paragraph, then, might look like the following illustration.

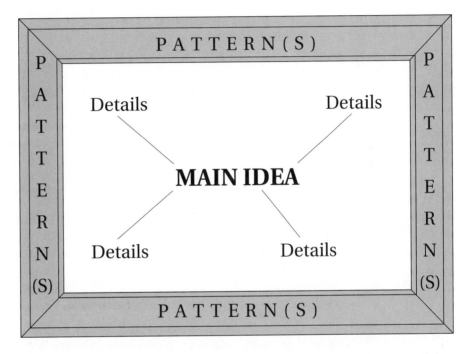

Details essentially explain, describe, support, or in some other way elaborate on the main idea. The purpose of this chapter is to further clarify these relationships between main ideas and details, and to give you practice with identifying the role details play in the main idea of a reading selection.

WHY ARE DETAILS NEEDED?

If you have ever had a conversation with friends who have just returned from a trip, you know that their excitement about their trip is expressed when they give you the details of what they saw, where they went, and so on. Without these details, you might not be convinced that the trip was so terrific. The details are necessary to give the fullest meaning to the statement "Our vacation was really wonderful." The main idea is supported by the details, as the following outline illustrates. Notice how each detail mentions some "wonderful" aspect of the trip.

Main idea: Our vacation was really wonderful.

Details: The weather never went above 80 degrees, and it was always sunny.

Our hotel room overlooked the bay.

There was so much unusual and delicious food, it was hard to decide what to eat.

The prices on gold jewelry were so much better than the prices back home.

The museums and galleries had exhibits of work of the natives from nearby villages.

The same principles that apply to sharing information when you speak apply to most of the writing assignments you will have in college, including when you write personal narratives about your experiences, theoretical papers in which you give researched evidence for some idea, and argumentative or persuasive papers in which you provide arguments for or against something. In all cases, support for your ideas is provided by the details. Without the details, your readers would have only the basic statement (the main idea or thesis). Your readers would never fully understand your theory or your experience, nor would they be able to agree or disagree with your arguments.

Sentences that provide details are usually referred to as *supporting sentences*. They may provide facts and statistics, offer reasons, give examples, add description, give steps or procedures, or in some other way answer questions about the main idea.

<u>ACTIVITY A.</u> Adding Supporting Sentences to Paragraphs

In each of the following paragraphs, the main idea is underlined. To each paragraph, add a sentence of details that you think would lend support for the main idea. Draw an arrow to where in the paragraph this additional sentence of details would go. (*Note:* What you add does not have to be true. Use your imagination.)

Example:

Visitors to Hawaii are often surprised to hear that English is not the only language spoken there. Even today, Hawaiians include much of their mother tongue, Hawaiian, in their speech. It is an interesting language to study. It is very musical. It is a dialect of the Polynesian language. Hawaiian contains only twelve letters, and each vowel is pronounced separately and distinctly.

*A **detail you could add:*** The language also uses one of the letters, the letter h, in 50 percent of its words.

1. People tend to over-rely on doctors for advice about the care of new-borns. One study showed that new mothers leaving the hospitals with their babies asked their doctors an average of nine questions about caring for their newborn. Questions ranged from concerns about how to diaper the baby to how often to feed it. Some parents wanted to know about the proper dress for the infant in various types of weather conditions. A very popular question was, "How often shall I feed my baby?" Let's hope these new parents remembered what they were told or sought help elsewhere once they left the hospital.

   A detail you could add: _____

   _____

2. One major criticism of the teaching profession in the Carnegie Report (1986) was that colleges have not adequately prepared undergraduates to teach in schools. The report urged that future teachers be required to have a strong liberal arts and disciplinary background. It suggested, further, that teachers be paid according to their students' performance. All in all, the report recommended that the U.S. educational system undergo a major overhaul in order to remain competitive with the rest of the world.

   A detail you could add: _____

   _____

3. Until the Industrial Revolution, workers in Europe were mostly inde-pendent. Then they became dependent on someone else—especially absentee owners—for their livelihood. This arrangement led to many abuses since employees were forced to work long hours at hard labor in dingy, windowless, and unventilated factories in return for low pay and no job security. Children were also unfairly exploited. Children as young as seven years of age were forced to lift heavy loads and work twelve to fourteen hours a day. When workers were hurt in an accident or became too old or sick to work, they were fired, with no pension.

   A detail you could add: _____

   _____

4. There is a 200-inch telescope at Mount Palomar. Attached to it is a piece of modern genius, a special magnifier called the Charge Coupled Device, or CCD. The CCD improves images or objects in space by gath-ering light more effectively. For instance, it is possible to see Uranus with its five moons in the distant night sky. The best portrait we have of Neptune was also made with a CCD. It shows major features such as the bright ice-crystal clouds in that planet's northern and southern hemispheres.

A detail you could add: _

_ _

5. He smiled at me and pointed to the sky. He made flying motions with his arms, then fluttered his hands more and more slowly as the wings of the bird he was imitating closed around its body, and it landed on the rim of the birdbath. He turned his head at an angle, then stretched forward as though to drink. His hands fluttered once again, his arms waved, the bird flew away. He shook snow from a bush, motioned me to look closely, pointed to a twig, put his hands together beneath his chin, then gradually widened them. I kicked away some snow from the ground. The earth looked like iron. I bent down and pretended my arm was a stalk that was growing up through the soil. I opened my fingers to sniff the petals of an imaginary flower. He let out a small shout of laughter and grabbed my hand and pressed it against his head. <u>I had understood that he was describing the coming of spring.</u>

Fox, P. "Unanswered Questions." May 6, 1988. *The Zena Sutherland Lectures, 1983-1992.* Ed. Betsy Hearne. New York: Clarion, 1993. 123.

A detail you could add: _

_ _

▶ **Thinking About Your Reading and Writing**

ACTIVITY B. Describing the Process

Describe the process you used to create sentences of details for the paragraphs in Activity A.

_ _

_ _

_ _

_ _

_ _

_ _

▢ **Working Together**

Share your additional sentences of details with those of a partner. Decide if your sentence and your partner's sentence could both be added to the same paragraph. Could they both be used in the same paragraph? Why or why not? What do you think accounts for this result? ●

Important details in an article or textbook chapter may serve different purposes. Depending on the main idea, authors may include details to:

- Offer reasons or arguments
- Provide description
- Outline steps or procedures
- Give single or multiple examples or illustrations
- Cite facts or statistics

It is also possible that within a single paragraph, the author will use a combination of these types of details in order to lend support to the main idea. Notice how these various alternatives have been applied in the following example paragraphs. The main ideas have been underlined.

Details That Offer Reasons or Arguments

Increasingly, the disposal of used materials has become a problem. Some used materials, such as organic wastes, can be returned safely to the environment—although as the population grows, the task becomes more difficult and more expensive. But some materials, such as plastics, are not easily recycled; nor do they degrade quickly when returned to the environment. Still other used materials—radioactive waste being the most dramatic but not the only example—are so hazardous for such a long time that how best to dispose of them is not clear and is the subject of widespread controversy. Solving these problems of disposal will require systematic efforts that include both social and technological innovations.

American Assn. for the Advancement of Science. *Project 2061: Science for All Americans.* Washington, D.C.: AAAS, 1989. 92.

Details That Provide Description

Looking out my window, I clearly knew that I was a long way from home. Outside my window the skyscrapers stood side-by-side against the gray sky. The marble edifice of the art museum I had briefly visited yesterday faced me, and to its left was the post office from which I had mailed the fateful postcard to Sandy saying, "I won't be coming back." Down the street, I could see the shopkeepers beginning to open their stores—so many of them. Not at all like the small-town Main Street to which I had become so accustomed.

Details That Outline Steps or Procedures

Homeowners can do home repair work themselves and save a great deal of money. For instance, hanging wallpaper is not difficult. The first step for hanging wallpaper is to select your pattern. You want to be sure that it does not clash with your floor design. After you have made your selection and it has been delivered to you, you will have to gather the tools you will need for hanging. For prepasted paper, you will need a sponge, scissors, a ruler, an edge roller, and an edge cutter or single-edge razor blade. Next, you should be sure you have a large bucket or a tub filled with water for dipping the paper. You will also need a large table on which you can cut the paper to the proper sizes. Once you have gathered your materials, you can finally begin to hang the paper, starting with an edge of a door and working your way around a room until all the areas have been covered. The process is easy, and the results are very satisfying.

Adapted from Ezor, Ed, and Jill Lewis. *From Paragraph to Essay: A Process Approach for Beginning College Writing.* New York: McGraw-Hill, 1984. 89.

Details That Give Single or Multiple Examples or Illustrations

Single

The Swiss psychologist Jean Piaget found that, around the age of seven or eight, children reach the step of "concrete operations." This stage is marked by the appearance of an ability that Piaget called *conservation.* An example of conservation is demonstrated with an activity using some beakers and water. Before age seven or eight, children believe that the amount of water in a short, wide glass changes when it is poured into a tall, thin beaker—they think there is more water in the beaker because it is higher, or less because it is thinner. An eight-year-old is able to "conserve" the amount of water and understands it remains constant despite the change in shape.

Multiple

Social Security has relieved children of the obligation to support their parents. Public schools and various public agencies have taken over many traditional parental responsibilities. In general, the social and economic ties between parents and children and grandchildren have loosened a great deal in America. People are far less likely than they once were to live in extended family units. Age groups have segregated themselves: children in the suburbs, single adults in fashionable city enclaves, older people in the Sunbelt retirement communities. Generations are less dependent on one another than in past decades, and this has allowed Americans pursuing their dreams to focus much more sharply on the present—on their own problems and interests.

Details That Cite Facts or Statistics

In 1986, nearly 11,000 people were employed as registered Washington lobbyists, with 3,750 of these serving as officers of 1,900 trade and professional organizations, including labor unions; another 1,500 employed by individual corporations; and about 2,500 representing organizations ranging from the National Right to Life Association to the Sierra Club. In addition, the six major national political-party committees, three Republican and three Democratic, headquartered in Washington, now employ roughly 1,200 people. And the creation and expansion of such ideological think tanks as the Heritage Foundation, the Center for National Policy, the Urban Institute, the American Enterprise Institute, the Cato Institute, and the Hoover Institution on War,

Revolution, and Peace have established whole networks of influential public policy entrepreneurs specializing in media relations and in targeted position papers. The number of special interest groups that have set up offices in Washington, D.C. is simply astounding.

Paragraphs That Have a Combination of Types of Details

Recent reports indicate that two out of every five women over thirty-five who are pregnant are now opting for genetic screening. Just ten years ago, this figure was one out of every five. Increasingly, women are opting for genetic screening during pregnancy, screening that enables physicians to detect some fetal abnormalities. The reasons for such increases are, perhaps, best understood by examining what can be learned from the tests that are done. Tests can reveal the condition of fetuses carried by women known to be at risk for specific diseases—such as women in their late thirties, who are more likely to have a child with Down's syndrome, a mental retardation caused by an abnormal number of chromosomes. Another disease that can be detected is Tay-Sachs disease, a fatal degenerative disorder of the nervous system. Doctors can use a number of procedures to make these genetic determinations, including blood examinations, ultrasound imaging, and amniocentesis. One woman reported that because of the early testing, her son was able to have a prebirth life-saving heart operation.

ACTIVITY C. Recognizing Types of Details

In each of the following paragraphs, identify the type of support provided by each of the numbered sentences as

reasons or arguments

steps or procedures

illustrations

description

single or multiple examples

facts or statistics

If sentences provide more than one type of support, indicate what combination is being used. Be prepared to justify your answers. The main idea sentence has been underlined in each case, and an example has been done for you.

Example:

(1) Until the mid-1980s, most states and the federal government had no formal statutes focusing on computer crime. (2) Most computer criminals were charged with illegal use of phone lines. (3) In 1984, at least partially in response to the computer invasions caused by the Milwaukee 414ers, the Federal Computer Fraud and Abuse Act was passed, making it illegal to tamper in any way with the federal government's computer systems. (4) This act was expanded in 1986 to include computer crimes against most private computers. (5) In

addition, the 1986 Electronic Communications Privacy Act was passed, making it illegal to intercept electronic information including bank transactions and electronic mail. (6) This new law also made it a federal crime to transfer information obtained through computer break-ins. (7) Providing others with computer information such as phone numbers, passwords, and the like, became the equivalent of trafficking in stolen goods.

Kershner, Helene G. "Specialized Technology." *Computer Literacy.* 2nd ed. Springfield: D. C. Heath, 1992. 243.

Type of support provided by sentence (3):   Example (of what has happened since the mid-1980s) and reason (why law was passed)

Type of support provided by sentence (5):   Example (of what has happened since the mid-1980s)

Type of support provided by sentence (7):   Reason (why it is considered a crime)

1. (1) Many questionable claims have been made for vitamin C that haven't been proved entirely. (2) Probably the most widely acclaimed value for vitamin C is that it is a preventive and cure for the common cold when taken in massive doses. (3) Famed chemist Linus Pauling, who wrote a small book on the subject, was largely responsible for this claim. (4) He recommended taking one or two grams of vitamin C a day to prevent colds and four grams a day to cure them. (5) His work was based mainly on subjective feelings about how he felt after he took the vitamin.

Adapted from Hoffman, Norman S. *A New World of Health.* 2nd ed. New York: McGraw-Hill, 1977. 185.

Type of support provided by sentence (2): _

Type of support provided by sentence (4): _

2. (1) If a particular genetic defect is known to cause a disease in humans, and if the same gene is knocked out in a mouse, the mechanism of the disease and the potential effectiveness of drugs and gene therapies can all be studied in the mouse model. (2) Knockout mice make great animal models for human diseases. (3) Last year, for instance, three research groups reported knocking out the gene that, when damaged, causes cystic fibrosis. (4) The knockout mice displayed some of the symptoms of the "human knockout": clogged lungs, digestive disorders, and early death.

Baringa, M. "Knockout Mice Offer First Animal Model for C.F." *Science.* 256:1046. Aug. 9, 1992.

Type of support provided by sentence (1): _

Type of support provided by sentence (3): _

3. (1) Women are now setting their corporate goals high, and more and more are achieving their ambitions. (2) <u>Women are making strides in the corporate world largely because of the changing attitudes of male corporate executives toward women.</u> (3) Companies now realize that females account for half of all prospective managerial talent in the country. (4) They also know that many of the best college graduates are women. (5) The attitude of men toward female managers seems to be changing, too. (6) According to a 1985 *Harvard Business Review* survey, the percentage of men who thought women were temperamentally unfit for management declined from 51 percent in 1965 to 18 percent in 1985. (7) Perhaps more important, 47 percent of the male respondents said they would feel comfortable working for a woman, compared to 27 percent in 1965.

Type of support provided by sentence (4): _____

Type of support provided by sentence (6): _____

4. (1) <u>The activity and prosperity of America's retirees have not gone unnoticed by the advertising industry.</u> (2) There was a time when advertisers behaved as though no one past middle age ever bought anything more durable than pantyhose. (3) No more. (4) Few marketing experts can ignore the fact that Americans over fifty earn more than half the discretionary income in the country. (5) Magazine publishers are betting on the favorable demographics. (6) Norman Lear's former wife Frances recently began publishing a glossy, upscale bimonthly magazine for women over forty. (7) Major firms are forming special groups to study the senior market, and at least one company that offers ageless ads has opened.

Type of support provided by sentence (4): _____

Type of support provided by sentence (6): _____

5. (1) <u>After food is ingested, digestion in different parts of an alimentary tract is achieved by mechanical and chemical means.</u> (2) Mechanical digestion, carried out, for example, through muscular grinding by teeth and stomach, achieves a progressive physical subdivision of ingested materials into fine particles suspended in water. (3) Chemical digestion then reduces these particles to molecular dimensions. (4) In the process, usable ions and molecules become separated out, and more complex molecules are broken up into smaller, usable ones.

From Weisz, Paul N., and R. N. Keogh. *Elements of Biology.* 4th ed. New York: McGraw-Hill, 1977. 172.

Type of support provided by sentence (2): _____

Type of support provided by sentence (3): _____

6. (1) Dr. George Cierny III, orthopedic surgeon at Atlanta's St. Joseph's Hospital studied the time it took twenty-nine patients to recuperate from leg-bone surgery. (2) His findings: Patients who smoked regained their ability to walk an average of six months later than nonsmokers. (3) "It may be that people smoking a pack a day mend their broken bones only while they sleep," says Cierny. (4) Research indicates that when a bone fractures, cells near the break produce a fibrous substance called collagen that patches the fissure. (5) The carbon monoxide and nicotine in cigarette smoke limit the amount of oxygen that reaches those cells, hindering their collagen-making ability.

Type of support provided by sentence (1): _____

Type of support provided by sentence (3): _____

Type of support provided by sentence (5): _____

7. (1) In Japan, employees' compensation is primarily determined by age and length of service with the company. (2) Wages based on productivity would embarrass the worker, a condition to avoid. (3) The fringe benefits given lifetime workers are considerably higher than in the United States. (4) This is because many of the benefits that government provides in the United States are provided by companies in Japan. (5) For example, benefits may include company-subsidized food services, housing, transportation, medical care, recreational facilities, training for more skilled jobs, cultural events, and saving plans. (6) Bonuses may run 25 percent of regular wages.

Type of support provided by sentence (2): _____

Type of support provided by sentence (5): _____

Type of support provided by sentence (6): _____

8. (1) Designed by the same architectural firm that designed the National Gallery of Art, the Thomas Jefferson Memorial was built in the style of Jefferson's own Rotunda at the University of Virginia. (2) Surrounding the statue are floors of Tennessee marble, walls of Georgia marble, and a coffered ceiling of Indiana limestone. (3) Each spring, the circular dome is framed by a ring of Japanese cherry trees on the banks of the Tidal Basin. (4) Restoration is currently taking place, but the twenty-nine-foot bronze statue of the brilliant statesman and excerpts from his famous works are still visible. (5) This memorial is truly a testimony to Jefferson's greatness.

Type of support provided by sentence (2): _____

Type of support provided by sentence (3): _____

9. (1) Lionel Portell was eight years old. (2) He has spent four hours every day watching TV for seven days per week, since he was two. (3) This is a total of 8,760 hours he has already spent viewing cartoons, sitcoms, and whatever else has attracted his eye. (4) There ought to be a limit on how much television a kid can watch. (5) It's bad for the eyes. (6) It's bad for the brain. (7) Little mental exercise is required. (8) There is an absence of problem solving and creative thinking, and communication is totally one-way. (9) There are better ways for kids to spend their out-of-school time.

Type of support provided by sentence (2): _____

Type of support provided by sentence (8): _____

Type of support provided by sentence (9): _____

10. (1) Sufferers from asthma and others who have difficulty breathing can use essence of mint. (2) This should be added to a half teacupful of warm water. (3) This mixture should be bottled and tightly corked. (4) When there is shortness of breath, a few drops sprinkled on a piece of cloth and held to the mouth and nose will bring relief. (5) Or the same mixture can be sprinkled on a pillow so that it will be inhaled during sleep.

Type of support provided by sentence (2): _____

Type of support provided by sentence (3): _____

Type of support provided by sentence (5): _____

DETAILS AS ANSWERS TO QUESTIONS

In Chapter 3, you learned that main idea sentences are fairly broad sentences; they are more general than sentences whose primary purpose is to provide details as support for the main idea. Recall also that these broad sentences raise questions in the mind of the reader and that the details often answer them. In Chapter 3, you were able to verify the validity of the main idea sentences you created by comparing details in the paragraphs to the questions raised by your main idea. You knew your main idea sentence was usable if the details answered some or most of the questions that resulted from your sentence.

You can also use the questions raised by main ideas to predict the content of the details in a reading passage. Since the main idea is often stated near the beginning of a reading selection, after you identify it, you should spend a few moments thinking about the information that probably will follow. In the next example, the main idea is stated in the first sentence.

Before you read the remainder of the paragraph, predict what will follow. What type of information can you expect to proceed from this main idea? Then read the rest of the paragraph to verify your predictions.

Example:

> You may be surprised to learn that Buenos Aires resembles a European capital. At first glance, the comparisons are evident: There are tidy plazas with Rodin statues in them, sidewalk cafés, *prêt-à-porter* windows where beautiful women gaze simultaneously at the clothes and their own reflections. A huge obelisk looms in the middle of the Avenida Nueve de Julio, and on either side are heavy-limbed subtropical trees and Parisian-style office buildings. You are in the heart of South America, but you can drink tap water and eat raw salads, and buy almost any new magazine or exquisite cosmetic. Throughout her convulsive and sometimes bloody history, Buenos Aires has kept her eyes fixed lovingly on Europe.

If you predicted that the example paragraph would contain details about Buenos Aires that illustrate its similarity to European cities, you were, of course, correct. Your prediction prepared you for the reading ahead and kept you focused while you read.

If you read with a questioning attitude, your goal will be to find the relationship between some of the more general sentences in the material you are reading and the remaining sentences. You will search for those details that elaborate on the questions raised by the more general sentences. And you will understand how those details provide support for the main idea. In Activity D, you will have an opportunity to think about this aspect of the reading process.

ACTIVITY D. Predicting Details from Main Idea Sentences

In these exercises, the main idea sentence is noted separately above the paragraph. Beneath this is a space for you to make predictions about the content of the details. You should base these on the questions the main idea raises for you. After you read the paragraph, decide how accurate your predictions were. Note this in the space provided below the paragraph. An example has been done for you.

Example:

Main idea sentence: Francis Bacon was known for his writing, his politics, and his influence on the scientific community.

Predicted content of details: The paragraph will discuss his writing and his politics, as well as how he influenced the scientific community.

> Francis Bacon was known for his writing, his politics, and his influence on the scientific community. He was a gifted writer and was recognized as an outstanding essayist. Some scholars also consider him as the true author of the plays attributed to William Shake-

speare. Bacon is reported to have been an ambitious and unscrupulous politician. Between 1618 and 1621 he was lord chancellor of England, under James I of England. Convicted of accepting bribes, he was dismissed and died in disgrace. Bacon is perhaps best remembered, however, as an early propagandist for the Scientific Revolution. His *New Organon* (1620), designed to replace Aristotle's logical works collectively called the *Organon*, called for a new approach to the study of nature. Science for Bacon was the means by which men could gain power over nature and use it for their own purposes. To do this, they needed a new instrument, a new method of approach. This new method was *empiricism*.

Witt, M. A. et. al. *The Humanities*. Vol. II. 3rd ed. Lexington: D. C. Heath, 1989. 8–9. Adapted.

Accuracy of your prediction: The details did discuss what had been predicted.

1. Main idea sentence: According to an early popular hypothesis that has since proved to be incorrect, it was believed that the stomach regulated the amount of food we ate.

Predicted content of details: _

_ _

_ _

According to an early popular hypothesis that has since proved to be incorrect, it was believed that the stomach regulated the amount of food we ate. Muscular contractions of an empty stomach were thought to control the sensations of hunger. It was assumed that a hungry animal would eat until its stomach was filled. By filling the stomach, the hunger pangs would stop, and so would food intake. But this hypothesis turned out to be invalid long ago. Even after the surgical removal of the entire stomach, hunger sensations continue to come and go, as before. Moreover, a "stomach hypothesis" of hunger control does not account for chronic overeating or undereating.

Accuracy of your prediction: _

2. Main idea sentence: Marketing strategies involving sales promotions must be used wisely, or serious consequences can occur.

Predicted content of details: _

_ _

_ _

As the automakers have learned, once a pattern of sales incentives is begun, it is extremely difficult to turn off. Marketing strategies involving sales promotions must be used wisely, or serious consequences can occur. Managers should be aware that sales promotion devices work in the same way as narcotics. They are so potent as reinforcers that consumers become dependent on them. Consumers simply stop buying when the incentives are removed. Furthermore, sales promotion devices can act as a large drain on profits. The extremely poor financial performance of General Motors during the fall of 1986, when the company employed a massive sales promotion campaign, illustrates this point.

Accuracy of your prediction: _____

3. Main idea sentence: Intermediate stages in evolution may occur very rapidly and may even be difficult to identify.

   Predicted content of details: _____

_____

_____

People think of evolution of a system as proceeding gradually, with a series of intermediate states between the old and the new. This does not mean that evolutionary change is necessarily slow. Intermediate stages in evolution may occur very rapidly and may even be difficult to identify. Explosions, for example, involve a succession of changes that occur almost too rapidly to track—whether the explosions are electric as in lightning, chemical as in automobile engines, or nuclear as in stars. What is too rapid, however, depends on how finely the data can be separated in time. Consider, for example, a collection of fossils of fairly rare organisms known to have existed in a period that lasted many thousands of years. In this case, evolutionary changes that occurred within a thousand years would be impossible to track precisely. And some evolutionary changes do occur in jumps. For instance, new biological developments do not arise only by successive rearrangement of existing genes but sometimes by the abrupt mutation of a gene into a new form. On an atomic scale, electrons change from one energy state to another with no possible intermediate states. For both the gene and the electron, however, the new situation is limited by, and explicable from, the previous one.

American Assn. for the Advancement of Science. *Project 2061: Science for all Americans.* Washington, D.C.: AAAS, 1989. 13.

Accuracy of your prediction: _____

4. *Main idea sentence:* It is obvious that Yom Kippur is a day that Jews anxiously await.

Predicted content of details: _

_ _

_ _

To the Jewish people, Yom Kippur, the Day of Atonement, is the most solemn religious holiday of the year. It is a day of great importance, the day they "heed the call of the shofar" and ask God to forgive them for their sins and transgressions. It is obvious that Yom Kippur is a day that Jews anxiously await. Sociologist David Phillips discovered something extremely interesting about Yom Kippur and the people who observe it. Studying the mortality records for Jews in New York and Budapest, he found a notable drop in the death rate just before the Day of Atonement. There was no such drop among non-Jews before the High Holy Day. Carrying his investigation further, Phillips also examined the mortality pattern around people's birthdays. What he discovered tied in nicely with his Yom Kippur findings: There was a significant dip in deaths before birthdays and a significant peak in deaths thereafter— which all means, according to Phillips, that "some people look forward to witnessing certain important occasions and are able to put off dying in order to do so."

Andrews, Lewis, and Marvin Karlins. *Psychology, What's in It for Us?* 2nd ed. New York: Random House, 1975. 147.

Accuracy of your prediction: _

5. *Main idea sentence:* One important element of poll-taking is that the questions asked must be asked fairly.

Predicted content of details: _

_ _

_ _

One important element of poll-taking is that the questions asked must be asked fairly. They need to be asked in a clear language, without the use of "loaded" or "emotional" words. They must give no indication of what the "right" answer is, but offer a reasonable explanation, where necessary, of the consequences of each possible answer. For example, in 1971 the Gallup poll asked people whether they favored a proposal "to bring home all U.S. troops (from Vietnam) before the end of the year." Two-thirds of the public agreed with that. Then the question was asked in a different way: Do you agree or disagree with a proposal to withdraw all U.S. troops by the end of the year "regardless of what happens there (in Vietnam) after U.S. troops leave?" In this form substantially less than half the public agree.

Wilson, James Q. *American Government.* Brief version. 2nd ed. Lexington: D. C. Heath, 1990. 85.

Accuracy of your prediction: _____

MAJOR AND MINOR DETAILS

Have you ever stopped to ask for directions when you were driving to an unfamiliar location? If you have, you are surely aware that some people are better "direction-givers" than others. One thing that can distinguish a good set of directions from a poor set is the kind of information provided. Two different sets of directions for the same destination, a local movie theater, follow. They are being given from the same location, a local gas station. As you read each set, think about which set you prefer, and why.

As you leave from the station, make a right. Turn left after you pass the Fiesta Food store, which you'll see because it has a new brick facing on it and the prices are really low, and then you go past a school for grades two through five; keep going, but don't turn left yet. You see there's a large ballfield, and across from that is the Central gas station. After that, you come to a red house on the right and a bowling alley next to it. Then there's the first traffic light. Turn left here. Go up about three blocks. You'll see a white mailbox and a sign reading "Katie's Kennels" on the first block. An ice cream store and drug store are on the next block. When you get to the third block, you'll see a big sign saying "Theater Parking." Go in there, and you'll be at the theater.

As you leave from the station, make a right. Turn left at the first traffic light. Go up about three blocks. Then you'll see a big sign saying "Theater Parking." Go in there, and you'll be at the theater.

If you are like most people who ask for directions, you would prefer the second set. It is short, to the point, and easy to remember. In fact, most of the information given in the first set is unnecessary. It is interesting, and does help to create a picture for you of the town, but to get to the theater, all you need to know is what is mentioned in the second set. It contains only the major details, whereas the first set contains many minor details.

Working Together

What are some of the minor details in the first set of directions? With a partner, underline all that you can locate.

A sophisticated reader of textbook material spends time sorting out important details from unimportant ones. The major details contribute directly to the main idea. The minor details usually elaborate on some other detail that supports the main idea. The next paragraph illustrates this distinction. In this example, the two sentences that state the main idea are underlined. The major details are in italics. Other details are only minor. Following the paragraph is a map that shows how the major details connect to the main idea and how the minor details serve other purposes.

Example:

There is no question that <u>groups can exert both negative and positive influences over an individual's behavior.</u> They *can be used to extinguish human spirit* and *encourage antisocial acts,* yet they *can also be employed to expand individual freedom and social responsibility.* Groups can encourage an individual to take drugs; to commit violent crimes; even to disrupt platform speakers at a rally or convention. On the other hand, groups can also be effective in working to build shelters for the homeless, encouraging AIDS research, or maintaining safety at a concert. Clearly, group power is similar to atomic power: <u>It can be used to improve or to hamper the quality of life.</u> In the final analysis, it is up to us to decide how group power will be exercised.

Adapted from Andrews, Lewis M., and Marvin Karlins. *Psychology: What's In It for Us?* 2nd ed. New York: Random House, 1975. 115.

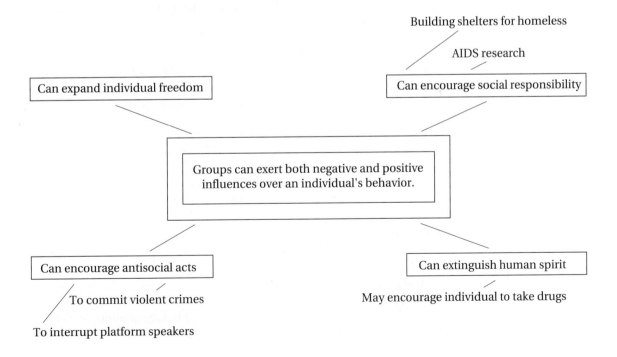

ACTIVITY E. Recognizing Major and Minor Details

Each paragraph includes a stated main idea, which is underlined, as well as sentences containing either major or minor details. In the spaces following the paragraph write whether each detail listed is major (MAJ) or minor (MIN). Be prepared to justify your answer.

1. In the United States a man cannot have more than one wife at a time, even if (as once was the case with Mormons) polygamy is thought desirable on religious grounds. For religious reasons, you may oppose being vaccinated or having blood transfusions, but if the state passes a compulsory vaccination law or orders that a blood transfusion be given a sick child, the courts will not on grounds of religious liberty prevent such things from being carried out. Many young children, however, have had to wait for transfusions until their case was heard in court. And in an issue that remains bitterly controversial to this day, the courts have allowed local authorities to close down schools operated by fundamentalist religious groups if the schools were not accredited by the state. This has upset many parents who feel their religious needs could not be met by the public schools. <u>Having the right to exercise your religion freely in this country does not mean that you are exempt from laws binding other citizens, even when the law goes against your religious beliefs.</u>

Wilson, James Q. *American Government.* Brief version. 2nd ed. Lexington: D. C. Heath, 1992. 59.

a. Many Mormons once believed it was proper to have more than one wife. _____

b. In this country, a man cannot have more than one wife, even if it is not opposed by his religion. _____

c. Hospitals will give life-saving transfusions even if it is against the patient's religion. _____

d. Some fundamentalist parents are dissatisfied with public schools. _____

e. Some fundamentalist schools were not accredited. _____

f. Some fundamentalist schools were closed down because they were not accredited. _____

g. There are religions that oppose vaccinations. _____

h. States may pass compulsory vaccination laws. _____

2. We all know people suffering from alcoholism. According to the National Council on Alcoholism, 9,000,000 Americans are afflicted. At least one out of 20 readers of this article is already in some stage of the development of the illness. Although there is a great deal yet to be learned about this disease, much knowledge is already available. <u>Yet, most educated Americans feel helpless when it comes to recognizing, understanding, or coping with alcoholism.</u> Medical schools, for example, are only beginning to address the problem of teaching their stu-

dents about alcoholism itself, as opposed to teaching only the physical complications of the disease. Schools of social work, clinical psychology, nursing education, and police science continue to turn out graduates substantially unequipped to deal with the large numbers of problem drinkers among their clients and students or to guide those in their care toward safe drinking practices. Few areas of the country boast adequate treatment facilities, even for those alcoholics and their families who come forward spontaneously in search of help. Nothing short of a massive national effort on the part of government and individuals alike will begin to make a meaningful impact on the problem.

a. At least one out of twenty readers of this article is already in some stage of the development of the illness. _____

b. Medical schools are only beginning to address the problem of teaching their students about alcoholism itself. _____

c. Schools of social work continue to turn out graduates substantially unequipped to deal with the large numbers of problem drinkers among their clients. _____

d. We all know people suffering from alcoholism. _____

e. According to the National Council on Alcoholism, 9 million Americans are afflicted. _____

f. Few areas of the country boast adequate treatment facilities. _____

g. Medical schools teach about the physical complications of the disease. _____

▶ **Thinking About Your Reading and Writing**

ACTIVITY F. Understanding Your Thought Process

Describe the thought process you used to determine whether a detail in Activity E was major or minor.

_____

_____

_____

_____

_____

Working Together

With a partner, return to the paragraphs in Activity C. Create maps for two paragraphs which show the relationships between the major and minor details in each.

CREATING VISUALS FOR IDEAS IN TEXTS

You can use the knowledge you now have about the relationships between main ideas, paragraph patterns, and details, and about distinctions between major and minor details to help you create visual displays of the information you read. These displays, sometimes referred to as *graphic organizers*, are frameworks that illustrate the important conceptual relationships between ideas in text. They will help you organize and recall information, and they are valuable study aids. The process of creating them will give you an opportunity to verify that you have understood the connections between ideas. (In Chapter 9, you will learn how to interpret and create graphic organizers that are used primarily for displaying statistics.)

There are different types of graphic organizers, each of which serves a different purpose. We discuss several types in the following sections. When you read, you will need to decide your purpose for making your visual before you begin to create it. Then you will know which type of visual design to use.

Concept Maps (for Key Vocabulary)

Academic text frequently contains new terms or concepts. Once you establish that the primary purpose of a section of the material you are reading is to define or explain a new term or concept, you can think about preparing a *concept map* for it. The basic layout for a concept map is shown in the

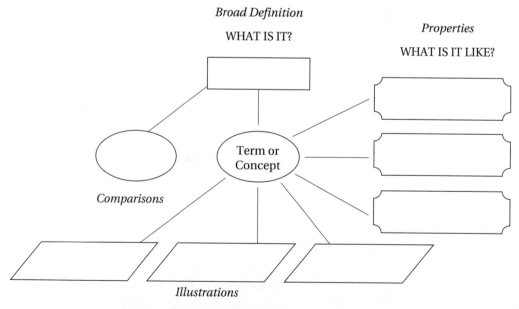

Broad Definition

WHAT IS IT?

Properties

WHAT IS IT LIKE?

Term or Concept

Comparisons

Illustrations

WHAT ARE SOME EXAMPLES?

figure. Notice that the term, or concept, is placed in the middle of the map. The broad definition for it appears at the top. On the right is space for indicating characteristics or properties of the term or concept. At the bottom is room for examples of it. On the left is space for writing another term or concept that is different from the one in the center but that will help you make comparisons with the new term.

Here is an example of material for which a concept map could be created. Read the material, and while you do so, think about what such a map would look like for this selection. Then study the example map that follows.

Example:

Optical Fibers

The revolution in ground-based communications has depended, not only on the invention of the laser but also on the development of the *optical fiber*. An optical fiber is a hair-thin, flexible thread of ultra clear glass one-tenth of a millimeter in diameter. Optical fibers also are known as *lightguides* because they serve as pipelines or conduits for laser light.

A glass optical fiber is made from silicon, the same material that is used to make microchips. Silicon is the main ingredient in sand, so it is very plentiful. An optical fiber has a glass inner *core* with an outer layer called the *cladding*.

The cladding is composed of a slightly different glass from the core. It acts like a mirror, totally reflecting the light beam traveling through the optical fiber back into the core of the fiber. The trapped light beam cannot escape from the optical fiber until it comes to the other end. For this reason, laser light traveling through an optical fiber does not lose its brightness.

Optical fibers have many advantages over copper wires for voice, information, or data transmission. Much more information can be sent by laser beam over a single optical fiber than by electricity over one copper wire. A single optical fiber can carry the same amount of information as a telephone cable containing 256 pairs of wires. A spool of optical fiber weighing only four and one-half pounds is capable of transmitting the same number of messages as 200 reels of copper wire weighing over eight tons!

Though an optical fiber looks fragile, it is stronger than steel and can withstand over 600,000 pounds of pulling force per square inch. Unlike ordinary glass, optical fibers are not brittle or easily broken. An optical fiber is flexible enough to be tied into a loose knot and still transmit laser light flawlessly.

The first commercial application of lasers and optical fibers to connect telephones in the United States was in 1978 at Disney World in Orlando, Florida. Vista-United Telecommunications linked telephones throughout the thousands of acres of the park using fiber optic trunk lines. In addition, alarm systems and lighting systems in the park use optical fibers.

Billings, Charlene. *Lasers: The New Technology of Light.* New York: Facts on File, 1992. 34–39. Adapted.

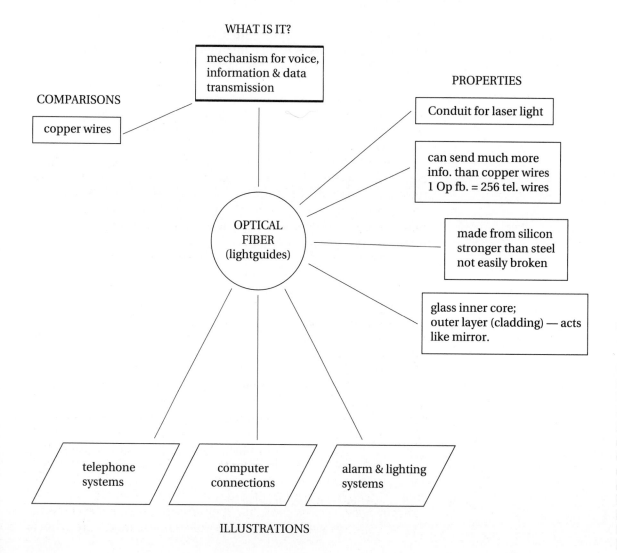

Semantic Webbing

This type of diagram is used to show the relationships between various ideas in the text, particularly between main ideas and details. If you decide to create a *semantic web* from text, it means that you believe the author's purpose for the material you are diagramming is to give a considerable amount of information about an event, process, or situation. The semantic web is useful as a self-monitoring tool, particularly if you create your web immediately after reading the material and without referring to the text. Once you have drawn it, you can verify that your web contains the important points made in the selection and that the relationship between these points has been clearly drawn. To identify prior knowledge they have on a topic, students sometimes create semantic webs before reading new material. This is always a good idea.

Read the example text. Then study the web above it. Notice how the lines drawn on the web show how the ideas are connected.

Example:

How hormones affect plants

What hormones do

cells contain receptors for hormones

degree of response varies

control when flowers bloom

regulate direction of growth

regulate rate of growth

hormones bind on molecules (receptor hormone complex)

PLANTS & HORMONES

Plants are able to use hormones to regulate their rate and direction of growth, to control the time at which they produce flowers and drop leaves, and even to coordinate the functions associated with germination. A hormone does not necessarily affect every cell of an organism in the same way. In fact, many cells cannot respond to a hormone message at all. In order to respond to the message carried by a particular hormone, a cell must contain a *receptor* for that hormone. Receptors are molecules to which hormones bind, forming a *receptor-hormone complex* that then affects cellular metabolism. Cells cannot respond to a hormone unless they contain the proper receptor. Those cells that do contain the receptor are known as *target cells,* and it is to such cells that the hormonal message is directed. The nature of the response depends on the amount of hormone that reaches the target cell, and it may also be influenced by the presence of other hormones that affect the same cell.

Levine, J. S., and K. Miller. *Biology.* 2nd ed. Lexington: D. C. Heath, 1994. 654.

Notice that the topic is in the middle of this map. Each important point (main idea) that is discussed and that is related to the topic is noted separately, and a line is drawn from it to the topic. The major details pertaining to each main idea have also been noted; lines extend between the detail and main idea. Minor details are drawn on lines that extend from the major details. Even someone who had not read the text would be able to see the relationship between the ideas on this web.

Hierarchical Array

When an author presents ideas in a hierarchy, he or she indicates that some ideas, or some details related to a main idea, are more important than others. You can diagram these relationships on a *hierarchical array.* This type of visual display is illustrated in two figures. In the example text, on which both displays are based, signal words tell you to expect that some details will have greater importance than others. This should alert you to read actively and to try to visualize the hierarchy while you read so that you are prepared to create the array immediately afterward.

Example:

Death Aboard Slave Ships

Death in the crossing was due to a variety of causes. The biggest killers were gastrointestinal disorders, which were often related to the quality of food and water available on the trip, and fevers. Bouts of dysentery were common and the "bloody flux" as it was called could break out in epidemic proportions. The increasing exposure of the slaves to dysentery increased both the rates of contamination of supplies and the incidence of death. It was dysentery that accounted for the majority of deaths and was the most common disease experienced on all voyages. The astronomic rates of mortality reached on occasional voyages were due to outbreaks of smallpox, measles, or other highly communicable diseases that were not related to time at sea or the conditions of food and water supply, hygiene, and sanitation practices. It was this randomness of epidemic diseases that prevented even experienced and efficient captains from eliminating very high mortality rates on any given voyage.

Although time at sea was not usually correlated with mortality, there were some routes in which time was a factor. Simply because they were a third longer than any other routes, the East African slave trades that developed in the late eighteenth and nineteenth centuries were noted for overall higher mortality than the West African routes, even though mortality per day at sea was the same or lower than on the shorter routes. Also, just the transporting together of slaves from different epidemiological zones in Africa guaranteed the transmission of a host of local endemic diseases to all those who were aboard. In turn, this guaranteed the spread of all major African diseases to America.

Klein, H. S. "Profits and the Causes of Mortality." *The Atlantic Slave Trade.* Ed. D. Northrup. Lexington: D. C. Heath, 1994. 118.

Model A

Causes of Death during Slave Trading

|

Gastrointestinal disorder

|

Small pox, measles & other communicable diseases

|

Length of time of crossing

|

Spread of endemic diseases to all who were aboard

Model B

Causes of Death during Slave Trading

Gastrointestinal disorder

Small pox, measles and
other communicable diseases

Length of time of crossing

Spread of endemic
diseases
to all who were aboard

In the first figure, the hierarchy is noted by the size of the print as well as the order in which the items have been placed beneath the heading. In the second, the distance of each item from the heading indicates its relative importance.

This type of diagram also works well for material that includes classifications. An essay about Indo-European languages, for instance, might result in your creation of a hierarchical array similar to the one shown here.

Indo-European Languages Today

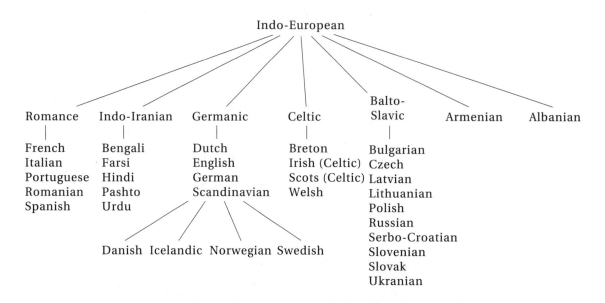

Linear Array

When there does not appear to be a hierarchical ordering of information, you can use a *linear array* of the details. Items are placed at the same level, beneath the heading. The language chart could have been arranged in this way, for instance, if only the main branches of the Indo-European language family had been noted. But once further subdivisions were added to show languages stemming from each major language group, the arrangement of details became hierarchical.

A linear array, sometimes called a *flow chart*, may also be used to show a sequence of events or a process. The example text discusses a process, and the linear array for the details appears beneath the text. Notice on the array that the connections between the parts of it are made clear by lines and arrows. It would be possible to understand the information on this visual without reading the text. When you create a visual such as this, be sure that you have included all the steps of the process.

Example:

Organizational communication is a complex system involving people's feelings, attitudes, relationships, and skills as well as the goals of management and the process of change, adaptation, and growth. Individuals can both send and receive information. Both the receiver and sender have their own personal frame of reference, developed over time. Each also uses his or her own communication skills, such as reading, writing, and listening abilities, that either strengthen or lessen understanding.

In the communication process between a manager and another organizational member, the receiver accepts the message and transmits either verbal or nonverbal feedback, thereby becoming the sender. Verbal feedback is a written or spoken response. Nonverbal feedback is a body movement or actions. Noise is the interference or the barriers that may occur at any point in the process, distorting understanding. The organizational environment also affects sending, receiving, and interpreting the message. The communication process is successful only when the sender and receiver understand the message to the same degree. Feedback permits clarification and repetition until the message is fully understood.

Adapted from Kinard, J. *Management.* Lexington: D. C. Heath, 1988. 349.

The Communication Process

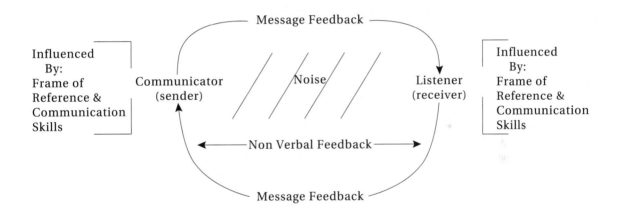

Visuals to Show Comparisons and Contrasts

As you know, authors often want to show contrasts or similarities between viewpoints, people, events, experiences, and so on. The similarities or differences often become more clear to the reader when displayed visually. If you create the visuals yourself, you will be able to determine whether you really know the comparisons or contrasts made. If you do not know them, you will not be able to complete all parts of the visual, which would indicate that you need to reread the material. In this section we show two ways to prepare visuals for text that includes comparisons and contrasts.

Comparison and Contrast Box.   Read the example text to note the contrasts being discussed. Think about the specific points made and try to visualize how you might place this information inside a box. Then look at the model to see how it has been done.

Example:

> Probably the basic disagreement on the causes of income inequality is between those who emphasize flaws in the economic system and those who emphasize flaws in those who are poor. Thus, many liberals, those on the political left, assert that the nation's economic system does not always create enough jobs, or the proper mix of jobs, so that all able-bodied individuals who want to work can find jobs at which they earn enough to provide adequately for those dependent upon them. On the other hand, many conservatives, those on the political right, tend to stress the disabilities that keep poor people from lifting themselves out of their poverty: low aspirations, low motivation, weak commitment to a conviction that one should work. They point to behaviors that make upward mobility impossible: dropping out of school, poor job performance, early parenthood, alcohol and drug abuse. They point out the obvious barrier created by lack of skills. Emphasizing the persistence of poverty despite more than twenty years of a war on poverty, some go so far as to argue that the very programs designed to reduce poverty had operated to perpetuate it.

Davis, B. *Poverty in America.* New York: Franklin Watts, 1991. 23.

Issue: Causes of Income Inequality

Left Point of View	Right Point of View
Flaws in the system:	Flaws in the people:
not enough jobs	low aspirations
wrong types of jobs	low motivation
jobs don't pay enough	behaviors —
	dropping out of school
	drug & alcohol abuse
	early pregnancies
	ineffective social programs

Note that the information in the box is written in short phrases; not everything has been written—just the most important points.

Venn Diagrams.   A second way to illustrate comparison and contrast information from text is by creating a diagram that illustrates both points of commonality and points of difference. This diagram, called a *Venn diagram*, is shown following the example text.

Example:

The one thing that all crystals have in common is that they are built up of repeated patterns. In other ways, crystals may differ widely. Some shatter easily. Others do not. Some are very hard. Some crumble at a touch.

These different properties of crystals are due to many causes. Let's look at some of them.

The way the atoms are arranged in a crystal affects its properties. Two crystals may be made up of the same kind of atom and yet have very different properties. The difference is caused by the way the atoms are arranged in each crystal.

The "lead" in a pencil is really a kind of crystalline material called graphite. Graphite is a form of the element carbon, so graphite crystals are made up entirely of carbon atoms.

Diamond is another form of carbon. Diamond crystals are also made up entirely of carbon atoms.

Diamond and graphite appear to be as different as Dr. Jekyll and Mr. Hyde. Or, as one scientist has put it, they are "beauty and the beast among crystals."

Diamond is the hardest material known. This is another way of saying that diamond will scratch or cut through all other materials. Diamond drills and saws are used to cut through rock. Diamond dust is used to grind and shape metal tools. Diamond crystals when cut and polished make brilliant gems.

Graphite is usually dull black in color and has a greasy feel. It is a very soft material. Like mica, graphite can be sliced easily into very thin sheets. The fact that thin sheets of graphite slide past each other very easily makes it useful for "oiling" moving parts in machines and makes it work in a pencil.

The difference between graphite and a diamond is the result of one extra atom of carbon in the building block of the diamond. Let's take a look at the building block of graphite first.

Weiss, M. E. *Why Glass Breaks, Rubber Bends, and Glue Sticks.* New York: Harcourt Brace Jovanovich, 1974. 24.

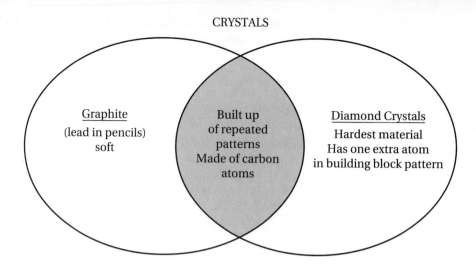

CRYSTALS

Graphite
(lead in pencils)
soft

Built up
of repeated
patterns
Made of carbon
atoms

Diamond Crystals
Hardest material
Has one extra atom
in building block pattern

The center part of the Venn diagram shows how the two types of crystals are similar; hence, the circles overlap. The left and right parts list the differences. This diagram could not have been prepared unless the reader understood the material.

▶ **Thinking About Your Reading and Writing**

ACTIVITY G. Thinking About Your Use of Visual Aids

Which types of visual aids discussed in this chapter will be most helpful to you in the courses you are taking this term?

ACTIVITY H. Determining Visual Displays to Use for Text

Decide which type of visual would be best for each of the following passages. Base your answer on the content of the passage, as well as on the purpose of each type of visual aid. Be prepared to justify your answers.

1. Decision-Making Strategies

There are two different schools of thought on the decision process—
analytical and *intuitive*. **Analytic,** or **systematic, decision making**
(sometimes called scientific decision making) is based on the theory that problem solving can be reduced to a systematic selection process. Proponents insist that decision theory should construct an ideal procedure for rational choice—a step-by-step, logical sequence for picking the best alternative as a solution to a business problem.

Intuitive decision making is based on the belief that good decision making is an art, not a science. Proponents contend that sound problem solving is largely intuitive and unconscious. They argue that good problem diagnosis and decision making result from an esoteric blend of experience, imagination, intelligence, and feeling joined almost unconsciously.

Considerable evidence suggests that managers use both approaches in solving problems and in making decisions. The analytical approach is more orderly, logical, and systematic; the intuitive approach is more prone to trial-and-error, or haphazard. Studies reveal significant differences in how the two types of decision makers approach problems.

Adapted from Kinard, J. *Management.* Lexington: D. C. Heath, 1988. 142.

Type of visual to create for this text: _

2. Drug Treatments for AIDS

Because AIDS is a condition that severely weakens the immune system and leaves the body open to a wide variety of opportunistic diseases, finding a single cure for it has been an elusive task. Instead, government agencies like the Centers for Disease Control (CDC) and the National Institutes of Health (NIH), along with private drug companies, have developed and adapted two categories of drugs to treat people with HIV infection and with AIDS. One category contains drugs that treat the opportunistic infections common to people with AIDS. The other category is made up of drugs designed to bolster the failing immune systems of people with AIDS thereby extending these patients' lives. The best known of the drugs in the second category is AZT or zidovudine. Other drugs include ddI, ddC, and acyclovir.

Most doctors have been pleased with the results of these drugs. According to Dr. Jay Lalezari, codirector of the HIV research unit at Mount Zion Medical Center in San Francisco, "Early results from a small study using AZT and ddC have yielded better results than anything else in the first decade of AIDS research." Results of drug trials from around the country, including a study done by Dr. Richard Moore of the Johns Hopkins School of Medicine in Baltimore, Maryland, show that AZT and other antiviral drugs have been effective at slowing the rate at which patients develop the symptoms of full-blown AIDS.

These drugs, however, have caused controversy for several reasons. Many people have charged that the drugs are harmful. Some argue that the sometimes debilitating side effects produced by these drugs—including nausea, diarrhea, and nerve and liver damage—negate their benefits. Others object to the drugs' limited effects—at some point the drugs stop being effective and the patient's vulnerability to infections increases. Still others contend that AZT is actually poisonous and destroys the immune system rather than bolstering it. Journalist John

Lauritsen, for example, maintains that AZT is "the most toxic drug ever approved or even considered for long-term use."

Many AIDS patients who concur with Lauritsen have turned away from conventional, government-approved drug treatments. These patients are experimenting with alternative medicines and treatments such as Chinese herbs, acupuncture, nutritional therapy, and massage, among others. While many doctors scorn these alternative methods, others have begun to incorporate aspects of alternative therapies such as improved nutrition and acupuncture into their standard treatments. The viewpoints in the following chapter discuss a variety of mainstream and alternative treatments for AIDS.

Biskup, M. D., and K. L. Swisher, eds. *AIDS: Opposing Viewpoints.* San Diego: Greenhaven, 1992. 158.

Type of visual to create for this text: _

3. Basic Elements of the Economy

The goods and services produced in each society derive from resources found naturally within it. (Of course, when barter and trade come into being, resources may be imported from and exchanged between other societies.) *Resources* are defined as everything needed for the production of goods and services. They include human energy used in producing goods and services as well as material objects. In economic terms, human energy is referred to as *labor.* Material objects may be found in nature or made by people. Those found in nature, such as land, minerals, and water, are collectively called *land* by economists. Those made by humans, such as machinery, factories, shoes, and pencils, are known as *capital.* Labor, land, and capital, in addition to *entrepreneurship,* are the *factors of production* and form the basic elements that must be combined in the production of goods and services. For example, when building a house, individuals are impelled by the spirit of entrepreneurship to use human energy—labor—to put a structure on a lot—land—using both natural material objects—wood and stone—and human-made material objects—nails, hammers, bricks, and so on. In economic terms, the result is a product which can be personally used or sold or traded for another product.

In addition to these basic factors, *technology, time,* and *efficiency* play important parts in production. The greater a society's skill and knowledge (its technology), the more effective its production of goods and services. Time is an economic resource that is scarce and precious: If production is to be effective, it must occur within reasonable time limits. If it takes five years to produce one hundred cars in a society of over two hundred million inhabitants, those cars will be of little value: The need is for immediate transportation. Efficiency, the ability to obtain the highest output from a given combination of resources in the least amount of time, is also an important factor.

Resources are versatile; they can be put to many uses. Land can be used to grow crops or for building factories, apartments, or shopping centers. Labor can be employed to harvest crops, to develop complex data systems, or to teach. But resources are also finite. Once used up or destroyed, they cannot always be replaced. Societies must therefore conserve resources and try to replace those depleted through production.

Perry, J. A., and E. K. Perry. *The Social Web.* 5th ed. New York: Harper and Row, 1988. 342–343.

Type of visual to create for this text: ------------------------------------

4. Modern Phyla First Known from the Cambrian

Many major living phyla probably trace their roots back to yet-unknown, soft-bodied ancestors that first evolved during the Protero-zoic era. Unfortunately, the dearth of fossils from that time still shrouds these origins in mystery.

By the beginning of the Cambrian, however, several major lineages of **invertebrates,** animals without backbones, began leaving recogniz-able fossils (*in* means "without"; *vertebrae* means "skeletal elements of the backbone"; hence *invertebrate* means "without a backbone"). Though modern members of these groups did not evolve for millions of years, the basic body plans that appeared during the Cambrian rep-resented evolutionary blueprints or archetypes for organizing body tis-sues. Within each phylum, variations on those blueprints could form new classes or orders, each of which could diverge in adapting to new ways of life—or disappear.

The Cambrian saw the debut of the first sponges, jellyfish, and sea anemones, several important groups of worms, and the ancestors of modern starfishes, sea urchins, snails, clams, and squid. But perhaps the best-known fossils from this period are the **trilobites,** the first rep-resentatives of the phylum Arthropoda, or "jointed-leg" animals, whose living members include crustaceans, spiders, insects, and a variety of other animals many people call "bugs."

Trilobites, the first animals to display the characteristics that made arthropods among the most successful of all invertebrate groups, rap-idly took over the early Cambrian seas. At first, their speed, agility, keen vision, and armor made them deadly and invincible predators. By the middle of the Cambrian, however, predators such as *Anomalocaris* and the giant sea scorpions called *Eurypterids* began to take their toll on the trilobite population. Neither trilobites nor their predators survive today; many died out by the end of the Cambrian.

Ordovician period

The closing days of the Cambrian ushered in one of the largest mass extinctions on record; nearly 50 percent of existing animal families, including many trilobites, became extinct. The Ordovician period that followed saw dramatic adaptive radiations within each major group that survived that extinction. Ancestors of modern snails, clams, and squid diversified extensively, as did aquatic arthropods. One group of early soft-bodied animals (not the corals of today) formed the first reefs.

Levine, J. S., and K. Miller. *Biology.* 2nd ed. Lexington: D. C. Heath, 1994. 506–507.

Type of visual to create for this text: _

5. The Shelter Network

Federal and state funding for battered women's shelters and related services is pitifully short-lived and small. The federal government has initiated no programs for battered women since 1984; and Minnesota, which has one of the most progressive and best-funded abuse prevention programs in the country, spends less to help battered women than to kill mosquitoes. One result is that there are only about a thousand shelters for battered women in the United States. Everywhere, women in need are turned away. In Philadelphia, Women Against Abuse rejects 75 percent of the women who seek shelter. In New York City, Sanctuary for Families turns away one hundred battered women and their children every week. In Seattle, five hundred men are arrested for battering every month, but only thirty-nine shelter beds are available for battered women. In Massachusetts, women's shelters turn away 71 percent of the women in need of shelter and 80 percent of the children. In all areas of the country, demand for temporary shelter, court advocacy, and peer support groups is rising, and budgets are being cut. Some shelters have had to discontinue support programs for children, while others have had to drop court advocates. Everywhere paid workers have cut their own salaries to make the money stretch farther; many carry on as volunteers. One Midwestern shelter laid off its custodian for lack of funds; later, when the shelter was criticized publicly for being dirty and unsanitary, she wrote to the local newspaper: "Until government and society commit themselves to ending violence in the home, there will always be battered women's shelters, they will always be full and there will always be dishes to wash and bathroom floors to mop. Token laws and band-aid funding are the real problem. If we're looking for solutions, why aren't we putting batterers in shelters and letting the women and children stay at home?"

Shelters were never meant to become permanent establishments, but because community institutions do not act effectively to defend women, shelters are the single most effective way of saving lives. More shelters should be established, and all of them should be staffed primarily by women who are survivors of abuse, whether or not they have professional credentials. And because so many battered women cite the lack of affordable housing as the single greatest obstacle to getting free of an abusive man, shelters must have additional funds and the cooperation of municipal housing authorities to help women find transitional and long-term housing. Overburdened federal, state, and local governments will be hard pressed to find more money for shelters, but they must rearrange their priorities to provide it. Elizabeth Schneider points out that money spent on shelters is well spent, for "shelter work contributes to community education, abuse prevention, and institutional change as well as the welfare of children."

Although shelters should be accountable for public funds they expend, they must be free to shelter any abused women and children in need. In 1992 an Iowa shelter became the subject of public controversy and an investigation by the state Division of Criminal Investigation after a former resident, who had risen through the ranks to become a staff member, was revealed to be a fugitive, sought for leaving Arkansas with her two children, of whom she had custody, in violation of custodial claims brought by her ex-husband. (Her children were returned to their father; she was arrested and taken to Arkansas to face prosecution.) But as long as women must run from male violence, as long as some find safety only underground, it should neither surprise us nor discredit a shelter that among the thousands of women it aids there is the occasional fugitive from "justice."

Jones, A. *Next Time, She'll Be Dead*. Boston: Beacon, 1994. 229–231.

Type of visual to create for this text: _

6. Understanding Cultural Differences

Understanding a foreign country's social and cultural aspects is as important to a company's effectiveness as is understanding its language. Knowing what to do is just as important as knowing what not to say. For example, each nationality views the concept of time differently, and many do not share our concern with time at all. Time is a valuable commodity in America; consequently, people rush to consummate business transactions. Greeks, however, feel time limits are insulting and reveal a lack of finesse. Arabs faced with a deadline feel threatened and backed into a corner.

Nonverbal cues also can offend foreign businesspeople. For instance, a face-to-face position that conveys friendship in one country can mean confrontation in another. South Americans, Greeks, and Japanese feel more comfortable standing or sitting close to strangers than do people of many other nationalities.

A stereotype is a mental picture used to identify certain groups of people. It usually contains a label given to the group and a mental list of traits associated with the group. When the label is applied to a national group, it becomes a national stereotype. Because the world is complex, such national stereotypes are used as a mental shortcut in thinking about groups of people. Being sensitive to national stereotypes will help international managers better understand the behavior of certain groups of people they meet but there is a danger in relying on these stereotypes. The international manager must remember that stereotypes are only broad generalizations about groups of people.

Creating Visuals for Ideas in Texts   **147**

Each person is an individual and will act and react in his or her own personal way.

Kinard, J. *Management*. Lexington: D. C. Heath, 1988. 483.

Type of visual to create for this text: _

7. Turn On Your Receiver

The word "perceive," which comes from the same roots as perception, can be used in all three of the above examples of "seeing." It literally means to interpret and translate into meaningful information the impulses that are picked up and recorded by our sense organs.

What the eye does is to engage in sensory reception, which is only one part of perception. The eye has evolved to do a special job and do it very well, to the advantage of the whole body. So, the *retina* of the eye contains light-sensitive *nerve cells* (called *rods* and *cones*) that are the receptors for light. Since the act of seeing involves picking up information in the form of light energy, these receptors are the first real contacts we have with the light of the real world outside of us.

The act of light energy striking the rods and cones of the retina of the eye is called *sensation*. Is this what we mean by perceiving? Probably not. So far, it's just a process of physics: light being focused through a double convex lens onto light-sensitive receptor cells. The same process operates in photography. But do we say that a camera "perceives"? Hardly.

Without going into great detail, we can say that the light energy reflected off the objects in the real world stimulates these rods and cones and triggers a pattern of electro-chemical changes along the nerve network, behind the eye. These bundles of nerves are called *optic nerves*, and the impulses are transmitted to the very back of the brain. Now we're getting close to the "seeing" part. Here, these impulses activate other cells that have had previous experiences. We assume they must be part of the memory system, though we don't really know.

In this part of the brain, the neural impulses are sorted, sifted, processed. And soon they "make sense." Now, they produce an image, even a picture, organizing the disconnected light energy so that it resembles the object outside, in the external world.

This translating process, where meaning is assigned to sensory impulses, is what is called perception. This is the part of the process that really deserves to be called "seeing."

Another way of putting it is that a message is picked up (say from a male object named Joe), which is simply light reflected off him and into my eyes. The rods and cones put that message of light into a code ("encode" it). Just as in secret agent stories, the code is for the purpose of enabling the message to travel more efficiently, with fewer interferences. In the brain, the message is decoded, or translated. I see Joe!

Brennecke, John H., and Robert G. Amick. *Psychology and Human Experience*. Beverly Hills: Glencoe, 1974. 195–196.

8. T'ai Chi

One of the best-known of the martial arts, t'ai chi is both a self-defense strategy and, more commonly in the West, a gentle exercise technique. In Chinese the words t'ai chi chuan mean "supreme ultimate fist," a reference, in part, to its lofty status among the martial arts.

T'ai chi consists of a series of postures performed in sequences. Known as forms, they vary in complexity, with some involving 18 postures and others more than 100. Students move from one posture to the next in a flowing motion that resembles dance. While not as physically demanding as karate and judo, t'ai chi takes a long time to master. Movements are learned slowly and carefully, creating a state of restful action in which the mind can concentrate on every motion. But the pace of class may quicken as students acquire proficiency and agility.

Tracing T'ai Chi's Roots.   The origins of t'ai chi are obscure. There are reports that it was being practiced some 5,000 years ago, and ancient Chinese drawings depict monks performing movements that look similar to t'ai chi. Some accounts of its origins describe the founder as a monk and kung fu student at a monastery in China in the thirteenth century. After witnessing a fight between a bird and a snake, the man noticed that the snake managed to avoid the bird's attack using swift, but subtle movements; from these observations, he developed the art of t'ai chi. Newer theories credit a Chinese general who, in the seventeenth century, improvised t'ai chi by combining martial arts with theories of traditional Chinese medicine.

Like aikido, the Japanese martial art, t'ai chi was influenced by the idea of Tao, which means "the way" or "the path," described by the Chinese philosopher Lao-tze. His philosophy, known as Taoism, stresses that humankind must attain harmony with nature and the universe. When in perfect harmony, things function effortlessly and spontaneously, according to natural laws. So, too, the body operates by the same principles. "When people are alive," Lao wrote, "they are soft and supple. When a plant is alive, it is soft and tender." T'ai chi practitioners believe that the qualities of softness and suppleness can be developed by cultivating the life force, qi, that flows through the body.

Clarity Through Contradiction.   Among the most intriguing aspects of t'ai chi are its various contradictions and seeming paradoxes. These are rooted in the Chinese notion of yin and yang, the law of complementary opposites. For instance, alert relaxation is essential to each movement. The body should remain supple and at ease, but not to the extent of going limp. Movement likewise entails opposition or contradiction. To move to the right, for example, you must first turn slightly leftward; to rise up, you must first sink slightly. The movement called push can be performed most effectively *without* the application of force: the arms and shoulders relax, the elbows hang loose, and the palms of the two partners meet without touching. All movement in t'ai chi describes circles, spirals, or arches. To achieve this effect is sometimes termed "curved seeking straightness." This refers to the necessary curvature of limbs.

Guinness, Al. *Family Guide to Natural Medicine.* Pleasantville: Reader's Digest. 1993. 230–231.

Type of visual to create for this text: _____

9. Artificial Hearts

If the heart is nothing more than a pump, then it should be possible to replace it with a mechanical device that pumps blood. This concept has been the inspiration for a number of research teams who have sought to develop an artificial heart to replace worn or damaged human hearts—and thereby to prolong the lives of patients suffering from severe heart diseases.

The first successful replacement of a human heart with a mechanical device was done in 1982 by surgeon William DeVries. DeVries removed the heart of Barney B. Clark, a patient who was suffering from acute heart failure, and replaced it with the Jarvik-7, a mechanical heart designed by William Jarvik. The heart was implanted into the chest and was driven by compressed air. Initially, the implant into Clark was successful; he regained consciousness and was able to talk and move about his hospital room. However, Clark suffered a number of seizures and strokes, and he died 112 days after insertion of the heart.

The Jarvik-7 helped one patient to survive for 620 days, and it was used in almost 200 patients as a temporary substitute for their own hearts while they waited for a heart transplant. Problems with clotting, infection, and seizures led the U.S. Food and Drug Administration to withdraw approval for the Jarvik-7 several years ago.

This does not mean that the effort to develop an artificial heart is over. The success of the Jarvik-7 has led a number of companies to develop ventricular assist devices that help a weakened heart to pump blood. These devices are implanted up against the left ventricle, the chamber that pumps blood directly to the body. Driven by compressed air or electric motors, these pumps squeeze the left ventricle in a way that assists the heart muscle's own efforts to force blood into circulation.

Ventricular assist devices are now widely used to help restore circulation in individuals with weakened heart muscles. In one case, a woman survived more than 5 years with a ventricular assist device until a suitable heart transplant was available. In other cases, the support provided by the device is sufficient to enable the heart to heal itself and regain enough strength to make a transplant unnecessary.

More than 65,000 Americans a year could benefit from devices that might replace or assist the heart. The success of ventricular assist devices is an indication that bioengineering is on the right track, and it may be only a matter of time before those patients can count on help from a machine that may literally make the difference between life and death.

Levine, J. S., and K. Miller. *Biology.* 2nd ed. Lexington: D. C. Heath, 1994. 704.

Type of visual to create for this text: _

10. Impeachment

There is one other way—besides death, disability, or resignation—by which a president can leave office before his term expires, and that is by impeachment. Not only the president and vice president but also all "civil officers of the United States" can be removed by being impeached and convicted. As a practical matter civil officers—cabinet secretaries, bureau chiefs, and the like—will not be subject to impeachment because the president can remove them at any time and usually will if their behavior makes them a serious political liability. Federal judges, who serve for life and who are constitutionally independent of the president and Congress, have been the most frequent objects of impeachment.

An *impeachment* is like an indictment in a criminal trial: a set of charges against somebody, voted by (in this case) the House of Representatives. To be removed from office, the impeached officer must be *convicted* by a two-thirds vote of the Senate, which sits as a court, hears the evidence, and makes its decision under whatever rules it wishes to adopt. Fifteen persons have been impeached by the House, and seven have been convicted by the Senate. The last conviction was in 1989, when two federal judges were removed from office.

Only one president has been impeached—Andrew Johnson in 1868—but Richard Nixon almost surely would have been had he not first resigned. Johnson was not convicted on the impeachment, the effort to do so falling one vote short of the necessary two-thirds majority. Many historians feel that the effort to remove Johnson was entirely partisan and ideological in nature, for he was not charged with anything that they would regard as "high crimes and misdemeanors" within the meaning of the Constitution. The Congress detested Johnson's "soft" policy toward the defeated South after the Civil War and was determined to use any pretext to remove him. The charges against Nixon were far graver: allegations of illegal acts arising from his efforts to cover up his subordinates' involvement in the burglary of the Democratic National Committee headquarters in the Watergate building.

Some Founders may have thought that impeachment would frequently be used against presidents, but as a practical matter it is so complex and serious an undertaking that we can probably expect it to be reserved in the future only for the gravest forms of presidential misconduct. No one quite knows what a high crime or misdemeanor is, but most scholars agree that the charge must involve something illegal or unconstitutional, not just unpopular. Unless a president or vice president is first impeached and convicted, many experts believe that he is not liable to prosecution as would be any ordinary citizen. (No one is certain, because the question has never arisen.) President Ford's pardon of Richard Nixon meant that he could not be prosecuted under federal law for things that he may have done while in office.

Wilson, James Q. *American Government.* 5th ed. Lexington: D. C. Heath, 1992. 358–359.

Type of visual to create for this text: _

Working Together

Compare your answers for Activity H with those of a partner. Then, with your partner, prepare visual displays for two of the preceding passages.

CHAPTER SUMMARY

Based on your reading of this chapter, list at least five points that were made that you believe will help you with future reading assignments.

1. _____
_____
_____
_____

2. _____
_____
_____
_____

3. _____
_____
_____
_____

4. _____
_____
_____
_____

5. _____
_____
_____
_____

Now that you have worked with the strategies necessary for understanding details, you can practice applying them to full-length reading selections. Choose (or your instructor may choose) a reading selection that is typical of what you will be expected to read for your other college courses, such as an essay or a textbook chapter. Use this selection to:

■ Recognize supporting sentences
■ Understand types of details
■ Understand relationships between main ideas and details
■ Distinguish between major and minor details
■ Create visuals from text

Decide the practice strategies you will use. Apply them to your selection. Then in a few paragraphs, write a description of what you did and how the strategies you used worked for you.

Name of material used: _____

Page numbers: _____

Your description:

Chapter 6

Using Contextual Clues and Other Strategies for Increasing Vocabulary

*I*magine you have seen a horrible movie on Friday night. The worst ever! The next morning, you are startled by a newspaper ad for that same film that includes quotations full of high praise from reviewers, such as "very appealing" and "for one and all." You wonder how this movie could have gotten such a positive response. A little investigation might reveal that the reviews from which the quotations had come had not been flattering at all. The words quoted in the ad had been taken *out of context*. In fact, the reviewers had actually said, "This movie is not very appealing." "An evening at home, rather than a night out to see this film, would be best for one and all." The moviemakers used only parts of sentences in their ads. The context, all the words originally surrounding the quoted portion, conveys critical information that moviegoers reading the ads did not receive. In much the same way, words in sentences take on particular meanings depending on the context in which they are used. In this chapter, you will learn how to analyze the context, as well as some other strategies, to help you comprehend the meaning of unfamiliar words.

Do you often feel frustrated by a need to turn to a dictionary during reading assignments to find the meanings of words unknown to you? If so, you might be surprised to learn that a dictionary is not always needed to define unknown words. Instead, you can often figure out the meaning of the unknown word by using the *context* in which the word has been placed—that is, you can use the words and sentences surrounding the unknown word to help you discern its meaning. This enables you to continue your reading without significant interruption to the flow of ideas that would occur if, instead, you took time to use a dictionary. This type of reading strategy is called *using context clues*.

You probably already use context clues, even without being aware of it. To see how you are able to determine the meaning of unknown words by using the context, complete both parts of Activity A.

ACTIVITY A. Learning What Context Clues Can Do for You

Fill in your responses to Parts 1 and 2 in this chart.

Part 1	*Part 2*	*Part 1*	*Part 2*
1._____	_____	6._____	_____
2._____	_____	7._____	_____
3._____	_____	8._____	_____
4._____	_____	9._____	_____
5._____	_____	10._____	_____

Your Score: _____% _____%

Part 1. For each numbered word, select what you believe to be the best definition. Place your answers in the chart above.

1. **myriad** (a) miracle (b) great number (c) skilled person (d) painting
2. **permeated** (a) appointed (b) allowed (c) spread through (d) harmed
3. **castigate** (a) punish (b) support (c) confuse (d) search
4. **indigence** (a) poverty (b) culture (c) innocence (d) knowledge
5. **dogmatic** (a) courageous (b) cruel to animals (c) weak (d) dictatorial
6. **feign** (a) destroy (b) pretend (c) graceful (d) emotional
7. **renounced** (a) refused to follow (b) announced with force (c) expected (d) encouraged

8. **shun** (a) frighten (b) a Danish coin (c) voice an opinion (d) avoid

9. **replete** (a) full (b) imaginative (c) brightly colored insect (d) cautious

10. **purge** (a) disease (b) remove (c) oppose (d) publicize

Part 2. Select the meaning for each **boldfaced** word from the choices that appear beneath each sentence. Place your answers alongside your answers for Part 1.

1. Because the sky was so clear, we were able to see a **myriad** of stars.
   (a) miracle (b) great number (c) skilled person (d) painting

2. When the smoke from the cigar **permeated** the lounge, the visitors apologized.
   (a) appointed (b) allowed (c) spread through (d) harmed

3. The dictator said he would **castigate** anyone who opposed him.
   (a) punish (b) support (c) confuse (d) search

4. The family's **indigence** meant they could not afford to buy a house or to send their children to college.
   (a) poverty (b) culture (c) innocence (d) knowledge

5. The **dogmatic** leadership style of the chairperson practically guaranteed that she would not be reelected for a second term.
   (a) courageous (b) cruel to animals (c) weak (d) dictatorial

6. If she could **feign** sleep, the child thought that she would not have to take her medicine.
   (a) destroy (b) pretend (c) graceful (d) emotional

7. The newest "pledges" of the fraternity **renounced** what they were asked to do, and later they protested in front of the frat house.
   (a) refused to follow (b) announced with force (c) expected (d) encouraged

8. In order to protect himself, the new boy in school had to **shun** the class bully.
   (a) frighten (b) a Danish coin (c) voice an opinion (d) avoid

9. The Christmas tree was **replete** with ornaments that had been collected over a fifty-year period.
   (a) full (b) imaginative (c) brightly colored insect (d) cautious

10. The prisoner was found wrongfully charged, and as a result, the courts had to **purge** his prison record.
    (a) disease (b) remove (c) oppose (d) publicize

The answers to Parts 1 and 2 are b, c, a, a, d, b, a, d, a, b. Check your work. How did you do? Did context clues help you? In a few sentences, describe the results you found.

WHAT IS THE PROCESS FOR USING CONTEXT CLUES?

You can best understand the answer to this question if you try to observe yourself and what you do when you read material containing an unfamiliar word. Read the following paragraphs, and try to figure out the meaning of the word that is italicized. As you do this, ask yourself, "What am I doing to get the meaning of this word?"

Paragraph 1:

Many researchers initially believed that unusual climatic conditions in the Antarctic atmosphere caused the ozone hole. Intensive studies showed, however, that although climate certainly contributes to the development of the ozone hole, the primary cause of ozone *depletion*, without question, is CFCs. Evidence to support that conclusion came from two intensive studies of the Antarctic stratosphere during the springs of 1986 and 1987.

—Adapted from Golub, Richard, and Eric Brus, eds. *The Almanac of Science and Technology.* Boston: Harcourt Brace Jovanovich, 1990. 32.

What do you guess is the meaning of depletion?

In a few sentences, explain how you formed this definition.

Paragraph 2:

It is difficult to form generalizations that apply to all Spanish-speaking people in the United States. Since the Hispanics of the Southwest have tended to remain quite rural and isolated until recently, they have encountered very little formal discrimination. The much larger Mexican-American group, however, has been discriminated against in every way, and there is growing impatience and militance in the barrio, or ghetto. On the one hand, there is the desire to merge with the dominant group. Some studies indicate that second- and third-generation Mexican Americans are undergoing rapid *assimilation*. In Los Angeles, for example, Mexican Americans are marrying out of their ethnic community to a much greater extent than ever before. Others are opposed to this and prefer to stay within their own cultural group.

What do you guess is the meaning of **assimilation?**

In a few sentences, explain how you formed this definition.

You may find that you have used a combination of strategies to figure out the meanings of unfamiliar words. Some of the strategies are listed next. Check all that you used.

◼ I used my prior knowledge of the word. _____

◼ I tried to pronounce the word. _____

◼ I looked for roots or prefixes in the word. _____

◼ I looked for definitions in the sentence. _____

◼ I looked for words in the sentence that had the opposite meaning. _____

◼ I looked at the other sentences in the paragraph for relationships to the sentence with the unknown word. _____

Working Together

Compare your responses to this checklist with a partner's. Did you use the same strategies? Why do you think your strategies were similar or different?

If you are skilled at using context clues, you will be able to figure out an approximate meaning of the unknown word. There are several different types of context clues. The next section introduces those that are most useful to readers of academic text.

WHAT ARE THE MOST USEFUL TYPES OF CONTEXT CLUES?

Contrast or Antonym Clues

One type of context clue is the *contrast clue,* or *antonym clue.* With this type of clue, the author provides you with a word or phrase that is the opposite, or antonym, of the word you may not know. If you know the meaning of the contrasting word, you will be able to figure out the definition of the unknown word. The antonym usually appears in the same sentence as the unknown word, or very close by. Signal words within the sentence containing the antonym may be used to alert you to it. Some of the contrast signal words you used for identifying paragraph patterns in Chapter 4 included *although, on the other hand, however, but, nevertheless, on the contrary, instead, yet, unlike, conversely, in contrast, _____ than _____*. These same words are often used to signal contrasts between individual words or concepts. Of course, a contrast may appear without signal words. You may still recognize a sentence, or a part of a sentence, as having a meaning opposite to the previous one. In such cases, you will rely solely on the context, without the signal word, to help you determine the meaning of the unknown word.

Example:

> The mood of the music on the radio was *somber*, unlike the cheerful tunes the child had been singing before she got into the car.

Antonym or contrast clue: <u>cheerful</u>

Meaning of unknown word: <u>sad</u>

Explanation: The word *unlike* is a clue to the contrast between *somber* and *cheerful*. Since we know what *cheerful* means, we can guess at the meaning of *somber*.

ACTIVITY B. Contrast and Antonym Clues

For each unknown word in italics, indicate the opposite or contrast clue available to you in the sentence(s). Then write the meaning of the unknown word.

1. He was *undaunted* when he had to speak in front of his class but was very fearful about giving a talk before the entire group of freshmen.

   Antonym or contrast clue: _____

   Meaning of unknown word: _____

2. The honor *bestowed* on the athlete was taken away once it was learned he had been on steroids.

   Antonym or contrast clue: _____

   Meaning of unknown word: _____

3. I would have *squandered* my whole week's earnings; however, my best friend encouraged me to save some of the money for next week's dance.

   Antonym or contrast clue: _____

   Meaning of unknown word: _____

4. Although she was *diminutive,* her booming voice made her seem much larger.

   Antonym or contrast clue: _____

   Meaning of unknown word: _____

5. The old man seemed *eccentric,* but to those who really knew him, he was perfectly normal.

   Antonym or contrast clue: _____

   Meaning of unknown word: _____

6. The castle was *fortified* at the front; however, the rest of it was unprotected.

   Antonym or contrast clue: _____

   Meaning of unknown word: _____

7. The young woman lived a *solitary* life, very different from her older sister who was surrounded by friends.

   Antonym or contrast clue: _____

   Meaning of unknown word: _____

8. Her story was *incongruous.* No one found it believable.

   Antonym or contrast clue: _____

   Meaning of unknown word: _____

9. The hero thought he was *invincible* until the dagger struck a blow to his heart and he died.

   Antonym or contrast clue: _____

   Meaning of unknown word: _____

10. The child's *skepticism* annoyed his elders because they thought he should just believe whatever he was told.

    Antonym or contrast clue: _____

    Meaning of unknown word: _____

Restatement or Synonym Clues

A second type of context clue is the *restatement clue,* or *synonym clue.* A word or phrase that has a meaning similar to a word you don't know placed in or near the sentence with the unknown word gives this type of clue. If you recognize the similar word or understand the meaning of the phrase, you will be able to approximate the definition of the word you do not know.

> ***Example:***
>
> > She made a *resolution* she would quit smoking, the fourth time she had made such a promise, so we were not convinced she would really stop.
>
> ***Restatement or synonym clue:***   promise
>
> ***Meaning of unknown word:***   promise
>
> ***Explanation:***   The phrase *such a promise* contains a synonym for *resolution*. The meaning of this phrase refers you to what has just been said. This makes it easy to figure out that *resolution* means *promise*.

ACTIVITY C. Restatement and Synonym Clues

For each unknown word in italics, indicate the clue available to you in the sentence(s). Then write the meaning of the unknown word.

1. The *agility* of the skater was demonstrated by her ability to move effortlessly on the ice.

   Restatement or synonym clue: -

   Meaning of unknown word: -

2. Jose's *gratitude* was immeasurable. He couldn't thank his girlfriend enough for helping him find a part-time job.

   Restatement or synonym clue: -

   Meaning of unknown word: -

3. After the injury to his leg, the tennis star quickly regained *mobility,* and he could move easily on the court.

   Restatement or synonym clue: -

   Meaning of unknown word: -

4. When the *decline* in production of American automobiles occurred, manufacturers looked for reasons to explain the reduction.

   Restatement or synonym clue: -

   Meaning of unknown word: -

5. She was so *incensed* at the animal trainer's cruelty she could not watch any more of the animal acts without being angry.

Restatement or synonym clue: _____

Meaning of unknown word: _____

6. There was such a *preponderance* of mail for the rock star it took her more than a week to answer just the large stack that arrived the day after Christmas.

Restatement or synonym clue: _____

Meaning of unknown word: _____

7. The United States was concerned about *combating* a food crisis world-wide while also fighting a drug war at home.

Restatement or synonym clue: _____

Meaning of unknown word: _____

8. The young child's table manners were so *exemplary* she was considered a model for others and was invited, often, to parties.

Restatement or synonym clue: _____

Meaning of unknown word: _____

9. His *effervescence* was contagious, and soon everyone shared his enthusiasm about the project.

Restatement or synonym clue: _____

Meaning of unknown word: _____

10. During the highly negative campaign, each candidate sought to *discredit* the other.

Restatement or synonym clue: _____

Meaning of unknown word: _____

Definition Clues

The *definition clue* is much like the restatement or synonym clue, except that the author *deliberately* provides the meaning of the unknown word. This is often done through the use of punctuation: commas, parentheses, brackets, or dashes that set off the definition. Helping words such as *that is, such as,* or *which means* are also sometimes used to signal the definition.

Example 1: Definition with commas

The doctor's income was *commensurate* with, or equal to, his ability as a surgeon.

Clue indicator: commas that set off the definition

Explanation: The unknown word *commensurate* is defined by the words between the commas.

Example 2:   Definition with parentheses

EEGs (tracings of the brain's brain wave activity) were first systematically used in the 1930s when researchers began to study eye movement.

Explanation: The words in parentheses provide a definition of EEGs.

ACTIVITY D. Definition Clues

For each unknown word in italics, indicate how the author signals that a definition is being provided.

1. The *Anasazi,* the group of American Indians living in the Southwest from 1000 to 1300 A.D., lived in cliff dwellings.

   Author's signal: _

2. It is a *universal* truth—one that all people accept—that success is usually the result of a combination of hard work and good luck.

   Author's signal: _

3. Our *forbearance,* or patience, made it possible for us to complete the entire experiment properly and to get satisfactory results.

   Author's signal: _

4. The *petiole* (the stemlike part of the leaf) joins the blade to the stem.

   Author's signal: _

5. *Photocopying* is the practice of making copies of parts of books, magazines, newspapers, or pamphlets.

   Author's signal: _

Illustration or Example Clues

To help readers understand particularly difficult concepts, important ideas, or words that may be used in a unique way, an author may provide *illustration clues,* or *example clues,* of the concept. These illustrations or examples enable the reader to create a definition for that concept or unknown word. Words that signal an illustration or example include *for example, for instance, such as, to illustrate.* These phrases are very common in academic text.

Example 1:

> Everyone in the scientific community knows that our weather system is *aperiodic*. Nature is full of others: animal populations that rise and fall almost regularly, epidemics that come and go on tantalizingly near-regular schedules.

Explanation: The unknown word, *aperiodic*, is explained through the other examples in nature that are given. These examples describe natural events that occur in cycles that are not quite regular. The word *aperiodic*, then, must refer to something that occurs in irregular cycles.

Example 2:

> Some people believe that morality in our culture has *retrograded*. For instance, young people are no longer waiting until marriage to have sex. News articles regularly report increases in all kinds of crime. Everywhere one can see growing evidence of crooked politicians. Perhaps the critics are correct.

Explanation: The unknown word, *retrograded*, is clarified through the use of examples. A close look at the examples shows they each refer to changes—change in attitudes toward premarital sex, growth in crime, and increase in crooked politicians. None of these changes are positive. Note also that the first example is introduced by the signal words *For instance*. Using all this information, we can determine that *retrograded* must mean going backward in a society or degenerating.

ACTIVITY E. Illustration and Example Clues

Use the information in each paragraph to define the italicized unknown word. Write your definition in the space provided.

1. The legend you may know as Lawrence of Arabia is actually T. E. Lawrence (1899–1935). He achieved fame as the result of his many *exploits* in Egypt. He helped organize the Arab revolt against the Turkish Ottoman Empire. His devotion to the Arab cause and his military genius led to the defeat of the Turks and the entry of the Arabs into Damascus, the capital of Syria. Lawrence was later killed in a motorcycle accident in England.

   Your definition: -

2. A popular way to use imagery is through *mnemonic* devices. The basic process of a mnemonic system consists in taking something that has known imagery content and then associating to it images of things to be learned. Such devices are used by stage magicians to learn the names of people sitting in the audience. A person good at this procedure can learn the names of 100 people after hearing them only once. The famous Roman orator Cicero was the inventor of an early system

called the method of loci. He used the images associated with walking to different parts of his garden to learn the order of ideas in his speeches.

Adapted from Grasha, Anthony F. *Practical Applications of Psychology.* 2nd ed. Boston: Little, Brown, 1983. 112.

Your definition: _____

3. Managers can improve their efficiency by *delegating* work. Delegating is important for several reasons. First, it frees a manager from some time-consuming duties that can be performed by subordinates. Second, decisions made by lower-level managers usually are more timely than those that go through several layers of management. Third, subordinate managers can reach their potential only if given the chance to make decisions and to assume responsibility for them.

Adapted from Kinard, Jerry. *Management.* Lexington, Mass.: D. C. Heath, 1988. 191.

Your definition: _____

4. My eighth-grade math teacher had few friends among the student population. We considered him a highly *captious* individual. For example, poor quality homework papers were often put on display, and the unfortunate souls who wrote them were never told how they could improve their work. If a student saw him in the hall and offered a kindly "hello," Mr. Boise only snapped back an unfriendly grunt along with some suggestion such as "You're late to class" or "Why don't you get a haircut?"

Your definition: _____

5. My elderly father had become more *sedentary* than I had originally thought. When I went to visit him, the changes in behavior were clear. He no longer went for his daily walk. He spent many hours sitting on the front porch watching the birds and listening to the rustle of the trees. He didn't visit friends as he used to. My husband and I became so concerned that we finally suggested he might want to come to live with us.

Your definition: _____

Experience or Common-sense Clues

A fifth type of context clue is the *experience clue* or *common-sense clue.* In sentences with this type of clue, the author describes a situation that you are probably familiar with or that you can imagine. By using your experience, or by considering what would make sense in the situation described, you will be able to figure out the meaning of the unknown word.

Example:

The low temperatures and cloudy sky *foreshadowed* the snowstorm that was soon to come.

Unknown word: foreshadowed

Experience or common-sense clue: low temperatures; cloudy sky

Meaning of unknown word: suggested; indicated beforehand

Explanation: In this sentence, the reader is told about three things: low temperatures, a cloudy sky, and a coming snowstorm. If the reader asks, "What is the relationship between these three things?" it makes sense to say that the low temperatures and cloudy sky are signs of the storm. Thus, *foreshadowed* must mean they are signs of, they suggest, they indicate beforehand.

ACTIVITY F. Experience and Common-sense Clues

For each unknown word in italics, indicate the clue given in the sentence. Then write the meaning of the unknown word.

1. In order to *coalesce* the two points of view, I needed to find their major similarities and to avoid discussing their differences.

   Experience or common-sense clue: _____

   Meaning of unknown word: _____

2. The judge *exonerated* the prisoner after learning that the man whom the prisoner had been found guilty of critically wounding had made several attempts on the prisoner's life while the prisoner was on probation.

   Experience or common-sense clue: _____

   Meaning of unknown word: _____

3. The "Homes of Our Ancestors" show at the New York Coliseum displayed *relics* from an earlier time that had recently been unearthed by local archaeologists.

   Experience or common-sense clue: _____

   Meaning of unknown word: _____

4. I was *repulsed* by the stories of conditions in the concentration camps during the Holocaust.

   Experience or common-sense clue: _____

   Meaning of unknown word: _____

5. A watch is such an *intricate* object that, even if you had all the parts of it in front of you, you wouldn't be able to figure out how to put it together without a watchmaker's diagram.

Experience or common-sense clue: _____

Meaning of unknown word: _____

6. So many employees of the town were going on vacation in July that the mayor had to appoint *surrogate* police officers for the month.

Experience or common-sense clue: _____

Meaning of unknown word: _____

7. The *cherished* photographs were wrapped carefully in tissue paper and placed in a velvet-lined trunk, which would be kept safely in the attic.

Experience or common-sense clue: _____

Meaning of unknown word: _____

8. Using statistics from last year, the World Wildlife Fund has been able to *conjecture* the rate at which humans will slash and burn tropical forests this year.

Experience or common-sense clue: _____

Meaning of unknown word: _____

9. In my private *niche* at home, I am able to read or listen to music for as long as I want without interruption.

Experience or common-sense clue: _____

Meaning of unknown word: _____

10. The Duke of Kensington *succumbed* to lung disease because his servants were ignorant about how to treat such an illness.

Experience or common-sense clue: _____

Meaning of unknown word: _____

▶ Thinking About Your Reading and Writing

ACTIVITY G. Reviewing Context Clues

Review each of the five types of context clues explained in this section. Then answer the following questions.

1. Which of these clues were most familiar to you?

----

2. How can knowledge of these clues help you with your writing?

ACTIVITY H. Defining Words Without Using a Dictionary

Without the use of a dictionary, define each of the italicized words in the following paragraphs. Then in the space provided, indicate how you obtained the definition. In some cases, something other than, or in addition to, context may have helped. If you used context clues, indicate which one(s) helped you.

1. In the field of primary health care, physicians are the most powerful, most influential, and most prestigious professional group. Innovative projects in which they are partners will generally proceed much more readily than those in which they are treated as *adversaries*. Admittedly, when physicians are partners with social workers in a project, the potential always exists for physicians to exploit the unequal balance of the partnership and to steer the direction of the project toward an endpoint that the social workers may view as undesirable.

   Word to define: *adversaries*

   Your definition: --

   The process you used: ---------------------------------------

   ----

   ----

2. It was soon common knowledge that Washington intended to appoint Hamilton as secretary of the treasury. Undoubtedly, this knowledge was

the primary motivation when Congress passed legislation that would prevent the president from granting the secretary too much power. The opponents of strong government feared Hamilton's views and his undoubted abilities, and they wished to *hamstring* him from the start.

Word to define: *hamstring*

Your definition: _____

The process you used: _____

_____

_____

3. *Tactics* is the art of employing forces in the presence of the enemy. Tactics is about the handling of all kinds of forces, not about the effect of forces on the course and outcome of campaigns of war. In the face of an intercontinental threat, no one can talk of an ICBM launch, or foreign tactics. In fact, all elements of the armed forces are both tactical and strategic instruments.

Word to define: *tactics*

Your definition: _____

The process you used: _____

_____

_____

4. America cannot make the productivity gains needed to succeed in the new economic era without doing more than simply redistributing capital assets and getting new technologies in place. Something equally difficult is necessary—the training and placement of employees in the appropriate jobs. A skilled work force to manage automated machinery, above all machinery based on the new "information" technologies, is essential to raising industrial and national competitiveness. In a global economy, it is a significant *inducement* to multinational corporations deciding to locate their production facilities in one nation or region over another.

Solomon, S. *Small Business USA: The Role of Small Companies in Sparking America's Economic Transformation.* New York: Crown, 1986. 79.

Word to define: *inducement*

Your definition: _____

The process you used: _____

_____

_____

5. Median family income, which had risen steadily in the postwar period, fell in real (inflation-adjusted) terms between 1970 and 1983. The *brunt* of that decline was borne by the traditional single-income household, which in 1984 had only three fifths of the buying power of the fast-growing, and visibly affluent, two-income families. Poverty rates climbed as well.

Ibid. 57.

Word to define: *brunt*

Your definition: _____

The process you used: _____

_____

_____

6. Fat babies have been thought to be healthy ones, which is not necessarily so. Fat babies are sometimes praised for being good babies because they seem to "fuss" less and are less active than thinner babies. Studies have shown that physical activity is habit forming. If we are in the habit of being active, we feel restless when inactive. If we are inactive and *indolent,* we feel more comfortable that way. Babies should be encouraged to be active and to play so that they will get into the habit of being dynamic rather than vegetative. This will definitely aid in fat prevention.

Word to define: *indolent*

Your definition: _____

The process you used: _____

_____

_____

7. As long as parents [in the United States] don't abuse or neglect their children, the law gives them the authority to make their own decisions about their children's welfare. However, parents' authority is not *absolute.* Children do not have to obey parents who order them to do some-

thing dangerous or illegal. Parents who mistreat their children can be charged with child abuse. Moreover, parents cannot allow their children to run wild or do anything they want. If they do, the parents can be charged with contributing to the delinquency of a minor. For example, a father who encourages his son to use drugs could be convicted of this crime.

McMahon, Edward T., et al. *Street Law: A Course in Practical Law.* 3rd ed. St. Paul, Minn.: West. 219.

Word to define: *absolute*

Your definition: _____

The process you used: _____

_____

_____

8. *Palimony* is the name given to support payments made by one ex-lover to another after an unwed couple splits up. In the past when an unwed couple split up, any property went to the person who had legal title to it. In relationships in which one partner was the wage earner and the other was the homemaker, the wage earner got the property. This was because the wage earner "owned" the property acquired through his or her wages.

Ibid. 212.

Word to define: *Palimony*

Your definition: _____

The process you used: _____

_____

_____

9. Scientists have long been mystified why anyone would ever do something unselfish for someone else. These displays of niceness, called *altruism,* don't seem to square with the Darwinian scheme of things. The point of the evolutionary game is to pass along your genes, and your best chance to do that usually means grabbing as much food and other resources for yourself and your *progeny* as you can. Animals with unselfish, generous impulses would seem ill-equipped to compete and likely candidates for a quick death. Darwin called it the survival of the fittest—not the nicest.

Word to define: *altruism*

Your definition: --

The process you used: --

Word to define: *progeny*

Your definition: --

The process you used: --

----

10. How do animals such as homing pigeons have such an amazing navigational ability? Experiments suggest that many animals use earth's magnetic field for guidance. People do the same with compasses, and many animals seem to have internal compasses. Embedded in their bodies are tiny crystals of an iron oxide called *lodestone*. Like iron filings attracted to a bar magnet, these crystals *orient* in the direction of earth's magnetic poles. By sensing this orientation, homing pigeons can determine the direction to their loft.

Word to define: *lodestone*

Your definition: --

The process you used: --

Word to define: *orient*

Your definition: --

The process you used: --

Compare your responses with those of a partner.

1. Which of your definitions were similar? _

   _

2. In what ways were the processes you used for defining words similar

   or different? _

   _

   _

   _

3. What reasons can you give to explain the similarities or differences in

   the processes you each used for defining words? _ _ _ _ _ _ _ _ _ _ _ _ _ _ _ _

   _

   _

   _ ●

INTELLIGENT USE OF THE DICTIONARY

Although context clues will enable you to determine the meaning of many unknown words, a good dictionary is still an essential tool for academic success.

There are several different types of "standard" dictionaries, dictionaries that contain alphabetical listings of words along with their pronunciations and definitions. An *unabridged dictionary* contains a great many of the words of the language as well as information about the origin and use of words. These huge dictionaries include more than 400,000 words. They are expensive and impractical for everyday use. Libraries typically have at least one unabridged dictionary.

Abridged dictionaries contain about half the number of words as an unabridged one. This type of dictionary serves college students extremely well for a number of reasons. They are usually hard bound, which makes them durable, and they contain all the general vocabulary information you will most likely need for your academic study.

There are also *pocket dictionaries*. As the name implies, these are very small and, thus, are not as useful for students. They have only one-quarter to one-half the number of words found in an abridged dictionary. Space limitations in pocket dictionaries also result in briefer definitions, and they offer less information about a word's origin or use. It is a handy spelling reference, though, and students often carry pocket dictionaries, along with their other reference materials, when they are preparing to write papers.

There are also *specialized dictionaries* that are devoted to the language of a particular field, such as music or technology. Such a dictionary may become useful to you when you start to take upper-level courses in your major.

Most of the information in this section is based on the typical contents of abridged dictionaries. A good dictionary is perhaps the most effective tool to use when you want to:

- Define words that cannot be defined from the context
- Check pronunciation
- Verify spellings
- Verify parts of speech
- Verify word usage

Before we look at each of these intelligent uses of the dictionary, we should review some of the basic facts about the dictionary. No doubt, you already know a great many of these facts from your earlier education. To determine your prior knowledge about the dictionary, complete Activity I.

<u>ACTIVITY I.</u> Identifying Your Prior Knowledge About the Dictionary

Several questions about standard dictionaries follow. For each, list any information that you already know. Include any details that come to mind, even if they seem unimportant to you.

1. What are some of the things you can learn about an individual word in a dictionary entry besides the word's definition(s)?

   _____

   _____

   _____

   _____

   _____

2. In what order is the information about a word usually listed in a dictionary entry?

   _____

3. What is a good strategy for locating words in the dictionary?

_____

_____

4. What is a good strategy for figuring out how to pronounce words in the dictionary?

_____

_____

5. What should you do when more than one meaning is given for a word in the dictionary?

_____

_____

6. What else, besides information about individual words, might you find in a good dictionary?

_____

_____

_____

Working Together

Share your knowledge with a partner. Add to your answers any information that your partner helped you recall.

How much were you able to recall? Probably quite a bit. You may have mentioned most of the following facts about dictionaries and dictionary entries:

■ The word being defined, the *entry word,* is written in boldface type. It is also written to show *end-of-line divisions.* These indicate where to hyphenate if this word must be broken at the end of a line you are writing.

- Entries indicate the correct pronunciation for the word being defined. *Diacritical markings* are used to show how it is pronounced. Alternative, acceptable pronunciations are also given. A key to the diacritical markings usually appears at the bottom of the page.

- Dictionary entries also indicate the function and usage of the word. A descriptor to show how the defined word commonly functions grammatically, perhaps as a noun [*n*] or as an adjective [*adj*], usually appears immediately following the pronunciation. Words that are no longer used in a language are noted as *obs*, meaning obsolete. If a word is seldom used, the entry reads *archaic*. In some cases, the entry about usage may indicate that a word's use is limited to a specific region of the United States (such as [New Eng] or [Northwest]) or to another part of the world (such as [chiefly Irish] or [Brit]). Word usage comments also may inform you that a word is *slang* or *nonstandard*. Words that are slang, such as the expression *main squeeze,* are used only for very informal writing or speaking situations. If the descriptor *nonstan* appears in the entry, it means that the word is disapproved by many people. Try to avoid using slang and nonstandard words in your formal writing assignments.

- Entries also inform you about word origin, or *etymology*. Often, you can understand the current usage of a word by knowing the word's history. Abbreviations are used to show the origins, the most common of which are [Gr.] Greek; [L.] Latin; [ME.]Middle English; [OE.] Old English. If the exact date or the century when the word was first used in a particular way is known, this may be shown, as in (12c) or (1599). If the word is no longer in use, the period when it was used may be indicated.

- Entries, of course, also provide the definition (or definitions) of the word. Some words have multiple meanings. Each definition is given in the entry. In such cases, you need to refer to the context in which the word was used in what you read so as to determine the appropriate meaning for your purposes. In some dictionaries, synonyms for the word are noted as well.

- *Inflected* forms of the entry word are often included. This part of the entry shows how the word is written in another form, as in a different tense or number. The entire word with the changed inflection is sometimes completely written. For instance, the inflected forms for the word *carry* may be shown as *carried, carrying*. Sometimes, though, only the added portion is shown, as in *-ried; -rying*. An inflected form may also be listed as a separate entry.

The following model illustrates how these parts of entries are arranged in one abridged dictionary for the word *universal*. Note that there are two different entries, each for a different part of speech. As you study this entry, note any additional information about dictionary entries that you did not have on your original list in Activity I.

Dictionary Entry:

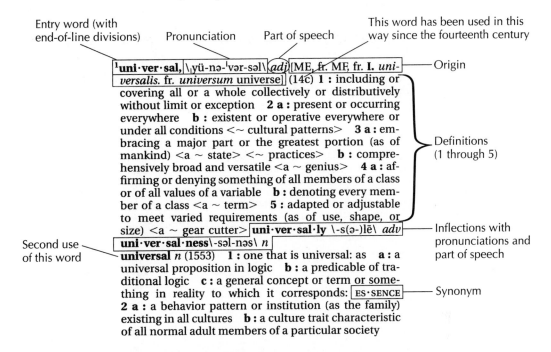

- Entry word (with end-of-line divisions)
- Pronunciation
- Part of speech
- This word has been used in this way since the fourteenth century
- Origin
- Definitions (1 through 5)
- Inflections with pronunciations and part of speech
- Second use of this word
- Synonym

¹uni·ver·sal, \ˌyü-nə-ˈvər-səl\ adj [ME, fr. MF, fr. L. uni-versalis. fr. universum universe] (14c) **1** : including or covering all or a whole collectively or distributively without limit or exception **2 a** : present or occurring everywhere **b** : existent or operative everywhere or under all conditions <~ cultural patterns> **3 a** : embracing a major part or the greatest portion (as of mankind) <a ~ state> <~ practices> **b** : comprehensively broad and versatile <a ~ genius> **4 a** : affirming or denying something of all members of a class or of all values of a variable **b** : denoting every member of a class <a ~ term> **5** : adapted or adjustable to meet varied requirements (as of use, shape, or size) <a ~ gear cutter> uni·ver·sal·ly \-s(ə-)lē\ adv uni·ver·sal·ness\-səl-nəs\ n

universal n (1553) **1** : one that is universal: as **a** : a universal proposition in logic **b** : a predicable of traditional logic **c** : a general concept or term or something in reality to which it corresponds: ES·SENCE **2 a** : a behavior pattern or institution (as the family) existing in all cultures **b** : a culture trait characteristic of all normal adult members of a particular society

■ Dictionaries may vary slightly in the order in which the entry contents appear, but the pronunciation, part of speech of defined word, and word origin are always near the beginning of the entry.

■ You also probably noted in your answers to Activity I that *guide words* appear at the top of each page of a dictionary. Guide words show the first and last words on the page and enable you to locate words quickly.

■ Many abridged dictionaries also include some very useful and interesting information in sections that are set apart from the definitions portion of the book. Within a single abridged dictionary, you may find such sections as

The English language (a history of its development)

Common Abbreviations (this section may also include symbols for chemical elements)

Foreign Words and Phrases

Biographical Names (names of notable persons, both living and dead)

Geographical Names (this section often includes basic information about the countries of the world and their most important regions, cities, and physical features)

Signs and Symbols (especially those used in the sciences and math)

A Handbook of Style (which discusses general rules for punctuation and grammar as well as models for writing bibliographies)

Forms of Address (which show the title to use in letters to officials in various capacities, such as an archbishop or ambassador)

ACTIVITY J. Recognizing Functions of Entries in Dictionaries

Here are some dictionary entries from an abridged dictionary. Several items on the entry have been numbered. In the space provided, identify the function of each numbered item.

1.

a.

trans·la·tion \tran(t)s-'lā-shən, tranz-\ *n* (14c)   **1 :** an act, process, or instance of translating: as   **a :** a rendering from one language into another; *also* : the product of such a rendering   **b :** a change to a different substance, form, or appearance : CONVERSION   **c (1) :** a transformation of coordinates in which the new axes are parallel to the old ones   **(2) :** uniform motion of a body in a straight line   **2 :** the process of forming a protein molecule at a ribosomal site of protein synthesis from information contained in messenger RNA—compare TRANSCRIPTION 3— **trans·la·tion·al**\-shnəl, -shə-nᵊl*adj*

b.

c.

a. _____

b. _____

c. _____

2.

a.

in·sol·vent\(ˌ)in-'säl-vənt, -'sȯl-\ *adj* (1591)   **1 a (1) :** unable to pay debts as they fall due in the usual course of business   **(2) :** having liabilities in excess of a reasonable market value of assets held   **b :** insufficient to pay all debts <an ~ estate>   **c :** not up to a normal standard or complement : IMPOVERISHED — b. **2 :** relating to or for the relief of insolvents — **in·sol·ven·cy**\-vən(t)-sē\ *n*— **insolvent** *n*

c.

a. _____

b. _____

c. _____

3.

a.   b.   c.

¹le·ver \'le-vər, 'lē-\ *n* [ME, fr. MF *levier*, fr. *lever* to raise, fr. L *levare*, fr. *levis* light in weight — more at LIGHT] (14c)   **1 a :** a bar used for prying or dislodging something   **b :** an inducing or compelling force :—TOOL <use food as a political ~ —*Time*>   **2 a :** a rigid piece that transmits and modifies force or motion when forces are applied at two points and it turns about a third; *specif* : a rigid bar used to exert a pressure or sustain a weight at one point of its length by the application of a force at a second and turning at a third on a fulcrum   **b :** a projecting piece by which a mechanism is operated or adjusted

a. _____

b. _____

c. _____

USING THE DICTIONARY TO DEFINE WORDS

If you have looked for context clues to meaning within the material you are reading, but have not found any, perhaps you should refer to a dictionary. This does not mean that you should look up *every* word you do not know. Intelligent use of the dictionary for the purpose of defining words means that you are able to make choices about which words to look up. Your decisions should be guided by your answers to these two questions.

1. Is the word essential to your comprehension of the material? Essential words usually meet one of the following criteria: They are words that (a) are repeated often in the material, (b) have specific technical definitions, and (c) are important to the main ideas in the material.

   As a general rule of thumb, look up words that cannot be defined through context whenever the flow of ideas is interrupted for you because you do not know the word's meaning or whenever the word is a technical term.

2. Is there, in the text you are reading, a glossary that can provide the definition? Glossaries of technical terms are often included in textbooks. When they are, you are better off using the glossary, instead of the dictionary, because the author tells you precisely how a term is being used in *that* text.

USING THE DICTIONARY TO CHECK PRONUNCIATION

If your goal is to read material quickly and to obtain meaning, you can safely ignore most of your questions about pronunciation—at least temporarily. Keep your reading going, and use a temporary pronunciation for the unpronounceable word. When you complete your reading, you can decide whether you should check pronunciation. If you believe that it will be important for you to be able to use the word in class discussions, you should learn how to pronounce it. Knowing the pronunciation of a word will also help you spell it.

USING THE DICTIONARY TO CHECK SPELLING

Any writing you submit to your instructors will be judged, in part, on the basis of your spelling and grammar. If too many words are misspelled, the worth of your ideas may be overlooked. The dictionary is a wonderful spelling reference. Use it to verify spellings whenever you are in doubt. Some students have begun to rely on spelling checkers that are included in many computer word processing programs. Spelling checkers compare the words in a document you write with words in an electronic dictionary. Such dictionaries contain as many as 100,000 words, and additional words usually can be added by the user. The spelling checker runs through the document, comparing each word to the words in the dictionary. If a match is found, it moves on to check the next word. If it does not find a match, the spelling checker either marks the word for later correction or asks the user to correct the error immediately. Some programs even offer suggested corrections, guessing at what the word is supposed to be. Spelling checkers have limitations, though, and should be used with caution. For instance, if the word *are* was typed instead of *art,* the spelling checker would not catch the error because both are legitimate words.

—Adapted from Kershner, H. G. "Using the Dictionary to Check Spelling." *Computer Literacy.* 2nd ed. Boston: D. C. Heath, 1992. 302.

USING THE DICTIONARY TO CHECK WORD USAGE

Every adult has four vocabularies: speaking, reading, listening, and writing. As adults, our speaking and writing vocabularies tend to be smaller than our reading and listening vocabularies. Thus, the words we use in our writing are ones we already have in our listening vocabulary. If you are uncertain whether a word can be used in a particular form, perhaps as an adjective, you will need to decide if this use of the word is correct. The first way to verify usage is to listen to how the word sounds in the sentence and form you intend to use. If it sounds correct to you, it probably is. If you are still uncertain, though, check the dictionary. A pocket dictionary may not give you this information; you may need to use either an abridged or an unabridged one.

▶ **Thinking About Your Reading and Writing**

ACTIVITY K. Personal Use of the Dictionary

Under what circumstances might you use a dictionary, even if you can define a word from the context? List any situations you can think of.

WORD STRUCTURE: A CLUE TO WORD MEANING

Anyone who is learning a second language knows the advantages of studying a new language that contains some words similar to ones in his or her native language. When words of different languages share a common *root*, it is easier to predict the meaning of the foreign word. Similarly, if you know the most common roots of your own language, as well as the most common *prefixes* and *suffixes*, you can often correctly guess the meaning of unknown words.

You are probably already familiar with the terms *root, prefix,* and *suffix;* these are the elements of a word's structure. To determine some of your knowledge, and to see how this information can be useful to you, complete Activity L.

ACTIVITY L. Recognizing and Using Word Structure

For each word listed, (a) identify the prefix, root, and suffix, as indicated, and provide a definition for the word. Then (b) think of another word with the same prefix and write its definition; then think of another word with the same root and write its definition. Your definitions may be approximations. If you can't answer one part of the question, continue to the next. Answers to later questions may help you with earlier ones you did not know. Write your answers in the space provided.

Example: *autograph*
a. *Prefix:* auto

   Prefix meaning: self

   Root: graph

   Root meaning: to write; to make a record of something

   Definition of this word: to write your own name
b. *Another word with the same prefix:* automobile

   Its definition: a car you drive yourself

   Another word with the same root: photograph (noun)

   Its definition: a record, on film, of someone or something

1. *monotonous*

   a. *Prefix:* _____

   Prefix meaning: _____

Root: _____

Root meaning: _____

Suffix: _____

Suffix meaning: _____

Definition of this word: _____

b. Another word with the same prefix: _____

Its definition: _____

Another word with the same root: _____

Its definition: _____

2. *invisible*

a. Prefix: _____

Prefix meaning: _____

Root: _____

Root meaning: _____

Suffix: _____

Suffix meaning: _____

Definition of this word: _____

b. Another word with the same prefix: _____

Its definition: _____

Another word with the same root: _____

Its definition: _____

3. *prediction*

a. Prefix: _____

Prefix meaning: _____

Root: _

Root meaning: _

Suffix: _

Suffix meaning: _

Definition of this word: _

b. **Another word with the same prefix:** _

Its definition: _

Another word with the same root: _

Its definition: _

4. *tricycle*

a. **Prefix:** _

Prefix meaning: _

Root: _

Root meaning: _

Definition of this word: _

b. **Another word with the same prefix:** _

Its definition: _

Another word with the same root: _

Its definition: _

▶ **Thinking About Your Reading and Writing**

ACTIVITY M. Your Conclusions About Word Structure

What conclusions can you now draw about using word structure to help you with meanings of unknown words?

_ _

No doubt you realize the extent to which words derive their meaning from prefixes, suffixes, and roots. The root is the basic unit of a word. It determines the meaning of the word. Many root words have their origins in Greek and Latin. The combination of prefixes and suffixes that are attached to the root create other words. These are always some variation of the root word. Note how, in the example that follows, the meaning of the root *scribere* remains central to the meaning of a wide number of other words in which it appears.

root: *scribere* (L) to write

scribe	[n]	an official or public secretary or clerk; a copier of manuscripts
	[v]	to work as a scribe; write
transcribe		to make a copy of (dictated or recorded matter) in longhand or on a machine
subscribe		to sign (as a document) with one's own hand in token of consent or obligation
inscribe		to write, engrave, or print as a lasting record
describe		to represent or give an account of in words
prescribe		to write or give medical prescriptions, to lay down a rule

The prefix is an element that appears before the root. It is possible for a word to have more than one prefix. When this occurs, the meaning of each prefix is needed to arrive at the complete meaning of the word. Note how the prefixes are combined for meaning in the following examples. The original root word is also indicated.

redistribute   to divide among several or many again
re: again
dis: apart
(root: fr. *tribere*—to allot; to give)

undiscernible   unable to recognize as separate and distinct
un: not
dis: apart
(root: fr. *cervere*—to sift; to sort)

preadmit   to give early entrance (as to a concert)
pre: before

ad: toward
(root: fr. *mittere*—to send)

inconclusive   leading to no conclusion or definite result
  in: not
  con: with, together, thoroughly
  (root: fr. *claudere*—to shut)

The suffix appears at the end of a word. Suffixes often serve to change the form of the word, as in this example:

animate	to give life to; full of life
animated	full of movement and activity
animation	the state of being animated; a motion picture made by photographing positions of inanimate objects
animatedly	in a lively way

When you are reading, you may encounter a word that, though unfamiliar to you, has a familiar word part. Such knowledge of word parts can be used to help you determine the unknown word's meaning. Certain academic subjects, particularly some of the sciences, have many words that share a common prefix or root. If you learn some of the most common prefixes and roots in the subjects you study, you will have a good start at defining many unfamiliar words. A prefix used often in biology or courses dealing with the human body appears next, along with words that use the prefix:

prefix: *gen* (also *gene*), born

words: **gene**   a unit of hereditary information

  genetic engineering   the use of recent technologies to "cut and paste" genes from one organism to another, introducing new genes and new characteristics into organisms

  genetic map   a presentation of the physical locations of genes on a chromosome

  genetics   a branch of biology that deals with the heredity and variation of organisms

  genotype   an organism's hereditary makeup

Levine, J. S., and K. Miller. *Biology.* 2nd ed. Lexington: D. C. Heath, 1994. A25.

Some roots, prefixes, and suffixes appear quite often in a wide range of reading material. These word parts can be combined into a small number of "master words" which, if memorized, can serve as a reference list for you for new words. The following list contains fourteen master words, each of which has a prefix and a root that form a part of many words in the English language. In fact, if you learn this chart, you will have the key to unlocking the meanings of more than 100,000 words!

Prefix	Its Other Spellings	Its Meaning	Master Words	Root	Its Other Spellings	Its Meaning
1. de-	—	down or away	detain	tain	ten, tin	have, hold
2. inter-	—	between	intermittent	mitt	miss, mis, mit	send
3. pre-	—	before	precept	cept	cap, capt, ceiv, cip, ceit	take or seize
4. ob-	oc, of, op	to, toward, against	offer	fer	lat, lay	carry, bear
5. in-	il, im, ir	into	insist	sist	sta	stand, endure
6. mono-	—	one, alone	monograph	graph	—	write
7. epi-	—	over, upon, beside	epilogue	log	ology	speech, science
8. ad-	a, ad, ag, al, an, ap, ar, as, at	to, toward	aspect	spect	spec, spi	look
9. un- com-	— co, col, con, cor	not with, together	uncomplicated	plic	play, plex, ploy, ply	fold bend
10. non- ex-	— e, ef	not out, formerly	nonextended	tend	tens, tent	stretch
11. re- pro-	— —	back, again forward, in favor of	reproduction	duct	duc, duit	lead, make shape
12. in- dis-	il, im, ir di, dif	not apart from	indisposed	pos	pound, pon, post	put place
13. over- sub-	— suc, suf, sur, sus	above under	oversufficient	fic	fac, fact, fash, feat	make, do
14. mis- trans-	— tra, tran	wrong(ly) across, beyond	mistranscribe	scribe	script, scriv	write

Leedy, Paul D. "Key to 100,000 Words." *A Key to Better Reading.* New York: McGraw-Hill, 1968. 19.

ACTIVITY N. Applying Your Knowledge of Word Structure

Review the Key to 100,000 Words. Then in the space provided, write any other words you know that have the same prefix or root as the master word. Write your definitions for each word. Develop your definitions from your knowledge of word parts, as well as from your prior experience with using each word.

Master Word	Definition	Word You Know	Definition

CHAPTER SUMMARY

Based on your reading of this chapter, list at least five points that were made that you believe will help you with future reading assignments.

1. _____

_____

_____

_____

2. _____

_____

_____

_____

3. _____

_____

_____

_____

4. _____

_____

_____

_____

5. _____

_____

_____

_____

Now that you have worked with the strategies necessary for using contextual clues and other strategies for increasing vocabulary, you can practice applying them to full-length reading selections. Choose (or your instructor may choose) a reading selection that is typical of what you will be expected to read for your other college courses, such as an essay or a textbook chapter. Use this selection to practice:

■ Identifying a variety of contextual clues
■ Getting meanings of words from context
■ Using the dictionary for a variety of purposes
■ Determining meanings from word structure

Decide the practice strategies you will use. Apply them to your selection. Then in a few paragraphs, write a description of what you did and how the strategies you used worked for you.

Name of material used: _____

Page numbers: _____

Your description:

Chapter 7

Strategies for Critical Reading and Thinking

*W*hat made you decide to attend this school? You probably investigated many colleges thoroughly before making your choice. In the process, you most likely reviewed such facts as costs, course offerings, housing, and tuition assistance opportunities. Sources of information for this choice may have included talking with college representatives and reading college catalogs. Perhaps you also sought opinions from students already attending this school. Once you had all this information, you could weigh the positive and negative points, think about what people said about the school, as well as what was suggested by what was said, and sort out reliable from unreliable sources. Then you made your decision. This process required you to engage in critical reading, thinking, and listening. All critical reading, thinking, and listening experience involves similar analytical and reflective processes: You make judgments about what you read, see, or hear. In this chapter, you will learn the types of criteria to use for making these judgments and how to apply these criteria to academic situations.

There are many definitions of critical reading, but all of them involve evaluating what you read with regard to:

its logic

its truth or accuracy

the merit of the ideas

the usefulness of the ideas

Evaluation of text in this way requires that you analyze what you read beyond identification of main ideas and details. Authors select the information they will give readers, and they decide how this information will be presented. They also determine which ideas to state directly and which to suggest indirectly. When you read critically, you draw conclusions and form judgments about what you read on the basis of what you are told as well as how the information is presented. You also examine the underlying ideas that are suggested by both of these. As a critical reader, you consider the logic of the ideas as well as how the information coincides or conflicts with your prior knowledge and personal beliefs. Further, you are aware that there are many viewpoints from which even a single subject or event can be discussed. You know that if you hear only one side of an argument or read about an event that is written from only one perspective, you are limiting your understanding and your ability to critically analyze it. The critical reader is an investigative reader. The value of being able to read with a critical eye is illustrated in Activity A.

ACTIVITY A. Critical Analysis of Three News Articles

Three accounts of the same event, each from a different newspaper, follow. Read all three news stories, and then answer the questions.

1. Queens Woman Is Stabbed to Death in Front of Home

—*The New York Times*, March 14, 1964, p. 26 © 1964 by the New York Times Company

A 28 year old Queens woman was stabbed to death early yesterday morning outside her apartment house in Kew Gardens.

Neighbors who were awakened by her screams found the woman, Miss Catherine Genovese of 82-70 Austin Street, shortly after 3 a.m. in front of a building three doors from her home.

The police said that Miss Genovese had been attacked in front of her building and had run to where she fell. She had parked her car in a nearby lot, the police said, after having driven it from the Hollis Bar where she was day manager.

The police, who spent the day searching for the murder weapon, interviewing witnesses and checking automobiles that had been seen in the neighborhood, said last night they had no clues.

2. "Help" Cry Ignored, Girl Dies of Knifing

Robert Parrella

—*The New York Herald Tribune,* March 14, 1964, p. 10
The World Journal Tribune

The neighbors had grandstand seats for the slaying of Kitty Genovese.

And yet, when the pretty diminutive 28 year old brunette called for help, she called in vain.

It wasn't until she had been stabbed 12 times and had crawled into a vestibule, that somebody called police, and even then Kitty lay for 10 minutes, bleeding and unbefriended, before they arrived.

"I wonder how many lives could be saved in this City if people who ask for help were not ignored?" Magistrate Bernard J. Dublin mused yesterday in Queens Criminal Court. "How many people could have been saved from death if when they call for help other persons did not run away."

Karl Ross, 31, a poodle clipper, of 82-65 Austin Street, Kew Gardens, a neighbor of Kitty's, finally did call police.

Mr. Ross had just testified that he recognized the girl, bleeding profusely after she had staggered into the vestibule of his apartment house. He returned to his apartment, he said, and called the police, and remained in the apartment until he heard them arrive, some ten minutes later.

A charge of breach of the peace was leveled against Mr. Ross later in the day by Detective Mitchell Sang, who said Mr. Ross tried to prevent him from questioning one of Miss Genovese's roommates, Mary Ann Zielonko.

Mr. Ross was sentenced to pay a $25 fine and serve five days on the breach of peace charge which was reduced from interference with an officer. The jail term was suspended.

Detectives on the case say that at least half a dozen neighbors heard Miss Genovese scream for help on Austin Street at about 3:30 a.m. yesterday. Several of the witnesses told police they saw a man bending over the girl, straighten up and run away.

The girl, they said, then staggered around the corner onto 82nd Street. Her slayer reappeared at that point, and then, not finding his victim, disappeared again. Finally, Miss Genovese returned to Austin Street and collapsed in the vestibule about 30 yards from her own apartment door.

Police, called by Mr. Ross, summoned an ambulance, and the girl was taken to Queens General Hospital, where she died a short time later. Assistant Queens Medical Examiner, Dr. William Bennison, said she had suffered 12 stab wounds in the chest, abdomen and back, inflicted by a very strong killer armed with a slender knife.

Police said Miss Genovese was manager of Ev's 11th Hour, a tavern at 1293-14 Jamaica Avenue, Hollis, and shared her apartment with Miss Zielonko and another waitress from the establishment.

Detectives are seeking to question a patron at the tavern with whom Miss Genovese had had dinner earlier in the evening. Although the girl's wallet was not found at the stabbing scene, investigators said they did not believe the motive was robbery.

3. Queens Barmaid, Stabbed, Dies

Thomas Pugh and Richard Henry

—*The New York Daily News*, March 14, 1964, p. 5

An attractive 28 year old brunette who had given up a more prosaic life for a career as a barmaid and residence in a tiny Bohemian Section of Queens was stabbed to death early yesterday.

Catherine (Kitty) Genovese, 5 feet 1 and 105 pounds was stabbed eight times in the chest and four times in the back and she had three cuts on her hands, probably inflicted as she tried to fight off her attacker near her apartment in an alley way, at 82-70 Austin Street at Lefferts Boulevard, Kew Gardens.

Late yesterday, police said the 30 detectives assigned to the case had not come up with any clues or a possible motive for the savage murder.

Had Teen Nuptial Annulled

Police of the Richmond Hill Precinct said Kitty had had her teenage marriage annulled two months after her wedding and, when her large family moved to Connecticut, she stayed in New York on her own.

She worked for an insurance firm, but gave that up for a barmaid's career. In August 1961, her travels with a "fast crowd" contributed to her arrest on a bookmaking rap.

Police pieced together this account of her last hours at 6 p.m. Thursday; she left Ev's Eleventh Hour Tavern, 193-14 Jamaica Avenue, Hollis, where she had been a barmaid and co-manager for one and a half years.

She and a male patron went on a dinner date to Brooklyn, and returned to Ev's at midnight. Her escort left (he was questioned by cops yesterday and his alibi freed him of suspicion in the crime).

Three Girls Shared Apartment

Kitty left the bar at 3 a.m. and drove her Fiat sports car seven miles to her home. She parked in the Long Island Railroad's parking lot next to the group of buildings where she and two other girls shared an apartment.

She walked along Austin Street, instead of going more directly to the apartment via a walkway at the rear of the building. Police said she apparently walked out front to have the protection of the street lights.

Gasps *"I've Been Stabbed!"*

Neighbors suddenly heard screams and the roar of an auto driving off. Leaving a trail of blood, Kitty staggered back toward the parking lot, around the rear of the structures, and collapsed in the doorway of 892-60 Austin Street, next to her home.

"I've Been Stabbed! I've Been Stabbed!" the Brunette Gasped

Kitty died in an ambulance en route to Queens General Hospital, Jamaica.

1. How does each author want you to feel about the event?

   Article 1: _____

   _____

   Article 2: _____

   _____

   Article 3: _____

   _____

2. What does each author do to get you to feel this way?

   Article 1: _____

   _____

   Article 2: _____

   _____

   Article 3: _____

   _____

3. What does the author of each article want you to feel about the person who is primarily involved?

   Article 1: _____

   _____

   Article 2: _____

   _____

   Article 3: _____

   _____

4. How do you know the author wants you to feel this way?

   Article 1: _____

   _____

Article 2: _____

_____

Article 3: _____

_____

5. Which article has left the biggest impression on you? Why do you think it has?

_____

_____

_____

Working Together

With a partner, discuss how a reader's reactions to this event might differ depending on which news story he or she has read.

▶ **Thinking About Your Reading and Writing**

<u>ACTIVITY B.</u> **Your Conclusions About Content and Language**

What conclusions can you draw from Activity A about the ways in which an author's content and language can influence a reader's beliefs and knowledge?

_____

_____

_____

_____

_____

It is not wrong for an author to try to influence readers. Authors write because they have something to say. They expect their readers to understand their ideas and, they hope, to agree with them. But critical readers and listeners will evaluate the ideas before accepting them. In the remainder of this chapter, you will learn strategies for making such evaluations, including strategies that will enable you to recognize:

■ when an author's content and language suggest unstated ideas

- When an author's content and language suggest certain biases
- when these biases and ideas are justified by reasons and evidence
- how the author's attitudes are similar to or different from your own and those of others
- what conclusions reasonably follow from ideas that you accept

We introduce these strategies separately so that you can have a clear picture of how to use each. However, these features of communication work simultaneously, in combination with one another, to produce the final effect on the reader or listener. For instance, if the newspaper articles in Activity A had differed from one another by only one sentence, the effect of any single article on you would probably not have been very different from that of any other single article. It was the totality—the headlines, the events discussed, the descriptions—that caused the striking contrasts.

DISTINGUISHING STATEMENTS OF FACT FROM STATEMENTS OF OPINION

Text material and lectures contain both factual information and opinions. Statements of opinion in academic text and lectures are also sometimes referred to as *thesis statements, theories,* or *hypotheses.* Your knowledge of the distinctions between these and statements of fact will help you evaluate the ideas of others. As a critical reader and listener, you will recognize ideas that are accurate, logical, and worthy of serious consideration, as well as those that you must question because they are unsupported, illogical, or seem inaccurate. Further, you will be more aware of whether the judgments you make about the ideas of others are grounded in fact or opinion or in a combination of these.

Factual statements are distinguished from statements of opinion in several ways:

- Facts can be proved to be true or false.
- Facts cannot be disputed. There is evidence to prove their truth.
- Facts are easily agreed-on ideas or are concepts that are held by everyone or that can easily be proved, such as, "The sun sets in the West" or "Maine is in the Northeastern part of the United States."
- Facts are based on direct evidence or actual observation. Examples, statistics, original documents, reports from research experiments, or eyewitness accounts are used to verify them.
- Facts are things that have occurred. They are not predictions.
- The truthfulness of facts can change over time. For instance, at one time it was thought that AIDS could be contracted only by homosexual males.

- Factual statements often begin with such expressions as, *The evidence for this is* _____, _____ *found, Statistical evidence for this appeared in a study by* _____.

Opinions, on the other hand, are not clear-cut or right or wrong, as are facts. Your academic reading and experiences in classrooms will expose you to many areas of controversy where opinions are voiced strongly. It is possible for people to disagree endlessly about an opinion and to never reach a conclusion. For instance, one person might say capital punishment is a good idea; another might say capital punishment should be abolished. Opinions are one person's view of the truth.

Frequently, there are opposing viewpoints or theories in academic writing. For example, there is disagreement over such issues as how the earth was first created and the seriousness of global warming. Psychologists and others have disagreed over the extent to which a person's genetic makeup influences his or her other personality and intelligence, compared to his or her environment. (These are called nature–nurture theories.) Critical readers recognize the possibility of such disagreements and will draw conclusions based on whatever evidence and facts they can find. Statements of opinion, then, have several features that will help you distinguish them from facts:

- Statements of opinion cannot be conclusively verified. Even if you agree with the author's opinion, it is still just an opinion although there may be good evidence for that opinion.

- Statements of opinion are often an expression of someone's values, personal beliefs, attitudes, or feelings. These are often based on hunches, inferences, or guesses. It is when you agree with the author's point of view that it is more difficult to make the distinction between fact and opinion statements. Try to avoid letting your own opinions influence your ability to determine which is which.

- Statements of opinion are subjective. The language of opinion statements is often vague or persuasive. The words used to convey the opinion may be open to many interpretations, like *love, peace, beneficial, dangerous.*

- Opinion statements often begin with such expressions as, *I believe, It appears, It seems, All would agree, I think* _____ *is true because, In my opinion.*

- It is possible for a single word to turn a statement of fact into a statement of opinion. For example, the phrase *sixteenth-century music* is a factual phrase. The descriptor, *sixteenth-century,* is factual because one could prove whether the music was of that period. However, the phrase *beautiful music* is a statement of opinion. Its descriptor, *beautiful,* is a matter of opinion to the listener.

ACTIVITY C. Creating Fact and Opinion Descriptors

For each pair, write one descriptor that makes a phrase factual and one that makes it an opinion. Several examples are done for you. Be prepared to justify your answers.

Factual		**Opinion**	
Sunday	picnic	*enjoyable*	picnic
broken	hand	*gentle*	hand
clerical	work	*tedious*	work
Aesop's	fable	*confusing*	fable
_____	damage	_____	damage
_____	country	_____	country
_____	business	_____	business
_____	parents	_____	parents
_____	law	_____	law
_____	textbook	_____	textbook
_____	highway	_____	highway

▶ Thinking About Your Reading and Writing

ACTIVITY D. Evaluating What You Know

What are some features of facts and opinions that you think will be useful for you to remember as you listen to lectures and do your reading assignments?

ACTIVITY E. Personal Facts and Opinions

In the space provided, write some factual and some opinion statements about yourself. As you do this, think about the criteria you are using to distinguish between fact and opinion.

Factual statements about you:

Opinion statements about you:

Working Together

Have a partner look at your personal factual and opinion statements in Activity E. Discuss whether they meet the criteria for each.

ACTIVITY F. Recognizing Statements of Fact and Opinion

Read each sentence and determine whether it is a statement of fact (F) or opinion (O). Mark your answer in the space provided. Be prepared to justify your answers.

1. Life on earth depends on two fundamental processes: matter cycling and the one-way flow of high-quality energy from the sun. _____

2. The work of Elisabeth Kubler-Ross, a physician, is often cited as having a major influence on American attitudes towards death and dying. _____

3. The tight end's personality changed for the worse when he made the varsity team. _____

4. The six-year-old girl was very mature for her age. _____

5. Smoking makes some people more sociable. _____

6. Smoking makes some people sick. _____

7. The release of huge amounts of explosive powder from an atomic bomb in only a fraction of a second creates a powerful blast effect. _____

8. It is unreasonable for a department head to expect that employees will come to work willingly during a holiday weekend. _____

9. Children write less creatively today than they did fifty years ago. _____

10. Citizens of affluent countries feel guilty when they see television programs showing starving children from other countries. _____

11. The score you achieve on some intelligence tests is called your IQ. _____

12. The first Muzak recording in 1914 was a medley of "Whispering," "Do You Ever Think of Me?" and "Here in My Arms" performed by Sam Lenin's orchestra. _____

Working Together

Compare your answers to Activity F with those of a partner. If you disagree, try to reach agreement by reviewing the criteria for factual statements. ●

At this point, you are ready for some good news and some bad news. The good news is that by now you have developed some useful strategies for determining whether an idea is a statement of fact or opinion. The bad news is that many statements that appear in academic text are neither all fact nor all opinion. Very often a statement contains a portion of fact *and* a portion of opinion. This is a particularly useful technique for writing an argumentative or persuasive essay, one in which you are trying to convince the reader to accept a certain idea or viewpoint. The opinions are mingled with the facts, so the sentence sounds factual. But, in reality, only that portion that states a fact is verifiable. The rest of it must be considered opinion and open to disagreement.

For example, a sentence may read: *The World Trade Center in New York City, which was bombed recently, is very likely targeted for more attacks in the future.* The part of this sentence that is fact is *The World Trade Center in New York City, which was bombed recently.* The rest, which reads *is very likely targeted for more attacks in the future,* is the author's opinion.

Here's another example: *Although the Navajo have written many myths, none is as popular as that of the Big Fly, which has been part of the culture for centuries.* Which part is fact? You should have recognized that there are two factual parts in this sentence: *the Navajo have written many myths* is a fact. Further, the segment of the sentence that reads *which has been part of the culture for centuries* is a fact. One can check to see whether the Navajo have, indeed, written many myths and whether this particular myth has been part of the culture for so long. The rest of the sentence is definitely opinion. It would be hard to prove that one myth is more popular than another, and views on methods to use to judge popularity would vary.

Fact and opinion also can become intermingled when someone else's opinion is quoted. The quotation marks give the opinion the appearance of fact, and it is a fact that someone made the quoted statement, but often the idea within the quotation marks is an opinion. For example, consider the statement, *"The United States should consider a complete halt in nuclear power plant construction because of unresolved safety questions," an Atomic Energy Commission safety expert said on September 21, 1974.* An individual made this statement when he resigned from the Atomic Energy Commission because he felt the Commission was ignoring questions of safety. It is a fact that the AEC safety expert made this statement, and perhaps one could argue that it is a fact that there were *unresolved safety questions* when the statement was made. But the solution recommended, *a complete halt in nuclear power plant construction,* is an opinion.

In Activity G, you will have a chance to identify those parts of sentences that are fact and those that are opinion.

ACTIVITY G. Recognizing Segments of Fact and Opinion in Sentences

In each sentence, *underline* those portions that you believe to be fact. Remember that you are claiming that what is not underlined is opinion. More than one part of a sentence may be factual. Be prepared to justify your answers.

1. Although everyone feels sad now and then, four to eight million Americans are treated yearly for clinical depression, and about 250,000 of these require hospitalization.

2. Authoritarian or despotic governments give the ruling group a total monopoly of decision-making power and cause the citizens of the society to live in fear.

3. By 1885, fewer than one thousand buffalo were left on the Midwest plains, and clearly there was little concern that the once-numerous quadrupeds were facing an inevitable complete extermination.

4. Ten years ago, John Graves Fletcher, a distinguished painter, designed the colorful, modernistic murals in our student union building, which houses all clubs, fraternities, and sororities, as well as a number of auditoriums and conference rooms.

5. Apple Computer Corporation has an ambitious plan to develop software that will run on all types of computers, from microcomputers and laptops to mainframes.

6. The statement that the per capita after-tax income of older Americans is $355 greater than the national average is misleading because it

causes people to think that the elderly are rich and to forget about the high medical costs experienced by people in this age group.

7. In 1981, a year when ninety-one police officers were killed in the line of duty in the United States, I realized that when we lower the penalty for murder, it signals a lessened regard for the value of the victim's life.

8. Current figures indicate that drug abuse costs American industry over $70 billion per year through lost productivity, a figure that would surely soar if legal restraints were removed.

9. Voters appeared impatient for change when, in one city, all five of the incumbents lost their bids for reelection.

10. Some scholars have spent decades studying the unplanned effects of social reform, and they have now reached the conclusion that everything has been tried, but nothing has worked.

▶ **Thinking About Your Reading and Writing**

ACTIVITY H. Reviewing Your Decision-Making Processes

Describe the thought process you used in Activity G to distinguish between fact and opinion. List as many of the steps you used in this procedure as you can.

Working Together

Compare the procedures you used in Activity G with those used by a partner. Add to your list in Activity H any steps your partner suggested that you believe will be useful to you.

EVIDENCE FOR STATEMENTS OF OPINION

Even though an opinion cannot be absolutely verified, it can be supported with evidence in a way that strengthens its force and makes it more believable. Critical readers will examine the type of evidence given for such statements to determine its value as support for the opinions or theories that are suggested. We next discuss several types of evidence commonly used in academic writing.

Expert Opinion

Expert opinion differs from other opinions because the person expressing the opinion knows quite a bit about the subject being discussed. Examples include Eastern European historians discussing the end of communism in Eastern Europe, music historians discussing the influence of the Beatles on contemporary music, economists discussing a recession, and a doctor giving medical testimony. When support for an opinion or theory is provided by an expert rather than by someone who knows little about the subject, that opinion carries more weight.

Informed Opinion

Authors and speakers preparing arguments or developing a thesis frequently conduct research or seek information from other sources that will help them prove their points. Informed opinions may include statistical reference, historical reference, the use of visual aids, and the use of personal experience.

Reference to Statistics Obtained Through Research.   For instance, if someone has the opinion that gun control legislation deters crime, statistics from states that have passed gun control legislation may be used to provide evidence that in these states there has been a reduction in crime. If someone wants to argue that one method of teaching mathematics to children is superior to another, the argument can be bolstered by citing mathematics test scores of the children using the favored method or by comparing these test results to those of children who were taught by a different method.

Here is one note about using facts in this way. Since in both examples a number of factors affect the situation being discussed, the facts cited as evidence are only partially useful. They do not give the whole picture. For example, crime might have dropped in cities that had passed gun control laws because the economy in those states was up, or children who were using the favored math approach might have been in school systems that also had very small classes. When statistics are used to support arguments, they must be considered with caution. The one voicing the opinion has chosen to include only particular statistics. Other statistics may support an equally strong argument against it.

Historical Reference.   The use of history to prove one's point is a fairly common strategy for creating the impression of an informed opinion. Phrases such as *history tells us* or *we know from the past* convince us that the opinion expressed is based on fact. Reference to historical documents, diaries, or speeches may be used as well. Critical readers will notice such references and will try to verify that the history as presented is both factually correct and unbiased.

The Use of Visual Aids.   Photographs, charts, and diagrams give arguments an air of validity. After all, the reasoning goes, if it can be graphically depicted, it must be so. Consider, however, the photos on the covers of supermarket tabloids. Wonderful graphics can be made on computers as well. But how valid is what they portray? Further, you must analyze whether there is any relationship between what is on the graphic display and the idea under discussion. For instance, if one is presenting an argument in favor of gun control legislation, one might use a graphic of a baby who has just been caught in the cross fire between two drug dealers. The impact on you is powerful. But how much support, beyond emotional appeal, does this photo lend to the key point? The critical reader will examine the source of the visual aid as well as the relationship between the graphics and the argument or theory itself.

The Use of Personal Experience.   How often have you remarked that you knew something to be true because you experienced it yourself? Perhaps you have said this when expressing such opinions as the food in a particular restaurant is bad, a certain band has a great sound, or someone you know is a terrific athlete. When you gave your opinion, did everyone agree with you? It is very common to use personal experience as evidence for one's own theories or opinions, but critical thinkers will not rely too heavily on this type of evidence for judging the merit of ideas. People interpret their experiences differently. Personal experience is subjective, as are opinions themselves. When personal experience is used as evidence, it is really a case of using subjective evidence to support a subjective idea.

Unsupported Opinion

Unsupported opinions often consist of *sweeping generalizations* and *stereotypes*. These are even less reliable than opinions based on personal experience. For example, to give support to the argument that towns ought to have curfews for teenagers, one might say, *Today's parents have little time for disciplining their children.* This statement is not backed by any statistical evidence or facts. It is a personal opinion intended to give strength to the argument that towns need curfews. Or if one is arguing that the news media should be controlled by the government, one might also say, *The stories in many local newspapers encourage crime.* This claim is unsupported. It is merely an unsupported personal opinion. Even a seemingly noncontroversial view, such as the Industrial Revolution had a major effect on the family life of Americans would not be well defended if the only support given for such a statement was *Men worked in factories for long hours and came home too tired to pay attention to their wives and families.*

How is this known? It remains just an unsupported opinion unless some evidence is offered, such as statistics, entries from diaries of people living at the time, or findings from other research studies.

ACTIVITY I. Identifying Support for Opinions

Several statements of opinion follow. Beneath each opinion statement are two other sentences that provide support for the opinion. Based on the type of support given, indicate whether the opinion is an expert opinion (EO), informed opinion (IO), or unsupported opinion (UO). Be prepared to justify your answers.

1. Sexual harassment in the workplace is far more common than most people suppose. _____

   ▨ One worker said she was sexually harassed by her boss nearly every day for six years.

   ▨ The American Civil Liberties Union noted that more than two hundred cases of sexual harassment are reported to them every day.

2. Senior citizens should not have to pay for public transportation. _____

   ▨ More than ten major cities now charge over $1.00 per ride for all users of public transportation.

   ▨ The real income of senior citizens has dropped by 7 percent in the last year.

3. Politicians have become extremely self-centered. _____

   ▨ Elected officials are more occupied with their own plans for re-election than with the public interest.

   ▨ Senators obviously spend more time campaigning in their home states than voting on important issues in Congress.

4. People with AIDS should not work in hospitals. _____

   ▨ A study done by my research team at Harvard found that the risk factor of being infected with AIDS when you were under the medical care of someone who was infected increased by 17 percent.

   ▨ An earlier study I conducted revealed that hospital workers who had AIDS took very few extra precautions, compared to those who did not have AIDS, when they worked with patients.

5. Unwed mothers are capable of making important decisions about their babies' futures. _____

   ▨ The Director of the Estridge Shelter for Unwed Mothers in Canton, Ohio, indicated that fifteen of the twenty women in her shelter were taking parenting classes and studying for their GED diplomas.

■ Last year, more than 78 percent of the unwed mothers in Detroit, Michigan, arranged for their three-year-olds to be in licensed day-care so that the mothers could work.

6. Prior to 1870, children were not encouraged to think independently. _____

■ One popular children's magazine I investigated, *Youth's Companion*, published from the mid-1800s until 1910, told children in 1856 to spend their time "thinking of ways they could achieve salvation."

■ Another periodical I examined, *Juvenile Miscellany*, first published in 1826, contained numerous stories of children who lived in fear of the dire consequences they would face if they did anything contrary to established rule.

7. Some actors and actresses pay a heavy price for stardom. _____

■ It is rumored that the legendary Greta Garbo once said she never married because "all those damn photographers would just follow us around then, maybe even to the bedroom."

■ The public craves all the latest gossip on their favorite stars, making them the target of tabloid smear campaigns.

8. In the middle and late nineteenth century, high schools developed as aids to the industrial system. _____

■ History was required in the curriculum to foster patriotism.

■ Laws passed by the states barred certain kinds of textbooks.

9. The minister reported that his research proved that during the early twentieth century, conditions in migrant labor camps in the United States were squalid and degrading. _____

■ "Shelters were made of almost every conceivable thing—burlap, canvas, palm branches," reported a minister describing a camp he had visited in the Imperial Valley of California.

■ Photos he had taken of the camps gave evidence that the growers felt no responsibility for the housing conditions or the welfare of their workers.

10. Through the training of their young, not only all humans but apparently all other primates as well pass on strong convictions of what is proper food and what is not. _____

■ Dietary laws of certain groups of Hindus and Buddhists prohibit eating meat of any kind.

■ DeGarine (1974) reports that in Polynesia in former times all species of fish that were offered to the gods, as well as all meat except poultry, were forbidden to women.

With a partner, provide different types of support to make each of the following statements an expert opinion, informed opinion, and unsupported opinion. Write your support in the space provided. (Be creative. Make up the support for an expert opinion and informed opinion if you wish.)

> ***Statement 1:*** Small businesses provide service for their customers that larger businesses just cannot offer.
>
> ***Support to make this an expert opinion:*** _
>
> _
>
> ***Support to make this an informed opinion:*** _ _ _ _ _ _ _ _ _ _ _ _ _ _ _ _ _ _
>
> _
>
> ***Support to make this an unsupported opinion:*** _ _ _ _ _ _ _ _ _ _ _ _ _ _ _
>
> _
>
> ***Statement 2:*** People who watch their diet will be happier than people who eat whatever they choose.
>
> ***Support to make this an expert opinion:*** _
>
> _
>
> ***Support to make this an informed opinion:*** _ _ _ _ _ _ _ _ _ _ _ _ _ _ _ _ _ _
>
> _
>
> ***Support to make this an unsupported opinion:*** _ _ _ _ _ _ _ _ _ _ _ _ _ _ _
>
> _ ●

ADDITIONAL CRITERIA FOR JUDGING FACTS AND OPINIONS

As you evaluate ideas presented in texts and lectures, you should consider some additional factors.

The Author's Qualifications.   Some authors are more knowledgeable about a subject than others because of the length of time they have been doing research, the experience they have had in the subject, or the formal training they have received in the subject. In textbooks, information about the author can often be found in the introduction or foreward. Periodicals sometimes offer a brief biography of the author.

The Source of the Material.   Hundreds of articles appear monthly in magazines, journals, and newspapers that are published by special-interest groups: religious organizations, groups with particular political leanings, senior citizens' organizations, women's rights associations, labor unions, environmental protection organizations, and so on. Publication affiliations are identified in the editorial box, which is usually placed in the first few pages of the publication. The critical reader understands that an article that discusses whether parents should be concerned about the type of music listened to by today's teenagers would be very different if it appeared in *Good Housekeeping* magazine than if it appeared in *Spin*. The special interests of the publisher and the audiences for those two magazines are quite different; they play an important role in the content and method of presentation of information. Critical readers consider this when they evaluate the ideas presented.

The *recency of the information* must also be considered. If the material was published some time ago, its age may affect its value. In many fields, such as the sciences, history, and anthropology, new information continually updates older theories and research findings.

The Author's Bias.   An author's opinion on an issue is a particular *bias, slant, position, perspective,* or *point of view.* The facts and opinions included are usually those that support that perspective. Thus, the details will reflect a particular slant. They will have been chosen because they support the author's point of view. At times, other positions are stated, but only to give the author a chance to show what is wrong with them. When you determine the extent to which the information is factual or subjective, as well as the source of the facts and opinions, you will be able to recognize author bias. Knowing the source of the material will also help you establish the author's bias, even before you begin your reading. If an author appears to be particularly biased, you may want to read additional material on the same subject written from another point of view. This will give you a fuller picture of the issues involved and the different sides of the argument. We discuss this aspect of critical reading more thoroughly in the next section.

RECOGNIZING POINT OF VIEW

An author's writing often reflects personal beliefs about the subject under discussion. When readers can identify these beliefs, they are determining the author's point of view or bias. A point of view may concern a very controversial topic, such as whether there should be mandatory testing for AIDS in the workplace. Or an author may express a point of view on something less controversial that is nevertheless a topic about which people may have differing opinions, such as the best way to make chocolate chip cookies. This bias is most often the result of the author's perspective on a subject. For example, an author may use one of several perspectives to discuss a plan by New York City's mayor to overhaul the mass transit system. The discussion may be written from the perspective of someone who lives in the city and who regularly uses the system; from the perspective of a Rochester, New York, resident who would have to pay toward the system but who does not use it; or from the perspective of a senior citizen who doesn't use the system but lives in New York City and would pay increased taxes. Whatever the author's perspective, the result is a particular bias toward the subject that reveals itself in the content.

Readers may sometimes recognize that an author's point of view differs from their own. It is always worthwhile to consider how an author's own experience and background have influenced his or her point of view and to assess how your own experience and background influence the position you take on the same subject. You also need to consider what other points of view are possible.

A single word can suggest much about your attitude or point of view toward a person or situation. For instance, if you refer to a person as a *dedicated worker,* you are saying something positive. But if you call that same person a *workaholic,* you are conveying a negative attitude about the same set of behaviors. Following a class debate, you might comment to a friend that the class debate was *stimulating,* or you might call it *argumentative.* One city dweller visiting a small town might call it *dull,* another person visiting the same town might describe it as *peaceful.* In each case, the descriptive word suggests a reaction to the same experience, and in each case, the reaction is clearly different.

In the example that follows, we illustrate a point of view on a controversial subject. Several questions about the paragraph are asked and then answered.

Example:

In sixteen of the past seventeen Gallup Polls on education, poor pupil discipline has been the most frequent criticism leveled against public schools. One may wonder if better discipline codes and more homework are adequate remedies for our current school problems or whether these dysfunctions are more profound and should be treated with more sensitive and complex remedies. Although literacy and student diligence are unquestionably worthy of pursuit, they are only part of the process of communicating serious morality. If we want to improve the ways we are now transmitting morality, it makes sense to analyze the way morality was transmitted before youth disorder became such a distressing issue.

■ What is the author's point of view? Behavior problems in school are a distressing issue. They are related to morality, and they cannot be solved simply by stricter discipline codes.

- What evidence is there that this is the author's point of view? The author says that more old-fashioned methods of teaching morality to children should be used. The author refers to Gallup Polls to prove the point that people are concerned about the behavior of today's youth.

- How does this point of view compare to your own on this subject? This question calls for a personal reaction. You may agree or disagree with the author's point of view for your own reasons.

- What other points of view are possible? Even if you agreed with the author, others might not. Some might suggest that it is parental neglect in the home that causes problems in the school, not the methods we use to communicate morality. Others might suggest that sterner discipline policies in school would solve the problem.

Notice that in the example the author uses specific words that suggest the point of view. Words such as *remedies, criticism, dysfunctions,* and *distressing* all convey the author's bias.

ACTIVITY J. Determining Point of View

Read each paragraph to identify the point of view, and then answer the questions that follow. Where you are asked to give evidence to support your own point of view, it may be from some source other than the paragraph.

1. What could be more disturbing than the photographs of the faces of victimized children over the past fifty years? Beginning with the children of the Holocaust and on through the devastation of the Second World War, Biafra, Vietnam, Laos, until our own time in Cambodia, their blank, bewildered stares flare out from their gaunt, malnutritioned bodies.

   What is the subject? _____

   _____

   What is the author's point of view toward this subject? _____

   _____

   What evidence is there that this is the author's point of view? _____

   _____

   How does this point of view compare to your own? _____

   _____

What evidence do you have to support your viewpoint? _____

_____

What other points of view are possible? _____

_____

2. Why did medieval people devote such time, energy, and money to the construction of huge and complex churches? It is hard to find anything comparable in the lives of modern people. We must try to remember that churches were not merely places to go on Sunday or decorations for a town; they represented a vital aspect of everyone's spiritual life. They were not only dwellings for God on earth but also a kind of bridge between the physical and spiritual realms. They began as heavy stone set on the ground, but they soared upward toward heaven. They contained something for everyone. For the common people, many of whom could neither read nor write, they offered a kind of visual religious education.

Witt, M., et al. *Humanities.* Vol. I. 3rd ed. Lexington: D. C. Heath, 1989. 204.

What is the subject? _____

_____

What is the author's point of view toward this subject? _____

_____

What evidence is there that this is the author's point of view? _____

_____

How does this point of view compare to your own? _____

_____

What evidence do you have to support your viewpoint? _____

_____

What other points of view are possible? _____

_____

3. There are four broad categories of electronic games: (1) coin-operated video games (the computerized answer to the pinball machine),

(2) games operated through the home television receiver, (3) software or personal computers, and (4) all other games, including those that are hand-held. Many of the computer games now on the market have an outer space or space warfare theme. Some emulate television game shows or card games. Computerized sports games—including auto racing, baseball, basketball, chess, football, hockey, motorcycle racing, pool, soccer, and tennis—are among the most popular. There appears to be something for anyone who wants to play an electronic game.

What is the subject? _____

_____

What is the author's point of view toward this subject? _____

_____

What evidence is there that this is the author's point of view? _____

_____

How does this point of view compare to your own? _____

_____

What evidence do you have to support your viewpoint? _____

_____

What other points of view are possible? _____

_____

4. Crime is caused by criminals; the fact is as simple as that. When a strong-arm robber slugs his victim in order to relieve him of his watch and wallet, he has committed a crime. No amount of elaboration on the question of whether or not the assailant came from an environment of poverty or a broken home makes the robbery itself any less a crime. Likewise, when a youthful demonstrator, intolerant of this country's pace in solving its social problems, throws a rock that strikes a policeman in the head, an aggravated assault has been committed. Apologists for criminal behavior may wring their hands as much as they like about the robber "striking out at a society which has brutalized him" or the demonstrator "merely expressing his idealistic young concern"; the fact remains that both are criminals.

Inbau, Fred E., and Frank G. Carrington. "Punishment Prevents Crime" in Bender, David L., and Gary E. McCuen, eds. *Crime and Criminals*. Minneapolis, Minn.: Greenhaven, 1977. 39.

What is the subject? _

_ _

What is the author's point of view toward this subject? _ _ _ _ _ _ _ _ _ _ _

_ _

What evidence is there that this is the author's point of view? _ _ _ _ _ _

_ _

How does this point of view compare to your own? _ _ _ _ _ _ _ _ _ _ _ _ _

_ _

What evidence do you have to support your viewpoint? _ _ _ _ _ _ _ _ _ _

_ _

What other points of view are possible? _

_ _

5. The corporation is a relatively new form of business ownership that didn't become really popular until about a century ago. Yet today it's the best-known and most powerful form of business ownership in the country. Although less than 15 percent of all U.S. businesses are corporations, they account for over 86 percent of revenues each year and receive 75 percent of all profits. This staggering financial record gives corporations tremendous economic and political clout. Corporations even influence campaigns by forming political action committees (PACs) to contribute to favored candidates.

Megginson, L. C., et al. *Business.* Lexington, Mass.: D. C. Heath, 1985. 66.

What is the subject? _

_ _

What is the author's point of view toward this subject? _ _ _ _ _ _ _ _ _ _

_ _

What evidence is there that this is the author's point of view? _ _ _ _ _ _

_ _

How does this point of view compare to your own? _ _ _ _ _ _ _ _ _ _ _ _ _ _ _

_ _

What evidence do you have to support your viewpoint? _ _ _ _ _ _ _ _ _ _ _ _

_ _

What other points of view are possible? _

_ _

Working Together

Compare your responses to Activity J with those of a partner. Look for differences in point of view.

Thinking About Your Reading and Writing

ACTIVITY K. Personal Response to Point of View

Do you think it is more interesting to read ideas that are similar to or that are different from your own? Explain your answer.

_ _

_ _

_ _

_ _

_ _

_ _

_ _

_ _

READING TO MAKE INFERENCES

Have you ever decided whether or not to see a movie based on the reactions of people coming out of the theater? Many people find this a useful way to judge whether or not to spend their money on seeing a film. Since strangers coming out of the theater most likely won't just come out and tell you their opinions, it is useful to know what to look for as audience indicators of a good movie: people laughing or crying (depending on the movie content) or people excitedly talking about it. Similarly, authors often don't tell you everything. Critical readers look for ideas that are *suggested* in text as well as for those that are directly stated. When you identified the author's point of view, you looked for words or phrases that suggested bias, as well as at the particular content the author chose to discuss. This was *inferential reading*. In this section, we discuss strategies for making other types of inferences: inferences about events, characters, or ideas that are suggested by the information stated in the text.

INFERENCES IN EVERYDAY LIFE

We are constantly making guesses, or inferences, about things we see, hear, and read. Imagine, for instance, that your attention is caught by a front-page photo in this morning's newspaper: A Jeep is turned over; shattered glass is all around it. The middle of the Jeep looks crushed. A car is close behind it. Standing beside the car is a young man looking off into the distance. Also next to the car is a firefighter. Across the street is a fire truck, its hose extending to the Jeep. Without reading the caption, you can already infer what has happened: a serious accident. Clearly, this was not some stunt being performed or some advertising ploy designed to capture the attention of Jeep buyers. Only one driver is in the photo, near the car; maybe the driver of the Jeep is trapped inside or has been taken to a hospital. That driver probably didn't survive. You wonder if there were any passengers. You also guess that there was a fire in the Jeep, caused when it flipped over. The man standing by the Jeep may have driven the car and may have caused the accident. It is hard to tell. But he doesn't look hurt. You are hypothesizing all this information through your interpretation of the picture. You still have not read any text. Now you read the article beneath the photo. It confirms some of your hypotheses and denies others: There was an accident and a fire; a young boy, not the driver, had been killed. Making inferences from text, without photos, works in much the same way.

FINDING SUPPORT FOR YOUR INFERENCES

An inference is an "informed guess" you make about something you read or experience. Your guess is based on what you know from your *prior experience* as well as from the *information given* in the text, photograph, cartoon, letter, situation, or dialogue about which you are making inferences. What you know (the factual details in the text as well as your prior knowledge) is considered to be the evidence or support for your guess. The inferences you make must follow logically from the available information. As more information becomes available, you may need to modify your original thinking. The following example illustrates how the process of making inferences works and how new information may cause you to reject inferences you made earlier. Read sentence 1. Then decide which statements beneath it could be appropriate guesses, based on the information in that sentence, as well as on your prior knowledge.

Sentence 1: The surgeon removed his gloves and quickly scanned the chart on the wall.

Possible inferences: [Decide which of these are logical. More than one can be selected. Put the letter(s) of your choice(s) in the space provided.]

a. The surgeon had just completed surgery.
b. The surgeon felt the surgery had gone poorly.
c. The surgeon was getting ready for his next patient.
d. The surgeon was in a hurry.
e. The surgeon had been cold.
f. The surgeon was an experienced pilot.

Supported inferences: _____

There is evidence that supports sentences a, c, d, and e. For sentence a, the evidence is that he was taking off gloves. You know that surgeons wear gloves. For sentence c, the evidence is that he is looking at a chart, which might be a chart of patients and surgery schedules. You know that hospitals use charts for patients. For sentence d, the evidence is the word *quickly,* which describes how the gloves were being removed. For sentence e, the evidence is that the surgeon was wearing gloves. He might have come inside from where he had been cold and then taken off the gloves.

Now read sentence 2, which gives additional information. From your choices of inferences that seemed logical based on sentence 1 and your prior knowledge, eliminate those that no longer make sense. In the space provided, list only those inferences that can now be supported.

Sentence 2: The airport where he was now waiting for his departure was freezing cold.

Supported inferences: _____

The sentences to be eliminated as logical inferences are a and c. In both cases, the sentences are contradicted by the fact that the surgeon is at an airport. You know that surgery is not performed at airports.

The sentence to be added as a logical inference is f. Sentence f is a logical inference because he is at an airport, and it is possible he will fly a plane. The charts he is looking at in sentence 1 might be connected to his flight. You know that airports keep various charts and records of flight schedules. We now have sentences d, e, and f as inferences that can be supported based on the information from the first two sentences.

Now read sentence 3, which gives additional details. Repeat the procedure you used with sentence 2.

Sentence 3: From the chart, he learned which instructor he had been assigned to for his first flying lesson ever.

Supported inferences: --

What sentences did you say are now suitable as inferences? Only d and e remain as logical inferences. Sentence 3 contradicts choice f, which, based on sentence 2, initially seemed possible.

You can see how important it is not to jump to conclusions. Every sentence *before and after* the sentence from which you make an inference contains information that will assist you in determining the extent to which your inference is valid. You will need to reject your inference if you can't find support for it in the material and if you have no prior knowledge to support it.

This process of making inferences while you read is applicable to any kind of text, regardless of length or subject matter. It works for both non-fictional (expository) and fictional (narrative) reading material. Activity L offers additional practice in applying this reading and thinking strategy.

▶ **Thinking About Your Reading and Writing**

ACTIVITY L. Understanding How to Make Inferences

In your own words, explain the process for making inferences.

ACTIVITY M. Identifying Possible Inferences

Beneath each paragraph are several possible inferences. For each possible inference, indicate whether it is supported (S) or contradicted (C) by the information given in the paragraph. If there is no information either supporting or contradicting the possible inference, write (?) to indicate that the inference is neither supported nor contradicted by the paragraph. Be prepared to cite evidence for your answers. Your evidence may include your prior knowledge but should also include information from the passage.

Example:

Major advertisers, eager to tap the estimated $134 billion in spending power wielded by Spanish-speaking Americans, have ventured into Spanglish to promote their products. In some cases, attempts

to sprinkle Spanish through commercials have produced embarrass-
ing mistakes. An ad for now-bankrupt Braniff airlines that sought to
tell Spanish-speaking audiences they could settle back *en* (in) luxu-
riant *cuero* (seats), for example, mistakenly said they could fly without clothes (*encuero*).

Possible inferences:

  S   a. Corporations will write specific ads for specific audiences.
          (The first sentence supports this inference.)

  S   b. Large corporations are willing to spend huge sums of
          money on advertising.
          (The first sentence also supports this inference.)

  ?   c. Spanish-speaking Americans object to having ads made
          that are designed to appeal especially to them.
          (There is no information about this in the paragraph.)

  S   d. It is sometimes difficult to translate concepts from one lan-
          guage to another.
          (The example given illustrates this inference.)

  C   e. Braniff intended its ad to be humorous.
          (It is suggested that this was an "embarrassing mistake.")

1. Farmers in the dairy and cattle business can be a pretty biased bunch
when it comes to the sex of a newborn calf. Dairy farmers hope for a
female (more milk); cattle farmers cheer for a male (more beef). In an
effort to help both constituencies, the U.S. Department of Agriculture
has developed a new way of separating livestock sperm with female
potential (cells that carry an X chromosome) from sperm with male
potential (cells that carry a Y chromosome). The result, after *in vitro*
fertilization with the presorted sperm, is healthy calves whose sex can
be successfully predetermined almost 90 percent of the time.

From "Predetermined beeves." *Discover.* Vol. 14. May 1993. 20.

Possible inferences:

       a. Male and female sperm can be distinguished by their
          chromosomes.

       b. Farmers' sex preference in cows is based on a profit motive.

       c. The U.S. Department of Agriculture engages in scientific
          activity.

       d. The federal government feels farmers should be satisfied
          with whatever calves they get.

       e. The farmers resent the involvement by the U.S. Depart-
          ment of Agriculture in cattle-raising issues.

2. Benedict Arnold had long considered himself unjustly treated by Congress. Time and again, his brilliant gifts had been overlooked and less
able officers promoted over his head. But such had also been the lot of

other competent commanders in the army, yet none turned traitor to his country. Arnold, however, feeling mistreated and suffering financial embarrassment due to his own reckless expenditures and the extravagances of his pretty wife, the former Peggy Shippen, entered into secret negotiations with Sir Henry Clinton. On the promise of a large sum of money and a command in the British army, he agreed to surrender West Point, key fortress to the Hudson River Valley and vital to communication lines between New England and the other states.

Possible inferences:

_____ a. Benedict Arnold easily forgave people.

_____ b. Benedict Arnold knew his negotiations with the British army were wrong.

_____ c. Benedict Arnold's wife encouraged him to be a traitor.

_____ d. Benedict Arnold was guided by his feelings more than by his intellect.

_____ e. Sir Henry Clinton knew of Benedict Arnold's financial problems.

3. When Mr. Pontellier learned of his wife's intention to abandon her home and take up her residence elsewhere, he immediately wrote her a letter of unqualified disapproval and remonstrance. She had given reasons which he was unwilling to acknowledge as adequate. He hoped she had not acted upon her rash impulse; and he begged her to consider first, foremost, and above all else, what people would say. He was not dreaming of scandal when he uttered this warning; that was a thing which would never have entered into his mind to consider in connection with his wife's name or his own. He was simply thinking of his financial integrity. It might be noised about that the Pontelliers had met with reverses, and were forced to conduct their menage [household] on a humbler scale than heretofore. It might do incalculable mischief to his business prospects.

Chopin, Kate. "The Awakening." In *The Awakening and Other Short Stories,* ed. Lewis Leary. New York: Holt, 1970. 313.

Possible inferences:

_____ a. Mr. Pontellier was concerned about his status.

_____ b. Mr. Pontellier loved his wife.

_____ c. Mr. Pontellier and his wife were wealthy.

_____ d. Mrs. Pontellier was having an extramarital affair.

_____ e. Mr. Pontellier did not want his wife to leave.

4. The ethical code that all doctors recite when they join the medical profession today goes back at least two thousand years. The Hippocratic oath defines what ethical behavior is when a physician works with his or her patients. The oath describes not only the methods that

Finding Support for Your Inferences   **223**

doctors should and should not use in treating the ill but also the code of conduct they should follow in working with patients. One part of the code says, for example, "Whatever, in connection with my professional practice, or not in connection with it, I see or hear, in the life of men which ought not to be spoken of abroad, I will not divulge as reckoning that all such should be kept secret."

Possible inferences:

_____ a. Ethical problems in medicine have concerned men and women for a long time.

_____ b. The concern for ethics in medicine originated in the United States.

_____ c. Some patients prefer doctors who have not taken the Hippocratic oath.

_____ d. Part of the ethical behavior of doctors is to respect a patient's right to privacy.

_____ e. Today, graduates of medical schools in Europe do not have to take the Hippocratic oath.

5. Because handguns are not accurate beyond ten to fifteen feet, they are not the weapons of sports enthusiasts. Their sole purpose is to kill or at least to disable a person at close range. But only a minority of persons killed with these weapons are criminals. Since handguns chiefly destroy the innocent, they must be outlawed—not simply controlled more strictly, but outlawed—to all except to law-enforcement officials. Attempts to control handguns are costly and ineffective, but even if they were cheap and effective, stricter controls would not take handguns out of circulation among criminals because licensed guns are stolen from homeowners and shopkeepers, and thus fall into criminal hands. According to researchers Wright, Rossi, and Daly, about 40 percent of the handguns used in crimes are stolen chiefly from homes that the guns were supposed to protect.

Possible inferences:

_____ a. Handguns would be effective for seagoing military operations.

_____ b. Criminals prefer to use handguns that are licensed to someone else.

_____ c. Innocent people may be blamed for deaths caused by their own handguns.

_____ d. Research on handguns is relatively unreliable.

_____ e. The people physically harmed most often by handguns are criminals.

6. Flying solo isn't necessarily a lonely ride, says Duane Alwin, a University of Michigan expert on single living and mental health. A large body of research indicates that unmarried people suffer more from depres-

sion, anxiety, and ill health than those who are married—the theory being that close relationships protect the married against stresses the unmarried face alone. But Alwin argues that solitary living itself can't be held responsible. People need strong ties with others to be happy, he says, but it can't be assumed that living alone prevents those ties from forming.

Seligman, J. "The Art of Flying Solo." *Newsweek* 1 Mar. 1993:70.

Possible inferences:

_____ a. Duane Alwin is married.

_____ b. The longer a person is married, the less he or she will feel depressed.

_____ c. Unmarried people are incapable of forming strong ties with others.

_____ d. Flying solo refers to being unmarried.

_____ e. Sometimes there is disagreement about psychological theories.

7. More than three thousand genetic disorders afflict humanity. On the average, most humans have at least five or six potentially harmful hereditary traits encoded in their genes in a recessive or "carrier" state. Cystic fibrosis, for example, is transmitted from parent to offspring by recessive genes. Only if both parents bear the same recessive gene can their children suffer the disease. The chance of this occurring is relatively low. In some areas of the world, however, certain mutant genes are common, and there is a high risk of having an afflicted child. In southern Italy and Greece, for example, there is a high incidence of the genetic blood disease called beta-thalassemia, a severe anemic condition.

Possible inferences:

_____ a. People in Japan have a greater chance of passing cystic fibrosis on to their offspring than people in the United States.

_____ b. If you have a recessive gene for Tay–Sachs disease, a fatal degenerative disorder of the nervous system, there is better than a 50 percent chance that your offspring will inherit it.

_____ c. Fetal abnormalities can be prevented by selecting marriage or parenting partners on the basis of their genetic makeup.

_____ d. In parts of the world where there is a great deal of incest, there is greater likelihood that children will inherit harmful diseases.

_____ e. Good prenatal care can help prevent cystic fibrosis.

8. Several aspects of Brazilian social structure impede the economic advancement of lower-class Brazilians. Most obvious are obligations

associated with kinship. Men who through hard work have become more successful within the community are expected to share their wealth with a larger number of people. Obligations associated with marriage also drain wealth from the enterprising man. In Brazil, the union with the most prestige is one that has been sanctified by both church and state. Poorer couples are generally involved in common-law unions wherein there is no written legal joining of the couple. Upwardly mobile young men may have civil and religious ceremonies when they marry. If they do this, however, they undertake obligations to care for the wife's relatives, which do not exist with the common-law union. Since there is no divorce in Brazil, these obligations are for life.

Possible inferences:

_____ a. Parents whose children are in common-law marriages will not have the same protection in their later years as parents whose children have sanctified marriages.

_____ b. There are fewer sanctified marriages in Brazil than anywhere else in the world.

_____ c. Brazilian culture encourages concern for others who are less well-off.

_____ d. It is acceptable for Brazilian men who are wealthy to be critical of relatives who ask for money.

_____ e. The church and state have a close connection in Brazilian culture.

▶ **Thinking About Your Reading and Writing**

ACTIVITY N. Contrasting Inference and Main Idea Processes

In a few sentences, explain how the thought processes you use to make inferences differ from those you use to find main ideas.

Critical readers are aware that several other features of a written work contribute to its overall effect. These features include the author's *style, tone,* and *mood.* We discuss each separately in this section, but as with all the elements of an article or essay discussed thus far in this textbook, they work simultaneously to create a single effect on the reader. Style, mood, and tone describe *how* something has been written, whereas events or ideas could be considered the *what* of an article or essay. *How* something has been written affects the reader's response to the text.

Author's Style

The author's style refers to the *types of words and sentence construction* the author uses in order to appeal to a particular type of audience. Some writers want to appeal to a wide audience and will use fairly common expressions, slang, or easy-to-read sentences. Other authors are addressing their comments to a more educated group. Their sentences tend to be longer, and their choice of words more sophisticated. If a writer expects the audience to have a great deal of knowledge of the subject, he or she may use more technical language. Authors who want to persuade their audience to respond in a certain way will use emotional language; others will not make any effort to appeal to their readers' emotions. Their purpose, then, influences the language authors use.

Writers, of course, generally do not tell their readers what style they are using. The reader must know what to look for within the text itself in order to determine the author's style. The process is similar to the one you used to search for evidence to make other types of inferences.

Example 1:

Long-haul drivers, away from family and hearth for weeks at a time, put in longer hours to make a decent living than any other workers in America. From up high in a big truck we can look down into your little cars and scope out the "seat covers" (passengers). Despite what we sometimes see, we often wish we were in this other, more normal world. We can watch couples argue with each other, watch ladies try to drive to work and paint their faces at the same time, watch the less affluent people with their windows rolled down in the summer (no AC) but looking so proud: black T shirt, the driver's beefy arm hanging out the window with the radio blasting. (It's amazing how healthy the males look and how sparky the females in those noisy, hot cages.) Our TV screen is the windshield and yes, we male drivers do leer sometimes, enjoying the view as we observe the multiethnic, sultry femucopia of south Florida, the aggressive, preening go-getters driving the D.C. beltway, the Chicago working girls as we pass the train platforms alongside I-94, or the sunbathers along any beach highway. But what every driver likes even more, when he can get it, is a little respect.

—Aalborg, J. "The View from the Big Road." *Newsweek*
20 Dec. 1993: 10.

The author of this paragraph does not use a very extensive vocabulary, and the language is informal. Words such as *scope out* and *AC* contribute to this informality. The sentences are not complicated, either. They are short and easy to read. The intended audience is probably, then, a large general audience—perhaps all of us who have wondered about the life of the long-haul driver. The style is very natural, down-to-earth. The examples that illustrate what the drivers see—all of us—connect the author to all of us. By relating so personally to us, the driver is able to keep our attention to the end when he asks for *respect*. The author's style, then, helps accomplish the author's purpose.

Example 2:

When an external magnetic field is applied to a diamagnetic substance, such as bismuth, the only magnetic moments induced in the substance are aligned *against* the external field. Correspondingly, a diamagnetic substance has a *negative* susceptibility. Furthermore, one finds that a diamagnetic sample is *repelled* when placed near the pole of a strong magnet (in contrast with a paramagnetic sample, which is *attracted*). Although the effect of diamagnetism is present in all matter, it is weak compared with paramagnetism and ferromagnetism.

The language of this passage is extremely technical. The author assumes that readers are quite familiar with the subject already. The sentences are fairly long and complex, but the author believes that this educated audience will be able to follow. Since the language is unemotional, the author's intention is probably just to convey information. By writing with a straightforward style, the author is able to accomplish this purpose.

Critical readers who are sensitive to an author's style will have another measure by which to evaluate the usefulness of an author's ideas. You will be able to select material that is suitable for your own purposes. For instance, if you are writing a research paper, you would want to use material that has, itself, been researched and has used authoritative sources to support personal opinions. On the other hand, if you are reading for pleasure, you might prefer material written for a wide, general audience rather than a specialized one. Many authors are sensitive to their audiences. A textbook author who is aware that students are taking an introductory course in the particular discipline, for example, will often use examples they can relate to in order to help them comprehend the subject matter. This is often not the case in textbooks written for advanced students who are expected to have more knowledge of the field.

Keep in mind, too, that an author's style should have a bearing on your reading rate. If the language is very technical, you will need to slow down. If the writing style is more like that of the first example, you can go at a faster pace.

ACTIVITY O. Identifying Author's Style

Read each paragraph, noting the style in which it is written. Then answer the questions that follow.

1. Our nation's economy today is a far cry from what the classical economists envisioned. In Chapter 9, we will survey and discuss the changes in size and influence of our various levels of government. Today, a third of the market value of all the production in the United States, called the *gross national product* (GNP), is spent by our local, state, and national governments.

   Who is the intended audience? _____

   How do you know? _____

   Is there any evidence that the author is trying to appeal to your emotions? If so, what is it? _____

   _____

2. Each year, thousands of plant and animal species disappear. The ozone layer in the upper atmosphere that protects us from ultraviolet radiation is thinning. The temperature of the earth appears to be rising, posing a threat of unknown dimensions to virtually all the life-support systems on which humanity depends.

   Who is the intended audience? _____

   How do you know? _____

   Is there any evidence that the author is trying to appeal to your emotions? If so, what is it? _____

   _____

3. Many people came in contact with Elinor, including some people of power and influence. Many tried to assist her. Could not someone, some agency, have done something to alter the course of her seemingly inevitable destruction? In many ways, Elinor chose the way she lived, she chose to stay in the terminal. But that's just too simple: She was a victim.

Who is the intended audience? -

How do you know? -

Is there any evidence that the author is trying to appeal to your emo-

tions? If so, what is it? -

- -

4. Cotton was grown in the American South, sold to English factories, where it was made into clothing, and then sent back to the United States, where it was bought by Americans. By the 1850s, tariffs on the clothing that was brought into the country greatly reduced the profits that the English could make on their products. As a result, the English naturally bought less cotton from the South. Southerners complained bitterly about the tariffs but could do nothing about them.

Who is the intended audience? -

How do you know? -

Is there any evidence that the author is trying to appeal to your emo-

tions? If so, what is it? -

- -

5. Any viewer of the United States who watched regularly the television reporting from Vietnam—and it was from television that 60 percent of Americans got most of their war news—would agree that he saw scenes of real-life violence, death, and horror on his screen that would have been unthinkable before Vietnam. The risk and intrusion that such filming involved could, perhaps, be justified if it could be shown that television had been particularly effective in revealing the true nature of the war and thus had been able to change people's attitudes to it. Is there any evidence to this effect?

Knightley, P. "The First Televised War." *Fields of Writing.* 3rd ed. Ed. Nancy R. Comley, et al. New York: St. Martin's, 1975. 632.

Who is the intended audience? -

How do you know? -

Is there any evidence that the author is trying to appeal to your emo-

tions? If so, what is it? -

- -

Compare your answers to Activity O with those of a partner. Did you agree on which paragraphs made emotional appeals to readers?

Inferring Mood and Tone

Words can be powerful descriptors of feeling. Mood and tone refer to the emotional atmosphere conveyed through written language. When readers analyze narrative text (short stories, poetry, plays, and novels), the terms *mood* and *tone* may be used interchangeably. A character's dialogue, for instance, may simultaneously suggest a tone and create a mood, as in the case of a dying soldier who bids a passionate farewell to his lover. However, when readers analyze expository text (essays, newspaper or periodical articles, and textbook chapters), the term *tone* is generally used. As with other elements of writing we have already studied in this chapter, the author may not tell you directly what mood or tone is present in the writing. You will need to analyze the word choice and the details of the writing to arrive at an understanding of its mood or tone. You will be able to further appreciate and understand mood and tone by looking at some everyday examples of them.

Your experiences communicating with others have no doubt made you sensitive to differences in tone of voice. If a friend is troubled, you might listen and talk sympathetically. If you are speaking to someone who has damaged your property, you probably sound angry. If a new co-worker asks you to explain some work-related procedure, you probably use an instructional or serious tone of voice. If you have very strong feelings in an argument, you may be passionate when you explain your point of view. We adjust our tone of voice to suit the situation and our purpose, as well as to convey our feelings in the situation. Authors of expository text, or narrators of a literary work, use tone to reflect serious, angry, sympathetic, instructional, argumentative or persuasive, humorous, or ironic attitudes.

Tone can influence our personal reactions to a piece of writing or toward a character. Consider, for instance, the difference in your reactions to someone who requests a favor and sounds sweet and grateful, compared to someone who sounds demanding and insistent. You should recognize that your response to what you read may be similarly influenced by its tone. Thus, to read critically, you will need to be able to separate the content of what is said from the manner in which it is said. Then you will be able to honestly assess whether the ideas have merit.

As a critical reader, you should try to match your purpose for reading to the author's purpose for writing. Doing this will help your comprehension. For instance, if an author writes an essay suggesting that people should never own pets and does so in a humorous vein, the reader who recognizes the humor will read it as a humorous piece and won't criticize the author for having outrageous ideas. However, readers who think this author is serious will misinterpret the entire essay. To accomplish this reader–writer match in purpose, it is essential to determine the author's tone.

The mood of a written work may refer to the frame of mind of a character, as reflected through the character's actions, dialogue, and tone of voice. Mood also refers to the general atmosphere that surrounds an incident or scene; it is created by description and details or events. To further understand this element of a writer's craft, imagine that you are getting ready for a first date with someone you find pretty exciting. Your date has planned the entire evening. You hope for candlelight and champagne; instead, you are treated to hot dogs and a football game. Obviously, there is a difference in the mood or atmosphere created by the details used to describe each of these situations.

Authors of narrative text use details for a variety of purposes, one of which is to create a particular mood for their story. The details work together to create an overall effect. Some examples of mood that you might find in narrative text are suspense or mystery, horror, gaiety or joyfulness, sadness, gloominess, anticipation or adventure, romance, loneliness, hopefulness, and frustration.

If an author has been successful at creating a particular mood, it will inspire the desired feeling in the reader. Notice the contrast between the following two example paragraphs, both of which are about the same event. One has been written with carefully chosen details so as to create a certain mood; the other seems flat by comparison. Note the difference in the effect each has on you, the reader.

Example 1:

It was unbelievably wonderful to be home. The first thing she did was to race upstairs, tear off her uniform, and put on some proper clothes—an old cotton skirt, a well-worn white shirt left over from school, her favorite red sweater. Nothing had changed; the room was just the way she had left it, only tidier and shiningly clean. When, bare-legged, she ran downstairs again, it was to go from room to room, a thorough inspection, just to make sure that there, as well, everything was exactly the same. Which it was.

Example 2:

It was good to be home. She first went upstairs, took off her uniform, and put on some proper clothes—a cotton skirt, a white shirt left over from school, a red sweater. Her room was as she had left it, only cleaner. After dressing, she went downstairs again to go through the house to make sure that there, as well, everything was the way she had left it. Which it was.

What mood is created by example 1? _

What details contribute to its effectiveness? _ _ _ _ _ _ _ _ _ _ _ _ _ _ _ _ _ _ _

There is an air of excitement in the first example that isn't present in the second. Some of the details that help create this mood are the phrases *unbelievably wonderful* and *nothing had changed*. We can tell how glad the girl is to be home and to be putting on her *favorite red sweater*. These details, and others you may have noticed, work together to create the mood.

ACTIVITY P. Identifying Author's Tone and Mood

In the space provided, indicate the tone or mood that has been used in each paragraph. Then explain why you believe this is the tone or mood of the passage.

> *Example:*
>
> All health-care workers must follow universal precautions and established infection control procedures to reduce infection risks to patients and themselves. Appropriate use and disposal of needles and sharp instruments are the most important risk reduction strategy. In addition, universal precautions include the use of gloves, masks, eye protection, and other barriers as needed for procedures that involve contact with blood and body fluids.
>
> *Tone or mood:* informative; serious
>
> *Explanation:* A good deal of information is given. There is not much emotional language.

1. Every new advance in medicine—every new drug, new operation, new therapy of any kind—must sooner or later be tried on a living being for the first time. That trial, controlled or uncontrolled, will be an experiment. The subject of that experiment, if not an animal, will be a human being. Prohibiting the use of live animals in biomedical research, therefore, or sharply restricting it, must result either in the blockage of much valuable research or in the replacement of animal subjects with human subjects. These are the consequences—unacceptable to most reasonable persons—of not using animals in research.

   Tone or mood: _____

   Explanation: _____

   _____

2. I speak from experience when I say that cigar smokers have suffered the scorn of Americans who think our habit is vile. We have seen the

steady disappearance of places where cigar smoking is acceptable. Now we are being told that the federal government wants to raise taxes on our cigars to help finance health care. Eventually, cigars will cost nothing because if the prices keep going up and there's nowhere to smoke them, nobody's going to smoke them. The whole thing makes me nauseous.

Tone or mood: _

Explanation: _

_ _

3. It was so lonely in that swampy river that it made you want to cry. All the sad sounds in the world suddenly started. A dove set up that woeful oo-hoo-oo-hoo-hoo across the swamp, and another one, sadder still began to answer him back. They sounded like two old widow women swapping miseries.

Tone or mood: _

Explanation: _

_ _

4. As terrible as the fear of existence is, the fear of nonexistence is even worse. Maybe if we only knew what happened to us after we died, it would all be easier.

    One speculation is that we go to the Land of the Umbrellas. You've probably seen them at the end of every rainstorm. Lying in the gutter, crumpled, skeletal, inside-out, bereft of personal history. Who did these umbrellas belong to? Where are they going? What use are they now?

    Others say that after death we go to the Land of the M&M's—the place where the M&M's go after they fall behind the cushions on the sofa. Or some say it's the Land of the Other Shoe. (Ever drive along the road and see one shoe lying on the pavement and wonder how it got there? You never see *both shoes;* the other shoe has gone to join the umbrellas and the M&M's.)

    In the end, it is probably foolish to speculate about such matters. In ancient times, the biggest fear was that you would have a terrible life and be reincarnated, and the next life would be even worse. Nowadays, life is Hollywood, and if your life's been bad, you don't have to worry about there being a sequel. Not if Part I didn't make any money.

Brush, S. "Life: A Warning." *The Big Book of North American Humor.* Eds. W. Novak and M. Waldoks. New York: HarperCollins, 1990. 178.

Tone or mood: _____

Explanation: _____

_____

5. And after all the weather was ideal. They could not have had a more perfect day for a garden party if they had ordered it. Windless, warm, the sky without a cloud. Only the blue was veiled with a haze of light gold, as it is sometimes in early summer. The gardener had been up since dawn, mowing the lawns and sweeping them, until the grass and the dark flat rosettes where the daisy plants had been seemed to shine. As for the roses, you could not help feeling they understood that roses are the only flowers that impress people at garden parties; the only flowers that everybody is certain of knowing. Hundreds, yes, literally hundreds, had come out in a single night; the green bushes bowed down as though they had been visited by archangels.

Mansfield, Katherine. "The Garden Party."

Tone or mood: _____

Explanation: _____

_____

6. "I knew it before I got out of bed," she says, turning away from the window with a purposeful excitement in her eyes. "The courthouse bell sounded so cold and clear. And there were no birds singing; they've gone to warmer country, yes indeed. Oh, Buddy, stop stuffing biscuit and fetch our buggy. Help me find my hat. We've thirty cakes to bake."

Capote, Truman. "A Christmas Memory."

Tone or mood: _____

Explanation: _____

_____

7. For three years there has been too much talk and far too little progress in finding an environmentally safe way of disposing of dredged soils so that our vital ports can remain open, active, and employing workers.

    The time has come for all the federal agencies involved to take a strong and decisive stand on the dredging issue. The bureaucrats have skillfully displayed their vast regulatory proficiency in exhaustively studying real or perceived environmental and health problems. Meanwhile, ships are being diverted from Port Newark-Elizabeth and jobs are being lost.

Unless intense pressure is placed on the EPA and Army Corps to advance this proposal [to address both the long-term and short-term problem of disposing of dredged soils], I fear that months from now the only movement we will see is not of dredged sediment, but of trade diverted from our port to Montreal, Halifax, Baltimore, or Hampton Roads. The federal bureaucrats need to come out of the bunker and face this issue head on. No more disclaimers, trial balloons, and "let's wait and see" approaches to this issue. There have been too many false starts and yellow lights on the road to progress.

Franks, Bob. Letter. *Highland Park Herald* 29 July 1994: A-4.

Tone or mood: _____

Explanation: _____

_____

8. He sat on a bench here, watching the leafy trees and the flowers blooming on the inside of the railing, thinking of a better life for himself. He thought of the jobs he had had since he had quit school—delivery boy, stock clerk, runner, lately working in a factory—and he was dissatisfied with all of them. He felt he would someday like to have a good job and live in a private house with a porch on a street with trees. He wanted to have some dough in his pocket to buy things with, and a girl to go with, so as not to be so lonely, especially on Saturday nights. He wanted people to like and respect him.

Malamud, B. "A Sinner's Reading."

Tone or mood: _____

Explanation: _____

_____

9. She looked up at him, the wide, young eyes blazing with light. And he bent down and kissed her on the lips. And the dawn blazed in them, their new life came to pass, it was beyond all conceiving good, it was so good, that it was almost like a passing-away, a trespass. He drew her suddenly closer to him.

Tone or mood: _____

Explanation: _____

_____

10. Alfred lowered the gun. One shot, and he would be cornered like a rabbit at harvest time. If he was going to kill the man, he would have to

do so silently. With the Colt in his right hand, he pulled off his shoes and crept cautiously across the tiles. A chimney stack obstructed his view for part of the way. By the time he rounded it Snits had raised the rifle to his shoulder and was settling himself into a firing position.

Tone or mood: _

Explanation: _

_ _

▶ **Thinking About Your Reading and Writing**

ACTIVITY Q. Mood and Tone in Films

Think about some movies or videos you have seen. In a few sentences, discuss what you notice about how filmmakers create mood.

_ _

_ _

_ _

_ _

_ _

_ _

_ _

_ _

🔲 **Working Together**

With a partner, discuss some films you have seen where the mood has been an important part of the film's effect on you. Compare the types of moods you prefer. ●

DRAWING CONCLUSIONS FROM YOUR READING

Critical readers often draw conclusions from what they read. Some of these conclusions are probability statements based on the information in the text. Others are suggestions of how an author's ideas can be applied to different situations. In this section, you will learn how to form conclusions and how to decide whether your conclusions reasonably follow from the text and from your prior knowledge.

What Are Conclusions?

We draw conclusions about our everyday experiences all the time. For instance, we go into Sam's music store and notice that the price of a popular CD is $11.99, which is $2.00 higher than in Lonny's music store. From this, we might conclude that Sam's has high prices on CDs. Our conclusion is verified by other instances of higher prices on CDs at Sam's. We try to remember whether Lonny's was having a sale when we looked at its prices. If it was not, we can predict, or conclude, that anytime we come to Sam's the prices on CDs will be higher. If a sale was being held at Lonny's, however, we cannot conclude this.

In drawing conclusions about CD prices, we are stating that something is a *probable outcome* based on evidence we have gathered. Drawing conclusions from texts or lectures uses the same process: We look at the facts or reasons (which may include opinions), we judge how accurate and unbiased they are, and we eliminate particularly biased or irrelevant information.

A conclusion may explain or predict what will probably happen, or what will result, based on what you already know. It is a *reasonable guess* about an outcome. Conclusions are based on facts and well-supported opinions. For a conclusion to be probable, it should follow logically from this information. When you draw a conclusion, you are tying together the various pieces of information you have into a broad statement of probability. The information you use to draw your conclusion may come from several sources, as in example 1. Or it may come from a single source, as in example 2.

Example 1:

Conclusion: In your search for a family dog, you have decided that *the golden retriever is the best kind of dog for a family to own.* Your reasons are:

a. The American Kennel Club rates the golden retriever as the dog with the best disposition.

b. A friend of yours says his golden retriever has never destroyed any of his property.

c. You have read a newspaper account of a golden retriever who rescued a baby who had fallen into a pool.

Example 2:

Conclusion: As a result of your reading about the code of medieval chivalry, you have concluded that *the honor of being called a chival-*

rous gentleman could be bestowed on only a few men. The basis for this conclusion is the information in the following passage:

A chivalrous gentleman was brave, straightforward, and honorable; loyal to his monarch, country, and friends; unfailingly true to his word; ready to take issue with anyone he saw ill-treating a woman, a child, or an animal. He was a natural leader of men, and others unhesitatingly followed his lead. He was fearless in war and on the hunting field and excelled at many sports, but however tough with the tough, he was invariably gentle to the weak; above all, he was always tender, respectful, and courteous to women regardless of their rank. He put the needs of others before his own.

In each example, the conclusion logically follows from the information gathered. They are acceptable conclusions. It may be that at a later date some other information will become known that will refute these conclusions, but since it is not now available, these conclusions are considered probable or likely to be true.

ACTIVITY R. Identifying Conclusions

Select the conclusion that *logically follows* for each paragraph. Underline the information in the paragraph that you believe supports your conclusion. Be prepared to justify your answers.

1. One research team found that teacher instruction related to seatwork assignments seldom included statements about what would be learned and how the assignment related to other things that students had learned. When teachers did pay attention to students who were doing seatwork, they most often monitored student behavior but not student understanding or performance. For instance, when providing feedback, teachers' comments and explanations were usually procedural (for example, "Read the sentence and then pick the word that completes the sentence"), with little attention to the cognitive demands of the task (strategies for selecting the appropriate word). Likewise, much teacher feedback focused on correctness of answers or neatness of work.

Adapted from Good, T. L., and Jere E. Brophy. *Looking in Classrooms.* 4th ed. New York: Harper & Row, 1987. 31.

   a. Teachers are aware of the limited value of seatwork.
   b. Seatwork makes students bored in school.
   c. Teachers need more training in how to instruct through seatwork.
   d. Schools will soon eliminate seatwork as a method of instruction.

2. The skillful blending of different textures in a room is just as important to the success of the scheme as the choice of colors and the mixing and matching of patterned and plain surfaces, yet it is often a neglected

subject. Textures are all too often put together haphazardly even when the rest of the scheme has been carefully balanced. The selecting of textures needs even more care and attention when a room is being decorated with mostly plain colors on the larger areas of walls, floor, windows, and on upholstered furniture. If all these surfaces are of the same texture, even if the colors are different, the final effect will be boring. Just as a successful scheme in mainly warm or cool colors needs a sharp contrast from the opposite side of the color wheel to bring it to life, so textures need contrast for emphasis.

Adapted from Blake, Jill. *Color and Pattern in the Home.* London: Design Council. 50.

a. The textures in a room can have a major impact on the final effect of its appearance.
b. When colors in a room are of the same hue, the effect is dramatic.
c. Textures and colors can be used to reflect certain period styles.
d. To give rooms a lavish appearance, you should use velvet and satin textures.

3. Compared to machine language programs, assembly language programs are much easier for people to write and fairly understandable to read. However, like the machine languages before them, assembly languages are machine-dependent. That is, different computers require different assembly languages, and programs written for one machine will not run on another. Moreover, assembly language programs cannot be executed (processed) directly by a computer. First, they must be translated or assembled, into machine-readable form (machine code) before they can be processed. Despite their considerable improvement over machine language programs, assembly language programs are still very detailed. They are usually quite long and, like machine language, are error prone. Each assembly language statement translates directly into a single machine language instruction. A thorough knowledge of the computer hardware on the part of the programmer is often required for writing efficient code.

Kershner, Helene G. *Computer Literacy.* 2nd ed. Lexington: D. C. Heath, 1992. 216.

a. If a company switches from machine language programs to assembly language programs, it will need to buy new computers.
b. It took a long time to develop assembly language programs because they are more complex than those programs using machine language.
c. Businesses were not very excited when assembly language programs first came on the market.
d. It is not a good idea to use machine language programs any more.

4. During World War II, when great numbers of trained technicians were in demand, it was assumed that those who had mechanical aptitude would make good airplane mechanics. A careful analysis of this as-

sumption proved otherwise. It turned out that a good shoe clerk in civilian life would become a better mechanic for military purposes than someone who had fixed cars most of his life and learned on a Model-T Ford. The critical trait was not mechanical aptitude but the ability of the trainee to follow instructions. The Army then worked out its instruction manuals so meticulously that the best recruit turned out to be a mildly obsessional person who could read and follow directions. The last thing they wanted was someone with his own ideas on how to fix equipment.

Hall, E. T. *The Silent Language*. New York: Anchor, 1981. 71.

a. The Army is not a good place for an engineer.
b. Instruction manuals printed by the Army are designed for people who do not read very well.
c. Specialized skills are not needed by the Army.
d. The Army gives careful consideration to job requirements.

5. Scientists had believed that natural chemical cycles involving nitrogen and hydrogen controlled the stratospheric ozone amounts in this part of the earth's atmosphere. Observations made by NASA's high-altitude ER02 plane, however, detected much lower levels of nitrogen oxides (NOx) than scientists expected. The measurements also showed higher than anticipated levels of chlorine monoxide (ClO), known to play a key role in destroying ozone in the polar regions.

a. Scientists had overemphasized the importance of chlorine monoxide and its effect on the ozone layer.
b. Scientists had overemphasized the importance of the nitrogen cycle in its effect on the ozone layer.
c. NASA was reluctant to conduct this study.
d. The ER02 plane is unreliable.

6. Gadgets are getting more complex to use because of technological advances which enable them to do more interesting tasks. A dial telephone or a pocket watch was simple to use, but each did only one thing. If all you want to do is order a pizza or tell the time, they're still fine. If you want to be able to forward your calls to your cellular mobile fax machine, you will pay a price in added complexity.

Rogers, Michael. "The Right Button." *Newsweek* 7 Jan. 1991, 48.

a. Manufacturers of gadgets are adapting their products to our more complex lifestyles.
b. Pocket watches are no longer appreciated for their traditional style.
c. People using dial telephones do not know how to use more complicated technological equipment.
d. It is apparent that most people wished our society would become less complex, especially with regard to technology for our homes.

7. Because we live in a highly specialized society, different social tasks are entrusted to different groups of individuals. Government, for example, is held responsible for safeguarding the public's health. This, in turn, makes government officials dependent on the skills and commitment of a certain category of medical person; if the latter cannot be induced to perform their tasks—such as, for example, finding a cure for AIDS—tens of thousands of citizens will find their lives endangered. Similarly, if the government wishes to develop more advanced nuclear weapons, put a man on the moon, or design a strategic defense, it makes itself dependent on the relative handful of individuals who possess the appropriate scientific and technical skills. Indeed, since the number of each of these is far smaller than the number of businessmen, each of them is proportionately more powerful than is each businessman. And unlike those who currently occupy the role of businessman, they cannot be readily replaced.

Vigel, David. "The New Political Science of Corporate Power." *The Public Interest.* No. 87. Spring 1987. 63–79.

    a. Businessmen feel pressured to increase their scientific knowledge.
    b. In highly specialized societies, people are more interdependent.
    c. Medical science has advanced over the years because of increases in government funding.
    d. The government should feel responsible when small businesses fail.

8. Toward the end of March, Alice Manfred put her needles aside to think again of what she called the *impunity* of the man who killed her niece just because he could. It had not been hard to do; it had not even made him think twice about what danger he was putting himself in. He just did it. One man. One defenseless girl. Death. A sample-case man. A nice, neighborly, everybody-knows-him man. The kind you let in your house because he was not dangerous, because you had seen him with children, bought his products and never heard a scrap of gossip about him doing wrong. Felt not only safe but kindly in his company because he was the sort women ran to when they thought they were being followed, or watched, or needed someone to have the extra key just in case you locked yourself out. He was the man who took you to your door if you missed the trolley and had to walk night streets at night. Who warned young girls away from hooch joints and the men who lingered there. Women teased him because they trusted him. He was one of those men who might have marched down Fifth Avenue—cold and dignified—into the space the drums made. He knew wrong wasn't right, and did it anyway.

Morrison, T. *Jazz.* New York: Knopf, 1992. 73–74.

    a. Alice Manfred thought her niece had been unwise.
    b. The man who killed Alice Manfred's niece had escaped.
    c. Alice Manfred feels very unsafe now.
    d. Alice Manfred felt that the courts were ignoring the horror of her niece's death.

ACTIVITY S. Reflecting on Drawing Conclusions

In a few sentences, describe the thought processes you used to reject or accept conclusions in Activity R.

ACTIVITY T. Evidence for Conclusions

The sentences that follow offer conclusions that could have been drawn from academic texts or lectures. In the space provided, indicate what type of evidence you would want to have before you accepted this conclusion. Be specific.

Example 1:

Conclusion: The use of AZT on AIDS patients has made many of them stronger.

Evidence you would need to accept this conclusion: Testimony from AIDS patients; statistics from medical research.

Example 2:

Conclusion: Increasingly, the Mundurucu people of the Amazon's rain forest are becoming Westernized.

Evidence you would need to accept this conclusion: Reports from anthropologists who have been there.

1. **Conclusion:** Women have an easier time moving into executive positions today than they did twenty-five years ago.

Evidence you would need to accept this conclusion: _ _ _ _ _ _ _ _ _ _ _ _ _ _ _

_ _

2. **Conclusion:** There is a strong correlation between academic achievement and family income.

   Evidence you would need to accept this conclusion: _ _ _ _ _ _ _ _ _ _ _ _ _ _ _

   _

3. **Conclusion:** Lee Harvey Oswald was acting alone when he assassinated John F. Kennedy.

   Evidence you would need to accept this conclusion: _ _ _ _ _ _ _ _ _ _ _ _ _ _ _

   _

4. **Conclusion:** America's wilderness and sensitive animal life are not threatened by big business, but by government.

   Evidence you would need to accept this conclusion: _ _ _ _ _ _ _ _ _ _ _ _ _ _ _

   _

5. **Conclusion:** Young men and women living in affluent communities have similar attitudes with regard to premarital sex.

   Evidence you would need to accept this conclusion: _ _ _ _ _ _ _ _ _ _ _ _ _ _ _

   _

6. **Conclusion:** The prison system in the United States is ineffective in changing inmates' attitudes toward crime.

   Evidence you would need to accept this conclusion: _ _ _ _ _ _ _ _ _ _ _ _ _ _ _

   _

7. **Conclusion:** Children who are adopted by gay couples fare as well in life as those who grow up with heterosexual couples.

   Evidence you would need to accept this conclusion: _ _ _ _ _ _ _ _ _ _ _ _ _ _ _

   _

Working Together

Compare your answers to Activity T with those of a partner. What differences were there in the evidence you each wanted? Add any of your partner's ideas that you liked to your own.

▶ **Thinking About Your Reading and Writing**

<u>**ACTIVITY U.**</u> **Your Conclusions About Conclusions**

What are some conclusions you can draw about how critical reading and thinking will benefit you in your college career?

_____

_____

_____

_____

_____

_____

_____

_____

_____

_____

_____

_____

RECOGNIZING FAULTY REASONING

Authors will often state conclusions directly. This is particularly true in argumentative or persuasive writing. The conclusion may be written as a separate paragraph, and it may be offered as an answer to a problem that had been discussed. You may view the author's direct statement of conclusions in a positive way, as something that will assist you with interpreting what you read. However, you should be aware that the conclusions drawn are not necessarily ones that follow from the evidence provided. *Faulty reasoning* may be used to convince readers to accept a conclusion or point of view. When this occurs, you should reject the conclusion unless some other evidence for it is found in the text or is known by you. Your ability to recognize incorrect or inconclusive arguments will help you evaluate the strength of your own arguments as well. Faulty reasoning includes:

1. Coming to conclusions without sufficient evidence or before the facts are known.

   Conclusion: The spokesperson announced that the deaths of four restaurant patrons were the tragic result of food poisoning.

   Explanation of faulty reasoning: It was later learned that the deaths were caused by bacteria that had been in the water pipes.

2. Ignoring evidence that might disprove the conclusion.

   Conclusion: The death penalty is a deterrent to crime.

   Explanation of faulty reasoning: Statistics show that the number of executions and the crime rate are both rising.

3. Using irrelevant issues as support.

   Conclusion: Because of an increasing concern about how children use their leisure time, more and more parents will buy computers for their children.

   Explanation of faulty reasoning: Although parents may be concerned about the use of leisure time, there is no evidence that they see computer ownership as a solution.

4. Suggesting that one thing is the cause of another when this relationship is doubtful or when there could be several causes.

   Conclusion: Dr. Peterson is obviously a boring teacher; Bianca fell asleep right in his class.

   Explanation of faulty reasoning: Several other causes are possible: Bianca may have been sick, on drugs, or overtired.

5. Attacking individuals who disagree rather than discussing the weaknesses of an opposing point of view.

   Conclusion: Legislators who do not support this proposal for improving the sewage treatment facilities in this community can't be trusted; one is being audited by the IRS.

   Explanation of faulty reasoning: The IRS is a governmental agency that collects taxes; it has no relationship to sewage treatment facilities. Further, being "audited" is not proof of guilt.

6. Simplifying the problem or suggesting that there are only two points of view.

   Conclusion: If the players don't agree to sign this contract, then it is clear they want to go on strike.

   Explanation of faulty reasoning: The players could reject this contract and continue negotiating without going on strike.

7. Suggesting that a serious consequence will follow if the author's ideas, proposals, or solutions are not accepted.

   Conclusion: If the railroad line is not improved, then taxes will have to go up to improve the highways needed to serve the large increases in car commuting that will inevitably occur.

   Explanation of faulty reasoning: A tax increase is always a serious consequence for taxpayers. There is no evidence that car commuting will increase, but the author makes readers feel threatened.

8. Appealing to the prejudices of people to support an argument.

   Conclusion: Those of us who understand God's will, will believe in the truth of my comments.

   Explanation of faulty reasoning: Few people listening would want to be called nonbelievers. Thus, they may feel it is necessary to support the conclusion.

9. Making a statement that assumes that the issue being argued has already been proved.

   Conclusion: The only way we can achieve customer satisfaction is to give our customers more options in color and design.

   Explanation of faulty reasoning: It is being assumed that customers are not satisfied.

10. Appealing to tradition. Arguing that because something has existed for a long time, it should continue in that way.

    Conclusion: Our parents didn't have sex education in school, and it shouldn't be mandated for our kids, either.

    Explanation of faulty reasoning: It is being argued that things should be done now as they were done in the past.

11. Appealing to the emotions and diverting attention from the important issue.

    Conclusion: Unless more funds are allocated for police protection, we will live in ever-increasing fear.

    Explanation of faulty reasoning: The important issue is why there is so much crime.

12. Making a comparison between two things that actually have nothing in common.

    Conclusion: Making teenagers perform community service is like drafting young boys into the military.

    Explanation of faulty reasoning: Although the government may require community service, as it did military service, the dangers and responsibilities are vastly different. The comparison has limited usefulness.

<u>ACTIVITY V.</u> Finding Errors in Reasoning

Find the reasoning errors in each of the following conclusions. Identify each error, and explain your answer in the space provided. For some sentences, you may be able to find more than one error.

1. The greediness of the promoters of the fight has caused them to reject our proposals for tougher safety standards.

   Reasoning error(s): --

   Your explanation: --

   ----

2. Since everyone fears associating with people who have AIDS, it is best to put AIDS patients in a separate wing of the hospital.

   Reasoning error(s): --

   Your explanation: --

   ----

3. Anyone who doesn't agree with this editorial must be pretty dumb.

   Reasoning error(s): --

   Your explanation: --

   ----

4. A free society cannot maintain its unity and order unless there is equal pay for equal work.

   Reasoning error(s): --

   Your explanation: --

   ----

5. A ban on smoking in the workplace is another example of government's intrusion into our personal lives.

   Reasoning error(s): --

Your explanation: --

----

6. The protests have been successful because only one week after the antiabortion activists started protesting at Oakdear Clinic, the number of abortions performed in the country dropped.

Reasoning error(s): --

Your explanation: --

----

7. Racism is not a major problem on this campus because two of my black friends have been accepted into nearly all-white fraternities.

Reasoning error(s): --

Your explanation: --

----

8. It is the most costly VCR, so it will be more satisfactory than any other.

Reasoning error(s): --

Your explanation: --

----

9. Our president can't tell us anything about foreign policy. He's never fought in a war.

Reasoning error(s): --

Your explanation: --

----

10. We now all appreciate the beauty of the musical *Hair*. We know this because more than ten million people have seen this show since it first opened.

Reasoning error(s): --

Your explanation: --

----

11. People who remain unemployed for more than six months are lazy and don't want to work.

    Reasoning error(s): -

    Your explanation: -

    -

12. Alcoholic beverages have always been banned at our local sports events, and they should remain that way.

    Reasoning error(s): -

    Your explanation: -

    -

13. A woman without a man is like a fish without a bicycle.

    Reasoning error(s): -

    Your explanation: -

    -

Working Together

With a partner, return now to Activity T. Review the evidence you said you would need to accept the given conclusions. Look for instances of faulty reasoning, and make any necessary changes.

CHAPTER SUMMARY

Based on your reading of this chapter, list at least five points that were made that you believe will help you with future reading assignments.

1.

2.

3.

4.

5.

Now that you have worked with the strategies necessary for critical reading and thinking, you can practice applying them to full-length reading selections. Choose (or your instructor may choose) a reading selection that is typical of what you will be expected to read for your other college courses, such as an essay or a textbook chapter. Use this selection to practice:

- Distinguishing between fact and opinion
- Evaluating evidence for statements of opinion
- Identifying point of view
- Making inferences
- Drawing conclusions
- Locating evidence for conclusions

Decide the practice strategies you will use. Apply them to your selection. Then in a few paragraphs, write a description of what you did and how the strategies you used worked for you.

Name of material used: _____

Page numbers: _____

Your description:

Strategies
for Reading Visual
Aids in Texts

$\mathcal{D}$o you like to take photographs? Why? Why do so many people take cameras with them when they go on vacation or to special events? Most say they enjoy taking photos because then they can share with others what they've seen. It also helps them remember the places they've visited and the people they've met. Although reading a textbook isn't exactly like going on vacation, authors often include visual information in their texts for some of the same reasons: to help explain information to the readers and to help them remember what they have read. A number of strategies can help you read visual aids in texts more effectively and use them to your best advantage. This chapter gives you opportunities to develop strategies that will work for you.

Pictorial displays, or visual aids, are often included in textbook chapters. They can be of great assistance to readers who know how to use them effectively.

ACTIVITY A. Determining the Value of Visuals

Read Selection A and Selection B. Then answer the questions that follow under the heading *Reflection.*

Selection A:

FEDERAL AID TO STATE AND LOCAL GOVERNMENTS, 1955–1989

Year	Total Federal Aid (in billions)	Federal Aid as Percent of	
		Federal Outlays	State and Local Outlays
1955	$ 3.2	4.7%	10.1%
1960	7.0	7.6	14.7
1965	10.9	9.2	15.3
1970	24.0	12.3	19.3
1975	49.8	15.0	23.0
1980	91.5	15.5	26.3
1982	88.2	11.8	21.9
1985	105.9	11.2	21.0
1989	106.5	10.0	na

Source: *Budget of the U.S. Government, Fiscal Year 1988: Special Analyses,* Table H-7.

Selection B:

During the 1960s, there was a significant increase in the federal government's role in funding goals that addressed social issues. Federal officials, not state and local ones, were the principal supporters of grant programs to aid the urban poor, combat crime, reduce pollution, and deal with drug abuse. This rise of federal involvement in social issues occurred at a time when the total amount of federal aid to states and localities had become so great that many state and local governments were completely dependent on it for the support of vital services. Whereas federal aid amounted to less than 2 percent of the total of state and local spending in 1927, by 1955 it had increased to 10.1 percent, by 1970 it amounted to 19 percent, and by 1980 to 26 percent. This trend declined slightly after the early 1980s but remained nearly double the 1955 level. States soon understood that if they wanted federal dollars, they would need to adopt the federal aid programs.

Wilson, J. Q., *American Government.* Brief version. 2nd ed. Lexington: D. C. Heath, 1990. 42.

Reflection:

What are some differences between the approaches you used to read Selection A and Selection B? _

_ _

Which presentation of this information do you prefer? Why? _ _ _ _ _ _ _

_ _

Which presentation do you think will help you remember this information longer? Why? _

_ _

In what way was the visual aid helpful? _ _ _ _ _ _ _ _ _ _ _ _ _ _ _ _ _ _

_ _

Working Together

Compare your answers to Activity A with those of a partner. What differences do you find in your responses?

WHAT ARE THE VARIOUS TYPES OF VISUAL AIDS?

There are several popular types of visual aids. Each type has its own unique features and purposes.

Charts

Charts summarize information through a combination of words and graphics. Often they show relationships between the items on the chart or comparisons between them. Charts enable the writer to explain complex ideas more concretely, and they enable the reader to visualize the relationships between abstract concepts.

Tree Charts.   *Tree charts* look like trees with branches. A tree chart showing the relationship between the sales division of a large company and the rest of the company might look like the following chart:

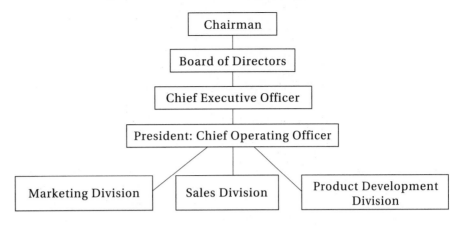

Flow Charts.   *Flow charts* show movement between events (a process) and may depict stopping out or correction points in this process. A flow chart designed to show the process for eating lunch might look like the diagram on the next page. The symbols on the chart are explained in a key or legend alongside the chart. Notice that several decision points can cause the flow to stop or to continue. These "stopping" or "rerouting" points are common on flow charts and are one reason they are useful for depicting processes.

Graphs

Graphs, especially *circle* (or *pie*), *bar,* and *line* graphs, are also commonly found in textbooks. The purpose of a graph is most often to show comparisons of quantitative information. There is always text, either directly on or surrounding the graph, and this information tells the reader what is being depicted. The reader then needs to see the relationship between the different pieces of information and determine the significance of it. For instance, by looking at the *circle graph,* we can see the differences that exist in the

1994 Entry-Level Incomes for Business (BA) Graduates

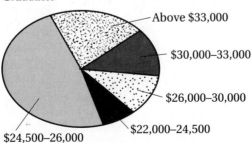

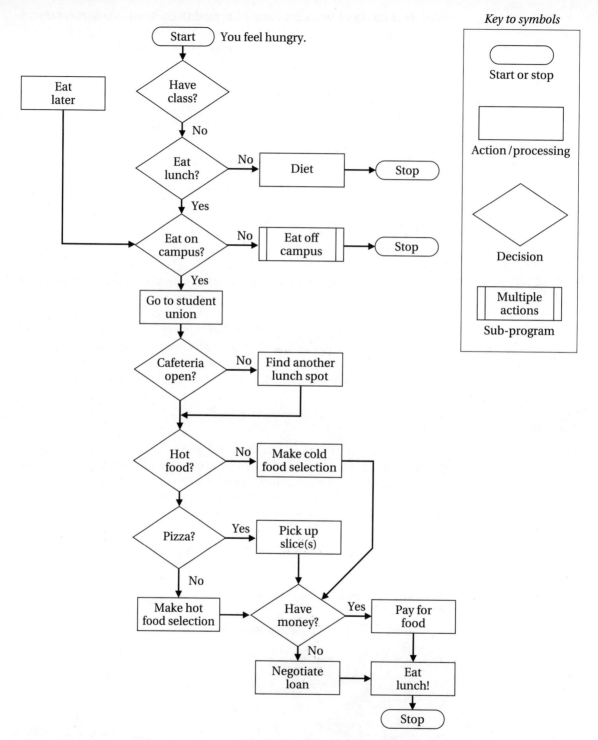

"Eating Lunch" Flow Chart   Source: Kerschner, H. G. *Computer Literacy.* 2nd ed. Lexington: D. C. Heath, 1992. 169.

entry-level incomes of individuals who graduated from four-year colleges with degrees in business in 1994. The information outside the graph tells us what we are looking at. We can draw several conclusions from the data, for instance, that some entry-level positions to graduates pay very high salaries and that most jobs pay an average salary that would enable a person first starting out, who had good budgeting skills, to live independently.

Bar graphs depict information that would be difficult for readers to follow in a textual discussion; they also make it easy for the reader to compare data, as the bar graph shown here illustrates. Notice that the meanings of the various shadings are provided in the legend to the graph. Footnotes

World Production and Consumption of Petroleum Source: *World Book Encyclopedia.* Vol. 15. 1991. 354. From *Energy Statistics Yearbook,* 1987, United Nations.

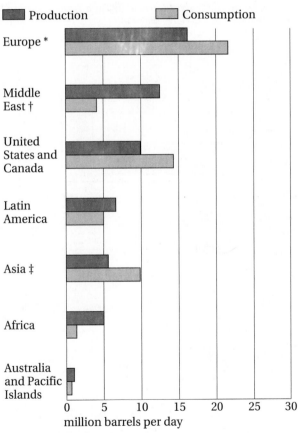

* Includes the Asian part of Soviet Union.
† Excludes Egypt and Sudan.
‡ Excludes the Middle East and the Asian part of the Soviet Union.

provide geographic explanations. The graph shows several relationships. The reader can compare production in one part of the world to production in another; comparisons can also be made between an area's production and its consumption, and that can be compared to similar ratios in other parts of the world.

Bar graphs may also be drawn horizontally, as in the following example. Once again, several comparisons are shown. One comparison is a comparison over time with regard to the form of transportation that has been used to carry domestic freight. Another comparison is the comparison between types of carriers, namely, air versus truck. In addition to the bar itself, which illustrates differences, the specific percentage volume contributed by each type of carrier to the total volume of domestic freight is provided by the notations alongside the chart, and a scale drawing of percentages is at the bottom of the "rails" bar.

Volume of Domestic Freight Carried by Each Transportation Mode Source: Megginson, et al. *Business*. Lexington: D. C. Heath, 1985. 414.

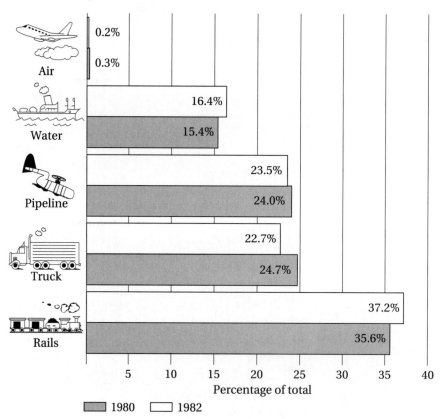

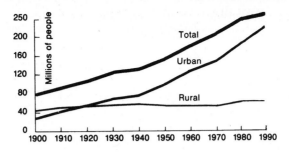

Population Growth *Population of the United States 1900–1990.* Source: Lachmann, R., ed. *The Encyclopedic Dictionary of Sociology.* 4th ed. Guilford, Conn.: Dushkin, 1991. 224.

Line graphs are useful for showing trends over time. Because line graphs can show small increases and decreases, they are sometimes considered the most accurate type of graph. As with all graphs, the information outside the graph is critical for you to read. It explains what the information on the graph represents. Above is an example of a line graph with three lines, each representing a particular kind of population growth in the United States: rural growth, urban growth, and a total for the entire country. On this graph, different line thicknesses are used to represent the different areas of growth. The information to the left and on the bottom of the graph inform the reader that the line placements represent millions of people between the years 1900 and 1990.

Tables

Tables are used to classify or categorize information, particularly when there are many numbers or several categories. The information on a table is usually arranged in columns, with the categories listed horizontally across the top and the items falling into each category listed vertically. As in the example, often several comparison points are being made on a single table. Footnotes also frequently appear on tables to give further explanation for some of the items.

AIDS DEATHS AND CASE-FATALITY RATES AMONG ADULTS AND ADOLESCENTS, OCTOBER 1990

Half-Year of Diagnosis		Cases	Deaths	Case-Fatality Rate*
Before 1981		78	30	82.1
1981	Jan–June	92	38	93.5
	July–Dec	199	85	91.0
1982	Jan–June	394	152	90.6
	July–Dec	685	282	88.6
1983	Jan–June	1,261	515	92.1
	July–Dec	1,631	917	91.4
1984	Jan–June	2,543	1,374	89.0
	July–Dec	3,334	1,917	89.8
1985	Jan–June	4,815	2,741	88.7
	July–Dec	6,187	3,730	87.0
1986	Jan–June	8,119	4,900	85.2
	July–Dec	9,760	6,231	82.3
1987	Jan–June	12,544	7,245	81.4
	July–Dec	13,947	7,611	74.5
1988	Jan–June	15,719	8,815	66.9
	July–Dec	16,003	9,999	59.9
1989	Jan–June	17,523	11,146	49.0
	July–Dec	16,839	12,280	39.4
1990	Jan–June	15,558	10,637	25.6
	July–Dec	5,000	3,565	13.1
TOTAL**		152,231	94,375	62.0

*Case-fatality rates are calculated by the Centers for Disease Control on a semiannual basis by date of diagnosis. For each six-month period, the rate represents the number of fatal cases reported, divided by the number of total cases diagnosed in that period, multiplied by 100.

**Total includes 165 adults and adolescents known to have died, but whose date of death is unknown.

Source: U.S. Department of Health and Human Services, Public Health Service, Centers for Disease Control, Center for Infectious Diseases, Division of HIV/AIDS, HIV/AIDS SURVEIL-LANCE, November 1990, Table 8, p. 13.

Time Lines

To show how something has progressed in stages or how something has evolved over time, a *time line* is particularly effective. Time lines often appear in scientific writing and may illustrate how scientific discoveries progressed from one stage, perhaps the stage where an illness is first identified, to a later stage, perhaps when a cure is found. More frequently, they are used to show historical developments in chronological order, as in the time line shown here.

Chapter 8   Strategies for Reading Visual Aids in Texts

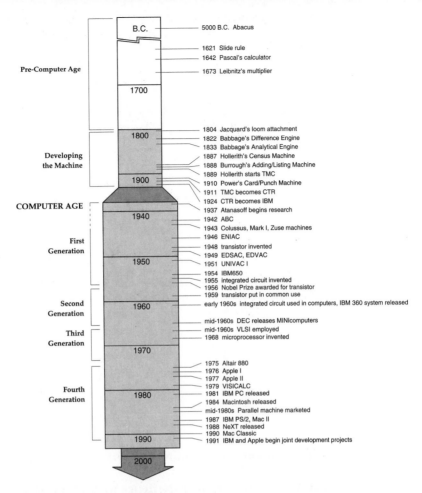

B.C.	— 5000 B.C. Abacus
	— 1621 Slide rule
	— 1642 Pascal's calculator
Pre-Computer Age	— 1673 Leibnitz's multiplier
1700	

Pre-Computer Age

Developing the Machine
- 1804 Jacquard's loom attachment
- 1822 Babbage's Difference Engine
- 1833 Babbage's Analytical Engine
- 1887 Hollerith's Census Machine
- 1888 Burrough's Adding/Listing Machine
- 1889 Hollerith starts TMC
- 1910 Power's Card/Punch Machine
- 1911 TMC becomes CTR
- 1924 CTR becomes IBM

COMPUTER AGE
- 1937 Atanasoff begins research
- 1942 ABC
- 1943 Colussus, Mark I, Zuse machines
- 1946 ENIAC
- 1948 transistor invented
- 1949 EDSAC, EDVAC

First Generation
- 1951 UNIVAC I
- 1954 IBM650
- 1955 integrated circuit invented
- 1956 Nobel Prize awarded for transistor
- 1959 transistor put in common use
- early 1960s integrated circuit used in computers, IBM 360 system released

Second Generation
- mid-1960s DEC releases MINIcomputers

Third Generation
- mid-1960s VLSI employed
- 1968 microprocessor invented

Fourth Generation
- 1975 Altair 880
- 1976 Apple I
- 1977 Apple II
- 1979 VISICALC
- 1981 IBM PC released
- 1984 Macintosh released
- mid-1980s Parallel machine marketed
- 1987 IBM PS/2, Mac II
- 1988 NeXT released
- 1990 Mac Classic
- 1991 IBM and Apple begin joint development projects

Years marked on timeline: 1800, 1900, 1940, 1950, 1960, 1970, 1980, 1990, 2000

The Major Events in Computer History Source: Kerschner, H. G. *Computer Literacy.* 2nd ed. Lexington: D. C. Heath, 1992. 68.

Photographs

Another popular type of visual aid in texts is the photograph. Some photographs depict situations that are true to life, such as urban street scenes, children in classrooms, or athletes in training. Art books depend heavily on photos of paintings. Other photos may be the result of special effects, such as photos of cells as seen from under a microscope or photos that are the result of computer graphic effects.

Diagrams

Technological or scientific writing often depends on drawings to explain complicated processes, structures, or sequences described in the text. In this example, a drawing has been used to assist the reader with understanding the structure of the ear. Each part is clearly labeled.

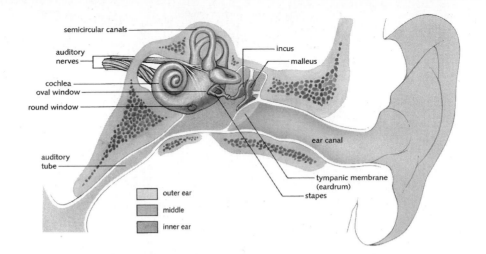

Phonoreceptors: The Mammalian Ear *Note ear bones in the middle ear cavity. The semicircular canals, are a part of the inner ear that detects changes in head and body position.* Source: Levine, J. S., and R. S. Miller. *Biology,* Second Edition. Lexington: D. C. Heath, 1994. 936.

▶ **Thinking About Your Reading and Writing**

ACTIVITY B. Your Prior Experience with Visual Aids

In the past, what types of visual aids have you found the most useful?

What types have been most difficult for you to read?

What do you do when you encounter a difficult one?

ACTIVITY C. Creating a Visual Aid Reference Table

Using the information from the preceding section, create your own table for handy reference to visual aids. In the space provided, create separate columns to list (1) the type of visual aid, (2) why it is used, and (3) its distinguishing features. Give a title to your table. When you have completed it, compare your table with a partner's.

ACTIVITY D. Constructing Your Own Visuals

Select one of the visuals from the preceding section and redesign it so that the information is displayed in another way. For instance, you might make a bar graph using data from the example line graph, or you might make a diagram to represent information originally given in flow chart format. Put your visual in the space provided.

Perhaps you commented in Activity A that it would be easier for you to recall information when it was presented in table format rather than in paragraph form. Most people would agree with you. Even when the paragraphs and sentences give valuable information, visuals allow us to organize that information in a way that is often easier to remember.

Another advantage of visuals is the effect they have on reader response to the information. The visual impact of an idea can be much more impressive than an idea stated in words. If an author wants to impress the reader with an idea, to make a more powerful statement, a visual might be used. Notice the difference in the effect between the two presentations of the same idea that follow.

Example 1:

In 1900, the population of Mexico was less than 15 million. By 1950, it had reached nearly 26 million, and by 1980, it was more than 70 million.

Example 2:

Growth of Mexico's Population, 1900–1980 Source: *Population Bulletin,* 20, No. 7 (Nov. 1964).

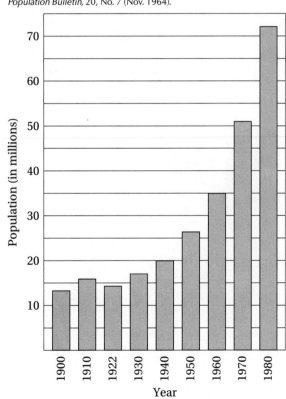

ACTIVITY E. Responding to Visual Aids

What is the visual impact of the preceding graph on you? Why do you think this graph has this impact?

Visual information can also help clarify material that sounds complex when stated in sentence form. Read the following paragraph. Then look at the diagram accompanying the text. Notice how the diagram helps the reader understand the complex process described in the text.

Example 1:

The tick vector of Lyme disease has a two-year life cycle in which it requires three blood meals. The larval form becomes infected from

Source: Tortora, G. J., B. R. Funke, and C. L. Case. *Microbiology An Introduction.* 4th ed. Redwood City: Benjamin/Cummings, 1992. 570.

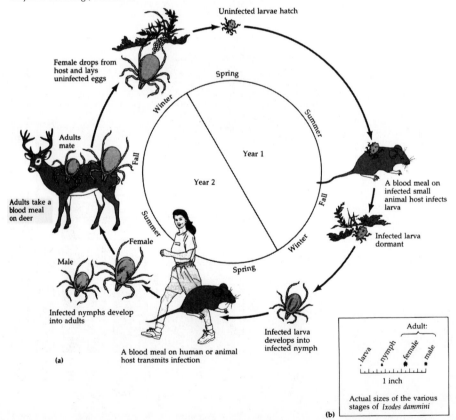

small animals, usually field mice, then enters a dormant stage until the following spring. Then it molts into a nymph, which is still infected. This is the stage at which it is most likely to infect humans. It is crucial to the maintenance of the cycle in the wild that the spirochete be able to remain viable in small animals to reinfect the larvae the following year. The field mouse is well adapted to this. The third feeding, by the infected adults that develop from the nymph, is taken from the deer. After this, the adults lay eggs, which are uninfected, that overwinter to develop into larvae the following spring.

Visuals can also substitute for written information. There is a saying that "a picture is worth a thousand words." For readers, pictures often can convey much more than words could ever describe. See how this might apply to the photo shown here.

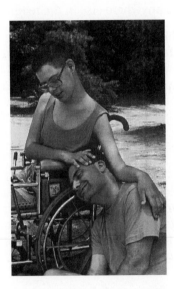

Source: Deborah Gilbert / The Image Bank, Boston

▶ **Thinking About Your Reading and Writing**

ACTIVITY F. Assessing the Impact of a Photo

Do you think this visual is "worth a thousand words"? Why or why not?

- -

- -

- -

For successful reading of visual aids, you should:

1. Preview the visual to get an overall impression and to make predictions.

2. Note details to gain more information and to verify your predictions.

3. Make connections between the visual aid and the text to see how each part is supported or extended by the other.

4. Make inferences from the visual to elaborate on your interpretation of the data and to see whether there is confirmation of your inferences in the rest of the text.

5. Draw conclusions from the visual to determine any wider application of the information and to see how your conclusions are further supported by information anywhere else in the reading selection.

In the remainder of this chapter, you will note that the strategies to use for reading visual aids differ somewhat from those you use for reading text that does not contain visuals. There are also, however, commonalities, and you will be able to apply your prior knowledge about reading strategies to the activities in this section.

PREVIEWING VISUALS

Visuals, like information conveyed through sentences and paragraphs, can be previewed. During your preview, your goal is to obtain an overall idea of the purpose of the visual and to determine how the data on it are organized. You also hope to be able to predict what sort of details you will find once you examine the visual more closely.

Previewing Graphs

To preview a graph, you need to:

1. Read the title of the graph. Treat it in the same way you would treat the title of a chapter or article.

2. Examine the lengths of the bars, divisions of a circle graph, or shape of the line(s). These features of a graph are similar to subtitles of text. They convey an overall impression of the information that will be provided through the details.

3. Look along the sides and bottom of the graph for any headings or labels that tell you more about the details displayed.

4. Look for any keys, legends, or footnotes on the graph that identify codes the author is using.

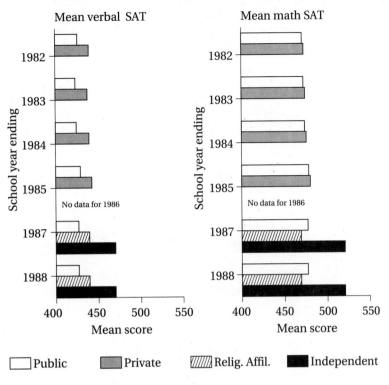

Mean verbal SAT

Mean math SAT

School year ending

1982
1983
1984
1985
No data for 1986
1987
1988

Mean score

Public   Private   Relig. Affil.   Independent

NOTE: As of 1987, private is reported as religiously affiliated or independent.

Mean Verbal and Math SAT, by Control of High School: 1982–1988
Source: College Entrance Examination Board, *The National Report of College-Bound Seniors, Profile of SAT & Achievement Test Takers,* various years.

5. Make predictions about what you will find when you read the information on the graph more closely.

On the above bar graph, some details have been eliminated. Follow the steps for previewing a graph to see what information you can obtain and what predictions you can make about the contents of the rest of the graph.

What information can you obtain from the graph in its present form? _____

_____

_____

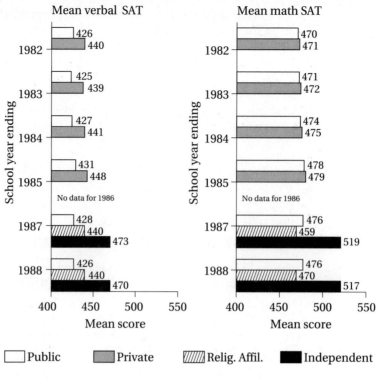

Mean verbal SAT

School year ending	Public	Private	Relig. Affil.	Independent
1982	426	440		
1983	425	439		
1984	427	441		
1985	431	448		

No data for 1986

| 1987 | 428 | | 440 | 473 |
| 1988 | 426 | | 440 | 470 |

Mean math SAT

School year ending	Public	Private	Relig. Affil.	Independent
1982	470	471		
1983	471	472		
1984	474	475		
1985	478	479		

No data for 1986

| 1987 | 476 | | 459 | 519 |
| 1988 | 476 | | 470 | 517 |

Mean score

☐ Public   ▨ Private   ▥ Relig. Affil.   ■ Independent

NOTE: As of 1987, private is reported as religiously affiliated or independent.

Mean Verbal and Math SAT, by Control of High School: 1982–1988
Source: College Entrance Examination Board, *The National Report of College-Bound Seniors, Profile of SAT & Achievement Test Takers,* various years.

Now look at the graph with the added details.

What additional information do you learn about SAT scores?

During your preview, you were able to recognize that this graph would be about math and verbal SAT scores, 1982–1988, in different types of high schools. You also should have been able to tell that private schools had higher verbal scores than public schools and that independent schools had higher scores than all other types of schools in both verbal and math. One prediction you might have made is that no more than fifty points in either math or verbal separated any two types of schools.

Once the details were added, your additional information should have included some of the following: Public school scores on the verbal portion declined slightly between 1985 and 1988 and in 1988 were at the lowest since 1982; public and private schools between 1982 and 1985 were very close on math. (You might have also concluded that this closeness was the result of the religious and independent schools being combined into this single private school figure.)

Previewing Tables

The aids for previewing that you will find on tables include the title of the table (often appearing at the top) and the subheadings that appear above each column on the table. These parts of the table should be treated in the same way as titles and subtitles in texts. Thus, to preview a table, you would:

1. Read the title.
2. Read the subheadings.
3. Use the title and subheadings to determine the focus of the table.
4. Look for any keys, legends, or footnotes on the table that identify any codes or symbols the author is using.
5. Make predictions about the specifics of the data in the table.

In the next example, you are first presented with a table that contains only the title and vertical and horizontal subheadings. Examine it to see what you learn from your preview. Then answer the questions that follow.

What is this visual about? _____

What information does the title provide?

_____

How are the title and the subheadings on this table related to one

another? _____

_____

_____

Chapter 8   Strategies for Reading Visual Aids in Texts

TABLE 1: BICYCLES AND PARTS, DOMESTIC SHIPMENTS AND TRADE, 1987–1993
(IN MILLIONS OF DOLLARS EXCEPT AS NOTED)

	1987	1988	1989	1990	1991[1]	1992[2]	1993[3]	Percent Change[4] (1987–1993)					
								87–88	88–89	89–90	90–91	91–92	92–93
Product shipments . . . .
Product shipments (1987$) . . . .
Apparent consumption[5] . . . . .
Imports . . . .
Imports to apparent consumption (%) . . . .
Exports . . . .
Exports to shipments (%) . . . . . .

[1]Estimated product shipments.
[2]Estimated trade and product shipments.
[3]Forecast.
[4]Percent changes are calculated on more detailed data.

[5]Apparent consumption = product shipments − exports + imports.
Source: U.S. Department of Commerce: Bureau of the Census; International Trade Administration (ITA). Estimates and forecasts by ITA.

What kinds of details will you most likely find on this visual?

Based on your prior knowledge, what do you expect the data to show (for instance, increases, decreases)? Why do you expect this?

Look now at the complete table on the next page, which includes all the previously missing details. How accurate were your predictions?

What additional information have you learned now that you have studied

the details of this visual?   --

During your preview, you no doubt recognized that this table would be about the imports and exports of bicycles and bicycle parts during the years 1987–1993. From the information beneath the title, you could tell that the details would be dollar amounts. One prediction you might have made, if you have any prior knowledge about the improved quality of American bikes, is that exports have increased and imports have decreased. Once the details were added, your additional information should have included the facts that although imports did increase slightly in some years, and there has been tremendous growth in exports, exports may now be at their peak and will level off.

Previewing Other Types of Visuals

All visuals contain elements that can be studied for making predictions before you make a closer inspection. When previewing time lines and flow charts, for instance, you can first read the major headings and the beginning and ending notations to see the period covered or the starting and finishing points of the process that are included in the visual. With a diagram or photo, you should first identify those features that stand out from the rest; then these can be used to make predictions about the remaining details. When you are reading a flow chart, you will want to notice the overall organization of the chart—such as how the hierarchy is arranged and how many branches stem from each of the major branches—before

TABLE 1: BICYCLES AND PARTS, DOMESTIC SHIPMENTS AND TRADE, 1987–1993
(IN MILLIONS OF DOLLARS EXCEPT AS NOTED)

	1987	1988	1989	1990	1991[1]	1992[2]	1993[3]	Percent Change[4] (1987–1993)					
								87–88	88–89	89–90	90–91	91–92	92–93
Product shipments	536.1	531.1	686.0	863.3	901.0	934.0		−0.9	29.2	25.8	4.4	3.7	
Product shipments (1987$)	536.1	500.1	618.6	764.7	796.6	825.8	860.1	−6.7	23.8	23.6	4.2	3.7	4.1
Apparent consumption[5]	1,255.3	1,151.1	1,321.6	1,499.7	1,471.5	1,536.2		−8.3	14.8	13.5	−1.9	4.4	
Imports	732.3	640.5	681.4	750.0	744.9	781.2	842.0	−12.5	6.4	10.1	−0.7	4.9	7.8
Imports to apparent consumption (%)	58.3	55.6	51.6	50.0	50.6	50.9		−4.6	−7.3	−3.0	1.2	0.5	
Exports	13.1	20.5	45.8	113.6	174.4	179.0	192.0	56.5	123.4	148.0	53.5	2.6	7.3
Exports to shipments (%)	2.4	3.9	6.7	13.2	19.4	19.2		58.0	73.0	97.1	47.1	−1.0	

[1]Estimated product shipments.
[2]Estimated trade and product shipments.
[3]Forecast.
[4]Percent changes are calculated on more detailed data.
[5]Apparent consumption = product shipments − exports + imports.
Source: U.S. Department of Commerce: Bureau of the Census; International Trade Administration (ITA). Estimates and forecasts by ITA.

you read the individually boxed headings. You will always want to look for keys, legends, or footnotes to the visual and to take note of any special effects the author has used to make distinctions, such as colors or shadings.

Whenever and whatever you preview, your goal is to obtain a general sense of the material before you do more extensive analysis. In this way, you are mentally preparing yourself for the detailed reading and analysis ahead.

ACTIVITY G. Previewing Visuals

In these exercises, the same visual aid appears twice. The first time it appears, it is incomplete, and you will respond to Predictions questions. The second time it appears, it is complete with all the details, and you will respond to Closer Analysis questions.

1.

MONEY INCOME OF HOUSEHOLDS—MEDIAN HOUSEHOLD INCOME IN CURRENT AND CONSTANT (1987) DOLLARS, BY RACE AND HISPANIC ORIGIN OF HOUSEHOLDER: 1970 TO 1987

Year	Median income in current dollars (dol.)				Median income in constant (1987) dollars (dol.)				Annual percent change of median income of all households	
	All house-holds*	White	Black	His-panic[†]	All house-holds*	White	Black	His-panic[†]	Current dollars	Constant dollars
1970										
1971										
1972										
1973										
1974										
1975										
1976										
1977										
1978										
1979										
1980										
1981										
1982										
1983										
1984										
1985										
1986										
1987										

Note: NA = not available. Minus sign (−) indicates decrease.
*Includes other races not shown separately.
[†]Hispanic persons may be of any race.
[3]Change.
Source: Gordon, S. D., and G. G. Dawson. *Introductory Economics.* 7th ed. Lexington: D. C. Heath, 1991. 277. Data from U.S. Bureau of the Census. *Current Population Reports,* Series P-60, No. 161, and unpublished data.

Predictions:

What predictions can you make about the type of information you will obtain from this visual?

What significant points do you expect the data to prove?

What is the relationship between the notations across the bottom of the visual and those along the side?

The next visual includes all the previously missing details. How accurate were your predictions?

MONEY INCOME OF HOUSEHOLDS—MEDIAN HOUSEHOLD INCOME IN CURRENT AND CONSTANT (1987) DOLLARS, BY RACE AND HISPANIC ORIGIN OF HOUSEHOLDER: 1970 TO 1987

Year	Median income in current dollars (dol.)				Median income in constant (1987) dollars (dol.)				Annual percent change of median income of all households	
	All house-holds*	White	Black	His-panic†	All house-holds*	White	Black	His-panic†	Current dollars	Constant dollars
1970	8,734	9,097	5,537	(NA)	25,563	26,626	16,206	(NA)	³6.9	³1.7
1971	9,028	9,443	5,578	(NA)	25,335	26,499	15,654	(NA)	3.4	−.9
1972	9,697	10,173	5,938	7,677	26,344	27,637	16,132	20,856	7.4	4.0
1973	10,512	11,017	6,485	8,144	26,884	28,175	16,586	20,828	8.4	2.0
1974	11,197	11,710	6,964	8,906	25,806	26,987	16,050	20,526	6.5	−4.0
1975	11,800	12,340	7,408	8,865	24,917	26,058	15,643	18,720	5.4	3.4
1976	12,686	13,289	7,902	9,569	25,328	26,531	15,776	19,104	7.5	1.6
1977	13,572	14,272	8,422	10,647	25,454	26,767	15,795	19,968	7.0	.5
1978	15,064	15,660	9,411	11,803	26,242	27,281	16,395	20,562	11.0	3.1
1979	16,461	17,259	10,133	13,042	25,775	27,024	15,866	20,421	9.3	−1.8
1980	17,710	18,684	10,764	13,651	24,426	25,770	14,846	18,828	7.6	−5.2
1981	19,074	20,153	11,309	15,300	23,835	25,184	14,132	19,119	7.7	−2.4
1982	20,171	21,117	11,968	15,178	23,750	24,865	14,092	17,871	5.8	−.4
1983	21,018	22,035	12,473	15,794	23,976	25,136	14,229	18,017	4.2	1.0
1984	22,415	23,647	13,471	16,992	24,526	25,874	14,740	18,592	6.6	2.3
1985	23,618	24,908	14,819	17,465	24,952	26,315	15,656	18,451	5.4	1.7
1986	24,897	26,175	15,080	18,352	25,807	27,131	15,631	19,023	5.4	3.4
1987	25,986	27,427	15,475	19,305	25,986	27,427	15,475	19,305	4.4	.7

Note: NA = not available. Minus sign (−) indicates decrease.

*Includes other races not shown separately.

†Hispanic persons may be of any race.

³Change.

Source: Gordon, S. D., and G. G. Dawson. *Introductory Economics.* 7th ed. Lexington: D.C. Heath, 1991. 277. Data from U.S. Bureau of the Census. *Current Population Reports,* series P-60, No. 161, and unpublished data.

Closer Analysis:

What additional information have you learned now that you have studied the details of this visual aid? _

_ _

_ _

2.

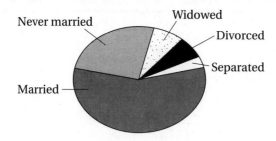

Singles in New Jersey, 1994 Source: New Jersey
Dept. of Labor.

Predictions:

Based on your prior knowledge, what labels do you expect to find

next to the labels by each section of the circle? _ _ _ _ _ _ _ _ _ _ _ _ _ _ _ _ _ _ _

_ _

What significant points do you expect the data to prove?

_ _

_ _

How are the different sections of the circle related to one another?

_ _

_ _

The next visual includes all the previously missing details. How accurate were your predictions?

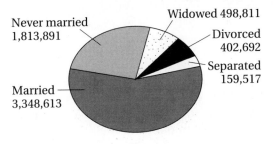

Never married
1,813,891

Widowed 498,811

Divorced
402,692

Separated
159,517

Married
3,348,613

Singles in New Jersey, 1994 Source: New Jersey Dept. of Labor.

Closer Analysis:

What additional information have you learned now that you have studied the details of this visual aid? _

_ _

_ _

▶ **Thinking About Your Reading and Writing**

ACTIVITY H. Sharing What You Know with Others

What advice can you now offer to another student about strategies to use when previewing visuals?

_ _

_ _

_ _

_ _

_ _

_ _

_ _

_ _

Working Together

Compare the advice you have written in Activity H with that of a partner. Discuss the value of each suggestion. Make any additions to your original thoughts that you now think should be included.

NOTING DETAILS

When you complete your preview of a visual aid, your next step will be to analyze all its details. As you do this, you will want to:

1. Identify any special effects the author uses to make distinctions between the various elements on the visual. Consider some of the methods used in the previous section:

    Colors, shadings, or patterns. The visual on SAT scores illustrates how various patterns are used to separate one type of school from another. You may also recall maps you have read that use different colors to reflect different temperature zones or topographical features.

    Broken or solid lines. If a line graph contains several lines, the author may distinguish between what each line represents by using a combination of broken and solid lines or by varying line thicknesses. In this chapter, the graph on population growth in the United States between 1900 and 1990 used line thicknesses to make distinctions.

2. Establish the nature or types of details included. Details may be names, dates, percentages, whole numbers, qualities, or almost anything. Often a combination of these is used. As you have seen in this chapter, when numbers are too large to express completely, the author may use a shortened form, which is then explained in the key.

3. Determine how the details are related to one another. In diagrams, each label may represent part of a whole. On a tree graph, they may show a hierarchy of importance. Details on a time line or flow chart show a sequence over time. Numbers may be used to show comparisons such as those between cities, ethnic groups, gender, age, or years.

4. Determine whether the details are presented in any particular order. This is obvious on tree charts or flow charts and time lines, but on tables, you often must determine an order for yourself, such as size, chronology, increases, or decreases.

5. Determine whether some details have more significance than others. For example, on the graph of Mexico's population, one year showed a sharp increase.

ACTIVITY I. Understanding Details on Visuals

Preview each visual, and then answer the questions that appear beneath it.

1.

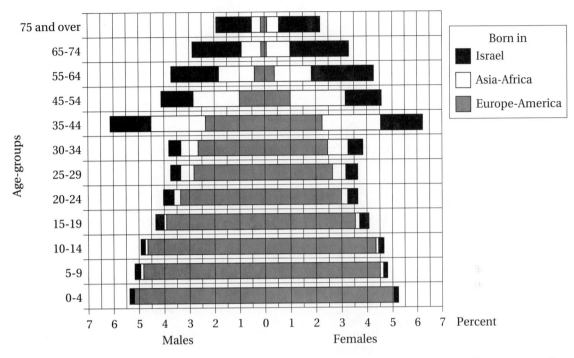

Source: Based on information from Israel, Central Bureau of Statistics, *Statistical Abstract of Israel, 1987*, No. 38, Jerusalem, 1987, 74–75. From *Israel, a country study*. Federal Research Division, Library of Congress. (ed. H C Metz) 1988.

What is the nature of the details? ---

What special effects, if any, does the author use to make distinctions

between details? ---
How are the details related to one another?

Which details, if any, give information that you consider to be particularly

significant? --

2.

TABLE 3. TWENTY-ITEM CHECKLIST CONSISTING OF REASONS FOR AND REACTIONS TO SHOPLIFTING PERCENT OF RESPONDENTS CHECKING EACH ITEM PRE AND POST GROUP (N = 143)

Items	PREGROUP		POSTGROUP	
	Number	Percent	Number	Percent
You felt remorseful when caught.	85	59	76	53
You do not understand why you shoplifted.	73	51	31	22
You shoplifted because you couldn't afford the items.	56	39	48	34
You were surprised that you were arrested for the shoplifting offense.	51	36	45	32
You shoplifted because you were frustrated.	50	35	76	53
You shoplifted because you don't have enough money to support yourself and/or your family.	44	31	39	27
You shoplifted because it was so easy to get away with it.	43	30	45	32
You shoplifted because you felt angry.	38	27	58	41
You knew you were going to be caught shoplifting.	37	26	51	36
You shoplifted because you felt sorry for yourself.	29	20	55	39
You shoplifted because you didn't see it as a serious crime.	26	18	32	22
You were relieved when you were caught.	25	18	51	36
You are very lonely.	24	17	29	20
You shoplifted because it was exciting.	20	14	32	22
You shoplifted because you wanted revenge.	20	14	33	23
You shoplifted because you felt that stores make too much money anyway.	13	9	17	12
You wanted to be caught.	11	8	26	18
You started shoplifting as a teenager and have continued to shoplift as an adult.	6	4	8	6
You shoplifted because you felt that you wanted to humiliate yourself.	5	4	5	4
You shoplifted because you had been drinking or using drugs.	4	3	9	6

Source: Kolman, A. S., and C. Wasserman. "Theft Groups for Women: A Cry for Help." *Federal Probation*. Vol. LV, No. 1 March 1991. 49.

What is the nature of the details? _

_ _

What special effects, if any, does the author use to make distinctions

between details? _

How are the details related to one another?

_ _

Which details, if any, give information that you consider to be particularly

significant? _

_ _

3.

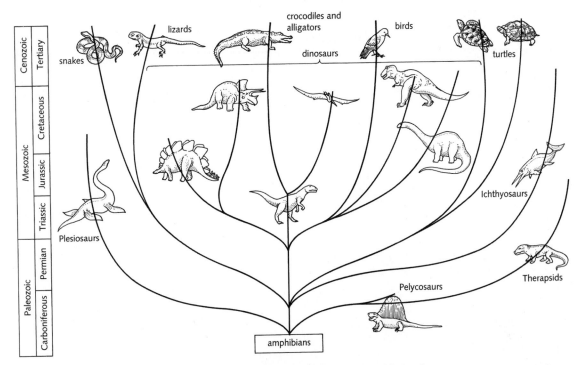

The reptilian radiation, showing both extinct and living forms. Source: Levine, J. S., and
R. S. Miller. *Biology.* Lexington: D. C. Heath, 1994. 519.

What is the nature of the details? -------------------------------

----

What special effects, if any, does the author use to make distinctions

between details? -------------------------------
How are the details related to one another?

Which details, if any, give information that you consider to be particularly

significant? -------------------------------

4.

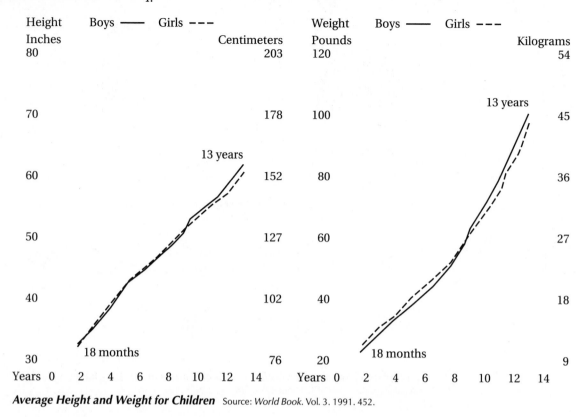

Average Height and Weight for Children Source: *World Book*. Vol. 3. 1991. 452.

What is the nature of the details? _____

_____

What special effects, if any, does the author use to make distinctions between details? _____
How are the details related to one another?

_____

Which details, if any, give information that you consider to be particularly significant? _____

_____

5.

Sulfur dioxide

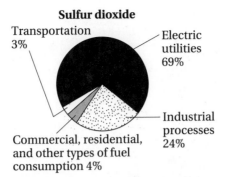

Transportation 3%

Electric utilities 69%

Commercial, residential, and other types of fuel consumption 4%

Industrial processes 24%

Nitrogen oxides

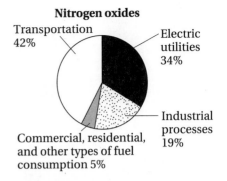

Transportation 42%

Electric utilities 34%

Commercial, residential, and other types of fuel consumption 5%

Industrial processes 19%

Sources of Acid Rain Pollutants Created by Human Activities Source: *World Book, Science Year,* 1993. 210. From U.S. National Acid Precipitation Assessment Program.

What is the nature of the details? _____

_____

What special effects, if any, does the author use to make distinctions

between details? _____
How are the details related to one another?

_____

Which details, if any, give information that you consider to be particularly

significant? _____

_____

6.

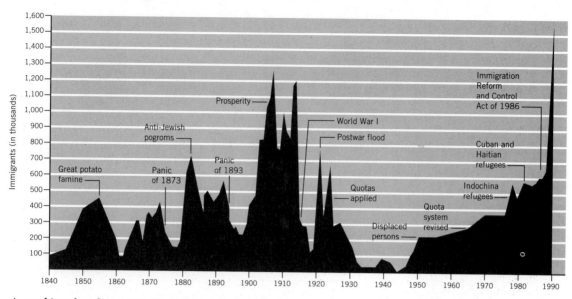

Immigrants (in thousands)

1,600
1,500
1,400
1,300
1,200
1,100
1,000
900
800
700
600
500
400
300
200
100

1840 1850 1860 1870 1880 1890 1900 1910 1920 1930 1940 1950 1960 1970 1980 1990

Great potato famine ——

Anti-Jewish pogroms ——

Panic of 1873

Panic of 1893

Prosperity ——

World War I

Postwar flood

Quotas —— applied

Displaced persons ——

Quota system revised ——

Indochina refugees ——

Cuban and Haitian refugees ——

Immigration Reform and Control Act of 1986 ——

Annual Immigration, 1840–1984 Source: Wilson, J. Q. *American Government.* 5th ed. Lexington: D. C. Heath, 1992. 499.

What is the nature of the details? _____

_____

What special effects, if any, does the author use to make distinctions

between details? _____
How are the details related to one another?

_____

Which details, if any, give information that you consider to be particularly

significant? _____

_____

7.

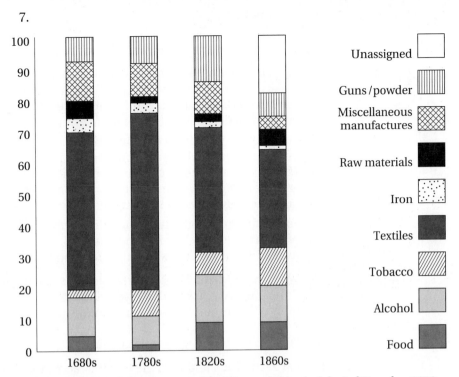

Estimated Relative Value of Imports into Western Africa in Selected Decades, 1680s–1860s Source: Eltis, D. "The Economics of African Participation in the Slave Trade." *The Atlantic Slave Trade.* Ed. D. Northrup. Lexington: D. C. Heath, 1994. 166.

What is the nature of the details? _

_ _

What special effects, if any, does the author use to make distinctions

between details? _
How are the details related to one another?

_ _

Which details, if any, give information that you consider to be particularly

significant? _

_ _

Visual aids most often accompany text for one of the following reasons:

 To give evidence for a point made in the text. For instance, the text may make the claim that poverty rates have increased in urban areas during the last decade. A table with poverty rates in urban areas during the last several decades would illustrate this point.

 To clarify or explain a complicated idea. The diagram of the life cycle of Lyme disease, which appeared earlier in this chapter, is an example. The idea presented is complicated because of the number of stages and species involved in the two-year period of the cycle. The visual helped clarify the events during the cycle.

 To add interest to the text. Sometimes visuals do not add a great deal of information to the reading material, but they do help maintain reader involvement. Photographs frequently are used for this purpose.

Whenever a visual aid is included in your reading material, you should decide its purpose. Visuals that give evidence or explain complicated ideas are often as important to know for exams as is the text itself.

ACTIVITY J. Connecting Visuals and Text

Look at each visual and read the text that accompanies it. Decide whether the purpose of the visual is to (1) give evidence, (2) clarify or explain a complicated idea, or (3) provide interest.

1.

Copper redhorse fish, unique to Great Lakes tributaries.

Source: Luoma, J. R. "Rare Species and Ecosystems Abundant in Great Lakes Region."
New York Times 22 May. 1994: C4.

A report by a private conservation group suggests that the Great Lakes region is a refuge for far more rare species and ecosystems than was previously known.

In a region with some of the world's most intense concentrations of heavy industry and agriculture, the study identified 100 species and 31 ecosystems, like freshwater marshes or dune systems, with groupings of plants and animals that are either imperiled or rare on a global basis. Fully half of these, it says, exist in the Great Lakes basin exclusively or predominantly.

Moreover, scientists who compiled the study said there were enough gaps in existing data, particularly about small aquatic organisms, that the real numbers were probably higher.

The study, described as the first to catalogue rare or unique forms of life throughout the 210,000-square-mile watershed of the Great Lakes, was conducted by the Nature Conservancy, a private group that specializes in assessments of biological diversity and protection of habitats. It was largely financed by the Environmental Protection Agency.

The purpose of this visual is to: _

_ _

2.

U.S. Military Spending as a Percentage of the Gross National Product* Source: Lachmann, R. ed. *The Encyclopedic Dictionary of Sociology.* 4th ed. Guilford, Conn.: Dushkin, 1991.

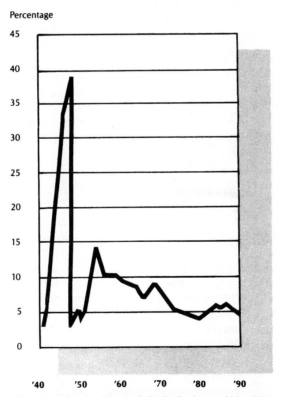

Percentage

*Figures for military spending are calculated in fiscal years, which end Sept. 30, 1990. GNP figures are calculated in calendar years.

MILITARY-INDUSTRIAL COMPLEX (MIC), a phrase coined by President Eisenhower in his farewell address to describe the large and growing connection between the military establishment and the private firms that do business with it. Because the military budget is so large (around $330 billion in 1990) and many of the biggest defense contractors do a majority of their business with the government, Eisenhower feared the complex would acquire "unwarranted influence" in government and would attempt to push defense spending even higher.

The purpose of this visual is to: _____

_____

3.

Income Differences

Employees usually judge the fairness of their pay by comparing it with that of their fellow employees. Whether they think their income is acceptable will depend on how they see their value relative to that of others with higher or lower incomes. Most employee dissatisfaction is over differences in pay between jobs and individuals. Differences in pay based on occupation, managerial responsibilities, length of service, and geographical location are generally accepted. Differences in pay based on age, race, ethnic group, and sex are now prohibited by law and public policy. Title VII of the Civil Rights Act of 1964 prohibits such discrimination, and the Equal Pay Act of 1963 makes it illegal to pay women less than men for the same general type of work.

However, women's earnings are still lagging behind men's. In fact, women's earnings were still only about 63 percent of men's earnings in 1980, as shown in the figure below. The percentage dropped to 61 in 1981 but rose to 63 in 1983. There are many reasons for this, including the fact that about two out of three new employees are women. They come into companies at

Slight Progress for Women Source: Megginson, et al. *Business.* Lexington: D. C. Heath, 1985. 252–253.

Women's Pay as Percentage of Men's

OCCUPATIONAL COMPARISONS

	Median Weekly Earnings		Women's Pay as Percentage
	Women	Men	of Men's
Secondary-school teachers	$357	$411	87%
Engineers	$479	$592	81%
Computer programmers	$382	$478	80%
College teachers	$415	$528	79%
Computer systems analysts	$428	$568	75%
Lawyers	$492	$653	75%
Editors, reporters	$325	$451	72%
Accountants	$325	$468	69%
Scientists	$378	$553	68%
Insurance agents, brokers	$284	$419	68%
Bank officials, financial managers	$336	$574	59%

the entry level and receive lower rates of pay in those low-level jobs. Also, in spite of all the public policy statements, women are still more heavily concentrated in lower-paid industries and jobs.

The purpose of this visual is to: -

- -

4.

A multinational company must often cope with a wide variety of work customs and even languages.
Source: Lachmann, R., ed. *The Encyclopedic Dictionary of Sociology.* 4th ed. Guilford, Conn.: Dushkin, 1991.

Coca-Cola in Amharic

Coca-Cola in Bengali

Fanta in Amharic

Fanta in Bengali

Sprite in Amharic

Coca-Cola in Chinese

Coca-Cola in Arabic

Fanta in Chinese

Coca-Cola in Cyrillic

Coca-Cola in Japanese

КОКА-КОЛА
Coca-Cola in Greek

Coke in Japanese

Coca-Cola in Hebrew

Fanta in Japanese

Coca-Cola in South Korean

Sprite in Japanese

Sprite in Thai

Coca-Cola in Thai

Coca-Cola in Turkish

Fanta in Thai

The purpose of this visual is to: _

_ _

MAKING INFERENCES FROM VISUAL AIDS

▶ **Thinking About Your Reading and Writing**

ACTIVITY K. Applying Your Prior Knowledge About Inferences

1. How might the strategies you learned in Chapter 7 for making inferences be applied to reading visual aids?

_ _

_ _

_ _

_ _

2. What should the reader of the visual aid do to make an inference?

_ _

_ _

_ _

_ _

▢ **Working Together**

Compare your answers in Activity K with those of a partner. Do you suggest similar strategies? Refer to Chapter 7 after you make your comparisons and see what else you can add. Then make your revisions to Activity K.   ●

In Chapter 7, you learned that inferences are statements about the unknown based on what is known. With your partner, you probably agreed that you can make inferences from visuals in the same way that you make inferences from text. When making them from visuals, of course, the numbers or features on graphs and tables, parts of the diagram, points on the time line, or details on the photograph become the evidence to support the inference in the same way that details in sentences or paragraphs provide evidence to support an inference about written material. The following figure illustrates this point. Although not stated on the graph, it is obvious

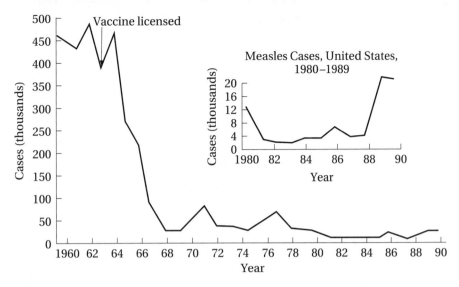

Source: Tortora, G. J., B. R. Funke, and C. L. Case. *Microbiology An Introduction.* 4th ed. Redwood City: Benjamin/Cummings, 1992. 527.

that once the measles vaccine was licensed and people realized its value, they took advantage of it, which resulted in the sharp drop in the number of measles cases.

ACTIVITY L. Making Inferences from Visual Aids

Use the details on each visual to make at least one inference about it. Beneath your inference, indicate your evidence.

1.

Who Do You Think State Government Serves?
Source: *The Boston Globe,* September 3, 1990. 1, 8–9.

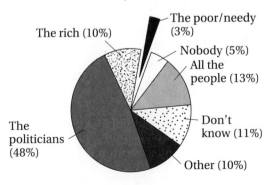

Your inference from this visual aid: _____

_____

Your evidence: _____

_____

2.

DRUGS AND BEHAVIOR
DRUG USE: 1974 AND 1985

Type of Drug	Percent of Youths (12-17)				Percent of Young Adults (18-25)				Percent of Adults (26 and older)			
	Ever Used		Current User		Ever Used		Current User		Ever Used		Current User	
	1974	1985	1974	1985	1974	1985	1974	1985	1974	1985	1974	1985
Marijuana	23.0	23.7	12.0	12.3	52.7	60.5	25.2	21.9	9.9	27.2	2.0	6.2
Inhalants	8.5	9.1	.7	3.4	9.2	12.8	(Z)	.9	1.2	5.0	(Z)	.6
Hallucinogens	6.0	3.2	1.3	1.1	16.6	11.5	2.5	1.6	1.3	6.2	(Z)	(Z)
Cocaine	3.6	5.2	1.0	1.8	12.7	25.2	3.1	7.7	.9	9.5	(Z)	2.1
Heroin	1.0	(Z)	(Z)	(Z)	4.5	1.2	(Z)	(Z)	.5	1.1	(Z)	(Z)
Analgesics	(NA)	5.9	(NA)	1.9	(NA)	11.4	(NA)	2.1	(NA)	5.6	(NA)	.9
Stimulants[1]	5.0	5.5	1.0	1.8	17.0	17.3	3.7	4.0	3.0	7.9	(Z)	.7
Sedatives[1]	5.0	4.0	1.0	1.1	15.0	11.0	1.6	1.7	2.0	5.2	(Z)	.7
Tranquilizers[1]	3.0	4.8	1.0	.6	10.0	12.2	1.2	1.7	2.0	7.1	(Z)	1.0
Alcohol	54.0	55.9	34.0	31.5	81.6	92.8	69.3	71.5	73.2	89.3	54.5	60.7
Cigarettes	52.0	45.3	25.0	15.6	68.8	76.0	48.8	37.2	65.4	80.5	39.1	32.8

(NA) Not Available.

(Z) Less than .5 percent.

[1]Prescription drugs.

Source: *World Almanac.* 1992. 201. From U.S. National Institute on Drug Abuse, NIDA Statistical Series.

Your inference from this visual aid: _____

_____

Your evidence: _____

_____

3.

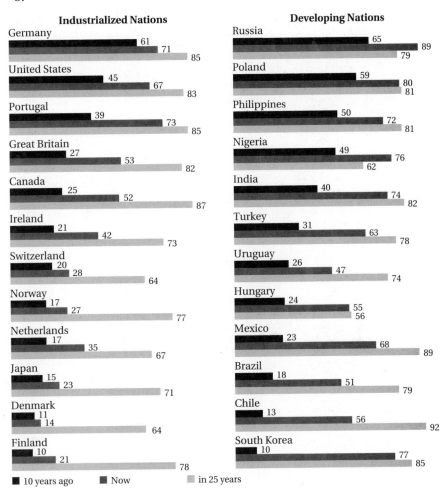

Industrialized Nations

Germany 61 71 85

United States 45 67 83

Portugal 39 73 85

Great Britain 27 53 82

Canada 25 52 87

Ireland 21 42 73

Switzerland 20 28 64

Norway 17 27 77

Netherlands 17 35 67

Japan 15 23 71

Denmark 11 14 64

Finland 10 21 78

Developing Nations

Russia 65 89 79

Poland 59 80 81

Philippines 50 72 81

Nigeria 49 76 62

India 40 74 82

Turkey 31 63 78

Uruguay 26 47 74

Hungary 24 55 56

Mexico 23 68 89

Brazil 18 51 79

Chile 13 56 92

South Korea 10 77 85

■ 10 years ago ■ Now ▓ in 25 years

Percentages of Respondents Who Say That Environmental Problems Affect Their Health "A Great Deal" or "A Fair Amount" Source: Dunlap, R. E., G. H. Gallup, Jr., and A. M. Gallup. "Of Global Concern: Results of the Health of the Planet Survey." *Environment,* 35. 9 (Nov. 1993): 14.

Your inference from this visual aid: _____

_____

Your evidence: _____

_____

4.

TEN LARGEST CITIES IN THE UNITED STATES, 1820, 1900, AND 1970

1820		1900		1970	
New York, N.Y.	123,706	New York, N.Y.	3,437,202	New York, N.Y.	7,771,730
Philadelphia, Pa.	63,802	Chicago, Ill.	1,698,575	Chicago, Ill.	3,325,263
Baltimore, Md.	62,738	Philadelphia, Pa.	1,293,697	Los Angeles, Cal.	2,782,400
Boston, Mass.	42,541	St. Louis, Mo.	575,238	Philadelphia, Pa.	1,926,529
New Orleans, La.	27,176	Boston, Mass.	560,892	Detroit, Mich.	1,492,914
Charleston, S.C.	24,780	Baltimore, Md.	508,957	Houston, Texas	1,213,064
Washington, D.C.	13,247	Cleveland, Ohio	381,768	Baltimore, Md.	895,222
Albany City, N.Y.	12,630	Buffalo, N.Y.	352,387	Dallas, Texas	836,121
Providence, R.I.	11,767	San Francisco, Cal.	342,782	Washington, D.C. (est.)	764,000
Salem, Mass.	11,346	Cincinnati, Ohio	325,902	Indianapolis, Ind.	742,613

Source: De Fleur et al. *Sociology: Man in Society.* Brief edition. Glenview, Ill.: Scott Foresman, 1972. Data from Bureau of the Census.

Your inference from this visual aid: _____

_____

Your evidence: _____

_____

5.

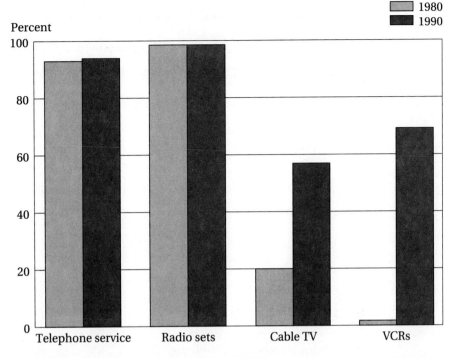

Households with Selected Media: 1980 and 1990 Source: *World Almanac,* 1992. Chart prepared by U.S. Bureau of the Census.

Your inference from this visual aid: _

_ _

Your evidence: _

_ _

Working Together

Compare your inferences for Activity L with those of a partner. You each may have made different inferences. Verify that your selected details provide evidence to support your inference.

DRAWING CONCLUSIONS FROM VISUAL AIDS

 Thinking About Your Reading and Writing

ACTIVITY M. Using Your Prior Knowledge About Drawing Conclusions

1. How might the strategies you learned in Chapter 7 about drawing conclusions be applied to reading visual aids? _

   _

   _

2. What should someone reading a visual aid do to draw a conclusion?

   _

   _

   _

Working Together

Compare your answers to Activity M with those of a partner. Do you suggest similar strategies? Refer to Chapter 7 after you make your comparisons to see what else you can add. Then make your revisions to Activity M. ●

As you work with visual aids in texts, you will need to draw your own conclusions from them. You will look for likely outcomes based on the data that are given. Conclusions move you beyond the text to thinking about applications and logical consequences or results that you can expect in the future based on the data given. Authors may state their conclusions from the data directly within the body of the text, but the visual will enable you to see how such conclusions were reached. Additionally, you may be able to draw other conclusions that the author does not state explicitly. These are often the most interesting conclusions because they are, truly, your own ideas, and the visual proves why your ideas are logical. The next example illustrates how information on visual aids leads to a variety of conclusions and applications.

Number of Banks

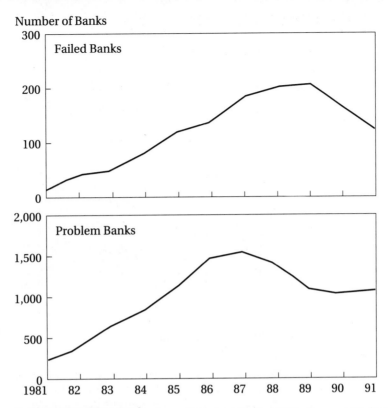

Failed and Problem Banks Source: U.S. Industrial Outlook 1993—Commercial Banking, p. 45–2. From the Federal Deposit Insurance Corporation.

The source of these data suggests that these "failed" and "problem" banks are insured by the federal government. This means that the federal government will feel pressure to address the problems of the U.S. banking industry. It is also logical to conclude that the banking industry will feel competition from other financial institutions, which will claim they can do a better job of handling people's money than the banks have done.

ACTIVITY N. Drawing Conclusions from Visual Aids

Beneath each of the following visual aids, write as many conclusions as you can draw from the information provided. Then indicate why you think these are logical conclusions.

1.

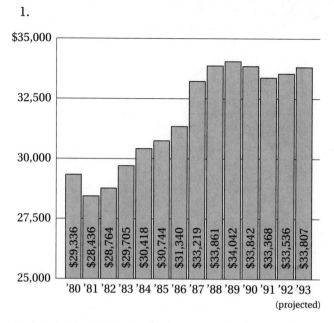

$35,000

32,500

30,000

27,500

25,000

$29,336 | $28,436 | $28,764 | $29,705 | $30,418 | $30,744 | $31,340 | $33,219 | $33,861 | $34,042 | $33,842 | $33,368 | $33,536 | $33,807

'80 '81 '82 '83 '84 '85 '86 '87 '88 '89 '90 '91 '92 '93
(projected)

Real, After-Tax Median Family Income   Source: *Reason* (Feb. 1994): 11. Data from Tax Foundation.

Your conclusions: _____

_____

_____

_____

Why is each conclusion logical? _____

_____

_____

_____

2.

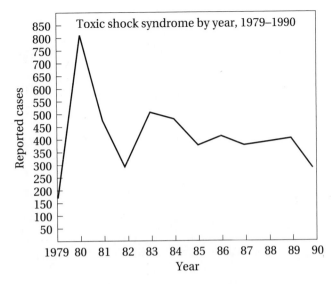

Source: Tortora, G. J., B. R. Funke, and C. L. Case. *Microbiology An Introduction.* 4th ed. Redwood City: Benjamin/Cummings, 1992. 385.

Your conclusions: _

_ _

_ _

_ _

Why is each conclusion logical? _

_ _

_ _

_ _

3.

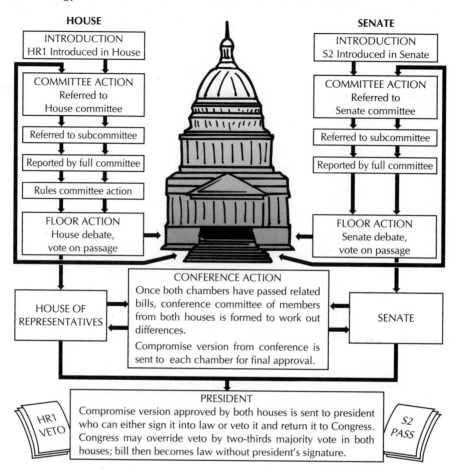

HOUSE

INTRODUCTION
HR1 Introduced in House

COMMITTEE ACTION
Referred to
House committee

Referred to subcommittee

Reported by full committee

Rules committee action

FLOOR ACTION
House debate,
vote on passage

HOUSE OF
REPRESENTATIVES

SENATE

INTRODUCTION
S2 Introduced in Senate

COMMITTEE ACTION
Referred to
Senate committee

Referred to subcommittee

Reported by full committee

FLOOR ACTION
Senate debate,
vote on passage

SENATE

CONFERENCE ACTION
Once both chambers have passed related bills, conference committee of members from both houses is formed to work out differences.

Compromise version from conference is sent to each chamber for final approval.

PRESIDENT
Compromise version approved by both houses is sent to president who can either sign it into law or veto it and return it to Congress. Congress may override veto by two-thirds majority vote in both houses; bill then becomes law without president's signature.

HR1 VETO

S2 PASS

How a Bill Becomes a Law Source: Wilson, J. Q. *American Government.*
Brief version. 2nd ed. Lexington: D. C. Heath, 1990. 201.

Your conclusions: _____

Why is each conclusion logical? -

- -

- -

- -

4.

rate per 1,000 of population

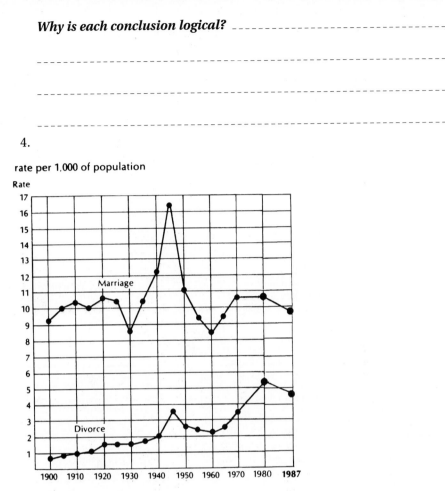

U.S. Marriage and Divorce Rates   Source: Lachmann, R., ed. *The Encyclopedic Dictionary of Sociology.* 4th ed. Guilford, Conn.: Dushkin, 1991.

Your conclusions: -

- -

- -

- -

Why is each conclusion logical? -

- -

- -

- -

5.

```
                           ┌──────────────────┐
                           │   Stockholders   │
                           └────────┬─────────┘
                           ┌────────┴─────────┐
                           │ Board of Directors│
                           └────────┬─────────┘
  ┌──────────────────┐     ┌────────┴─────────┐     ┌──────────────────┐
  │  Vice-President  │─────│ President and    │─────│  Vice-President  │
  │ for Administration│    │ Chief Executive  │     │  for Planning    │
  └──────────────────┘     │     Officer      │     └──────────────────┘
                           └────────┬─────────┘
                           ┌────────┴─────────┐
                           │    Executive     │
                           │  Vice-President  │
                           └────────┬─────────┘
```

Vice-President of Production	Vice-President of Sales	Vice-President of Personnel	Vice-President of Finance
Scheduling	Sales	Employee Relations	Treasurer
Purchasing	Advertising	Employment Manager	Accounting
Transportation			
Engineering			
Research			

Structure of a Typical Corporation   Source: Gordon, S. D., and G. G. Dawson. *Introductory Economics.* 7th ed. Lexington: D. C. Heath, 1991. 94.

Your conclusions: -

- -

- -

- -

Why is each conclusion logical? _

_ _

_ _

_ _

CHAPTER SUMMARY

Based on your reading of this chapter, list at least five points that were made that you believe will help you with future reading assignments.

1. _____

_____

_____

_____

2. _____

_____

_____

_____

3. _____

_____

_____

_____

4. _____

_____

_____

_____

5. _____

_____

_____

Now that you have worked with the strategies necessary for reading visual aids, you can practice applying them to full-length reading selections. Choose (or your instructor may choose) a reading selection that is typical of what you will be expected to read for college courses, such as an essay or a textbook chapter, which also contains visual aids. Use this selection to:

- Preview visuals
- Note details of visual aids
- Make connections between visual aids and text
- Make inferences from visual aids
- Draw conclusions from visual aids

Decide the practice strategies you will use. Apply them to your selection. Then in a few paragraphs, write a description of what you did and how the strategies you used worked for you.

Name of material used: _____

Page numbers: _____

Your description:

Strategies
for Active Listening
and Notetaking

*H*ow might you experience a football game differently if you were a player in the game or a spectator watching it? In which situation would you obtain the greatest inside knowledge about what had happened during particular plays? Which experience would result in more information about why your team won or lost the game? In which circumstance would you have greater connection to the emotions and reactions of the other team members? No doubt you realize that in answer to most or all of these questions, being in the game would give you an advantage over watching it. College students have a choice to make when they attend classes and do their reading assignments—they can be in the game, or they can be spectators. The experiences and knowledge you gain as a student will largely depend on which choice you make. In this chapter, you are introduced to strategies for listening and notetaking that will help you become an active player in academic life.

Good listening does not come automatically to most people. It is a skill that is learned, practiced, analyzed, and practiced some more. We are constantly bombarded with noises that compete for our attention. We *hear* all these sounds. But when we *listen*, we make a decision about which sounds will get our attention. Hearing that is purposeful and directed is called *listening*.

In your earliest grades in school, your teachers tried to instill in you the habit of being a good listener. Consider, for instance, how many times you sat in a circle in the classroom while the teacher told you and your classmates to "Shhh." Can you recall some special signals your teacher may have used to tell you that it was time to listen? Maybe the lights were momentarily turned off, or two fingers were raised, or perhaps your teacher rang a small bell that sat on his or her desk. These school practices were designed to help children learn that there was time to talk and time to listen. In some families, listening is very important, and children in them are frequently told they must listen to their elders. In other families, it appears that no one listens to anyone else—everyone seems to be talking all the time without concern for whether they are being heard.

In adulthood, our needs and interests in various situations guide our listening habits. We are more aware that listening is a voluntary activity and that we can deliberately "tune in" or "tune out" as we choose. When we tune out, communication stops and messages sent to us become undeliverable. But when we choose to listen, all sorts of knowledge and understanding become possible for us. Your decision whether or not to be an effective listener can have a major impact on your success in college and career.

The amount of time college students spend listening in classes, as opposed to other in-class activities, is considerable. Some estimates suggest that students spend more than 50 percent of class time listening to their instructors. Given this situation, you can understand why it is necessary to develop effective listening strategies.

▶ **Thinking About Your Reading and Writing**

ACTIVITY A. Your Listening Habits

Think about the listening habits you developed in your early life. How have they helped or hindered your ability to listen in a college classroom?

_____

_____

_____

ACTIVITY B. How Good a Listener Are You?

Here are some characteristics of listeners. Rate yourself on each item by placing a check in the column that most applies to you.

	Always True of Me	Sometimes True of Me	Never True of Me
When I Listen I			
1. Look at the speaker.			
2. Make predictions about what will be said.			
3. Think about what I already know about the topic.			
4. Look at the speaker's body language.			
5. Intend to understand.			
6. Stay awake.			
7. Ask for clarification when I don't understand.			
8. Select what is important.			
9. Take notes.			
10. Become distracted easily.			
11. Try to restate what the speaker has said in my own words.			
12. Fake attention.			
13. Evaluate my personal biases on the topic.			
14. Focus on the speaker.			
15. Summarize what's being said.			
16. Daydream.			
17. Look for the speaker's organization.			

When I Listen I

18. Use speaker's pauses as time to think.
19. Try to identify the speaker's purpose.
20. Concentrate on content, not delivery.
21. Listen for speaker bias.
22. Set a purpose for listening.

▶ **Thinking About Your Reading and Writing**

ACTIVITY C. Analyzing Your Listening Strengths

How did you do? Put the item numbers you placed in each category on the following lines:

Always True of Me _____

Sometimes True of Me _____

Never True of Me _____

Only items 10, 12, and 16 suggest *negative listening behaviors.* They are behaviors that interfere with effective listening. All the other statements are *positive listening behaviors.* You can evaluate your own listening behavior by noting the number of the positive behaviors that are true of you sometimes or all the time. We explain the reasons these are considered positive behaviors in the next section.

INDICATORS OF POSITIVE LISTENING

Connecting with the Speaker

Communication is a two-way process between speaker and listener or reader and author. Speakers often look at their audience for evidence that their ideas are being communicated successfully. One source of evidence is the audience's actions while listening. Listeners who make eye contact with the speaker, who sit in an attentive posture, who nod in recognition of some ideas, or who take notes, signal that they are connecting with the speaker and that speaker–listener communication is occurring. Professors are usually aware of those students who are making an effort to become involved in the lecture or discussion and those who are dozing off or who seem inattentive. Students may try to fake attention, but they can easily be detected. Even though these students may appear to be looking at the speaker, their eyes are often glazed over, and it is clear to the observer that these listeners' minds are elsewhere.

If you analyze the speaker's body language, it may help you stay engaged. Your analysis may also reveal particular body language signals that the speaker uses to send important messages to listeners. For instance, if the speaker is pacing back and forth across the front of the room but suddenly stops to face the audience, it probably signals that an important point will be made. If the speaker's hand makes a pounding or other forceful type of motion, this, too, is to emphasize an important idea. Sometimes speakers will move closer to the audience when they really want to get a point across. Arms folded across the speaker's chest may mean a disagreement with an idea being suggested, one that the speaker will refute in later remarks. Voice changes, such as increased volume, or a slowed rate of speech, or repetition of a point, also signal key points.

You will find that many benefits result from effective listening. The extent to which you try to stay engaged with the speaker can affect the speaker's own enthusiasm and effort to *keep* you interested. This give-and-take between listener and speaker builds mutual rapport. Speakers are more willing to answer questions and to provide requested clarifications for an attentive audience. Further, your efforts to stay involved with the speaker will have a bearing on how much you will remember of what you have heard. In a college classroom, this may have a tremendous impact on your grades; tests often measure what was discussed in class as well as what you have read. The rapport you establish with your professor by being a good listener can also carry over into other facets of classroom activity and may be the basis for your instructor to have a positive feeling toward you as a student.

Maintaining Concentration

Positive listeners are able to stay focused on the speaker, no matter what is occurring in the surrounding environment. Often the environment in which a lecture is given is not ideal—construction, bad weather, or loud conversation may be occurring outside the classroom. Imagine how distracting such noise is for someone trying to lead a discussion or to give a lecture. Of course, it is equally difficult for listeners to pay attention to what is happening inside the classroom when distractions such as these are outside. Nevertheless, both speaker and listener are obligated to attempt to stay focused and to ignore the distractions. How can you do this? *Concentration* is the key to success in such a situation. This means you must be able to focus your attention on a single task—in this case, on the speaker.

We have become so used to being able to "change the channel" when we don't like the program before us that we sometimes have difficulty concentrating when a lecture seems boring or unrelated to other things that are more meaningful for us. Some strategies to help you keep focused while listening follow.

Think About How the Information You Hear Relates to What You Already Know About a Subject.   Some instructors assume their students have considerable background on a topic, either because of students' prior knowledge or because they believe students have completed related assigned reading. We have discussed the importance of prior knowledge at many points in this text. If you connect new knowledge from a lecture to information you already have, it will help you understand and remember it.

While You Listen, Sort Out Main Points from Lesser Ones.   We have already mentioned some ways in which you can do this:

1. Look for body clues that are signals to important ideas.
2. Follow the organizational plan to identify shifts in topic or focus or details to support key points.
3. Notice whether the speaker uses a different tone of voice to signal important points.
4. Recognize a speaker's special efforts to point out major ideas. Sometimes visual aids are used to clarify or emphasize these.
5. Note when your professor refers to pages in the text that may further explain some point being made or when you are given such hints as, "This would be a good topic of discussion for a test."

Stay Focused by Making Predictions About What Will Be Said Next.   As you try to follow the speaker's direction of thought, you may be able to make some predictions about key points to be made, types of supporting evidence that will be used, and point of view. You will keep mentally active as you listen for verifications.

Form Questions While You Listen.   Active listening includes active questioning, either about points that seem unclear or about which you would like more information or about arguments being made that could be refuted by other evidence.

Try to Identify the Speaker's Point of View, Even When It Isn't Expressed Directly.   This will require "listening between the lines." Your speaker may not tell you directly the point of view being taken, but body language signals, as well as remarks about other points of view on the subject, are indicators you can use to determine the speaker's position. You will need to listen actively as you seek evidence to verify your conclusions about the speaker's biases.

Evaluate the Message.   Your analysis of the speaker's remarks should proceed in much the same way as if you were evaluating an author's writing. If the talk is anything more than mere recitation of facts, you will want to analyze the evidence offered as proof of the speaker's position. As you learned in Chapter 7, evaluation of messages includes noting whether the proof provided is merely more opinion or whether factual evidence is available, and it involves asking yourself such questions as, How authoritative is the source? What other opinions on this subject are possible?

Take Notes. Notetaking is an important skill in college, one that we discuss later in this chapter. It is one of the best ways to maintain your concentration during a lecture and to keep yourself actively involved in what is being said.

Listening with the Intent to Learn

Listeners who have positive attitudes will enter the lecture hall or classroom each time with an *intent* to listen. This intention requires that several things occur before and during the lecture:

Come Prepared to Listen and Learn. This means you should do the assigned readings before you arrive in class, and you should have brought the tools necessary for effective listening: your text and a course notebook and pen or pencil for writing important ideas during the lecture.

Be Aware of Barriers to Effective Communication During the Lecture and Try to Remove These. One barrier might be that of dialect or accent. When the speaker's native language is different from the listener's, yet the speaker is using the listener's language, it is up to the listener to make every effort to identify the pronunciation differences that occur regularly so as to be able to quickly make listening accommodations.

Another barrier might be the physical appearance of the speaker. If the speaker's appearance is somehow disturbing, or if he or she seems very nervous or uncomfortable, the listener will need to listen hard and to shut out the physical distractions caused by the speaker. Being aware of the distractions is the first step toward ignoring them.

Technical language used by the speaker can also be a barrier to communication. In such cases, advance reading and use of context are the two best strategies for overcoming the difficulty. If you have done these but still are unable to understand some of the language used, it may be appropriate to ask for clarification.

It may also be the case that you are unfamiliar with the speaker's style. When the speaker is one of your professors, you do have the advantage of having many class sessions during which you can adjust to the particular approach and language used. One area of difference may be the way in which the speaker organizes the lecture. Chapter 5 introduced you to organizational patterns in writing. These patterns are also often used in speaking situations. Although the speaker might digress from time to time, you may still be able to discern an overall pattern of organization that, once identified, will help you follow the speaker's ideas. Another difference you will notice is that some professors will use long, complex sentences with many embedded ideas. You will need to process this information rather rapidly, sorting out important ideas from unimportant ones. Fortunately, rate of speech is slower than rate of thinking, so you will have some time to weigh the importance of each element of the lecture. Some instructors may help you in this by identifying what the lecture goals are at the start of each class session. This will certainly facilitate communication.

A final barrier to communication may be the result of the instructional style the speaker uses, particularly if it is different from what you have been used to. Different instructors include student activities in their course presentations to different extents. In some classes, there will be a great deal of collaboration, and students will be expected to learn important concepts of the course as a result of these activities and exchanges with other students. At the other extreme, the professor will remain at the center of activity, and the students will participate actively only as listeners. In all instructional settings, you will need to ask yourself, What is the instructor expecting me to do in order to learn the major concepts of this course?

Listen for Speaker Bias But Keep an Open Mind.   The intent to learn requires that the listener believe there is something to be gained from listening. How do you typically respond to a speaker whose ideas are in total disagreement with yours? If you are like most of us, you get angry and want an opportunity to explain to everyone why the speaker is wrong. This tactic is not one that promotes good listening because your mind is so focused on your rebuttal that you really don't listen to what the speaker is saying. In the speaker's ideas, there may be some points you haven't considered, or there may be points that serve your interests because you can easily argue against their logic or significance. But if you don't listen to the speaker, if you are so wrapped up in developing your plan of attack, you will miss the opportunity to hear these other ideas. College students frequently discover that their ways of thinking about events change from when they first enter their academic program to when they graduate. There are many influences on your attitudes. Your personal biases are the result of your experiences and your memories of them. These are valuable sources of evidence for your present perceptions and biases. However, your instructors may have some new insights to offer that will help you rethink your ideas and, perhaps, modify them. By keeping an open mind, you are allowing yourself to find support for your beliefs or to change your ideas to more defensible and logical ones. Intelligent responses are easier when you have listened to what has already been said.

Recognize Confusions.   Since effective listeners plan to learn from lectures or discussions, they must recognize when they are confused and when learning is, therefore, not occurring. In most classrooms and lecture halls, there is opportunity for students to ask questions. Don't hesitate to ask them. Some professors assign "one-minute papers" after a lecture in which students write some of the main ideas they obtained from the lecture, as well as any questions they still have about the topic that was discussed. Use this opportunity to give feedback to your instructor and to ask for further explanation. If there is no chance to ask questions during the class session, make an appointment to see your instructor afterward. You will show yourself to be a serious student. You will be respected for seeking clarification, and you will demonstrate that you are working hard at reaching understanding.

▶ Thinking About Your Reading and Writing

ACTIVITY D. Controlling Your Listening Experience

To what extent are listeners in control of how much they benefit from a learning situation? Write your response in the space provided. Be specific.

Working Together

Compare your ideas in Activity D with those of a partner. How do you differ in your definition of what it means to be "in control" of a learning situation? Make any changes to your response in Activity D that you feel are appropriate.

ACTIVITY E. Analyzing Instructional Styles

Complete the chart for two of your instructors. For each category, write a few sentences that characterize each instructor. Then explain how this instructional style affects you as a listener.

1. Instructor A. (name not required)

    Speech complexity: _____

Body language: --

Assumptions about prior knowledge of students: ---------------------

----

Clarity of presentation: ---

Organization: ---

Opportunities for student involvement: -----------------------------

----

Listening strategies I should use in this class: ----------------------

----

Overall characterization of style: ----------------------------------

----

How this instructional style affects me: ---------------------------

----

----

2. Instructor B. (name not required)

Speech complexity: --

Body language: --

Assumptions about prior knowledge of students: _ _ _ _ _ _ _ _ _ _ _ _ _ _ _ _ _

_ _

Clarity of presentation: _

_ _

Organization: _

_ _

Opportunities for student involvement: _

_ _

Listening strategies I should use in this class: _ _ _ _ _ _ _ _ _ _ _ _ _ _ _ _

_ _

Overall Characterization of Style: _

_ _

_ _

_ _

How this instructional style affects me: _

_ _

_ _

EFFECTIVE NOTETAKING FROM BOOKS AND LECTURES

One noticeable difference between academic life in high school and college is the extent to which students are expected to be independent learners. In high school, your teachers may have put a lecture outline on the chalkboard, and they may have deliberately pointed out important points for you. This is often not the case in college. Usually, you must decide for yourself what notes to take and how to write them. Further, in some college courses, outside reading assignments are never discussed in class. Nevertheless, you are expected to read, understand, and remember information from them, and these assignments may form an important basis for exams and class lectures on related topics. The overall result is that your ability to effectively mark your textbooks and to take notes from them can have an impact on your course grades.

Because notetaking and textbook marking skills are seldom taught to students, you may believe that there aren't any specific strategies to use. It may appear as though some students just have a knack for good note-taking, and others don't. This, however, is seldom so. There are numerous strategies for effective marking of textbooks and taking notes. This section describes those that have been found to be most beneficial to college students. As you work with them, you should adapt them to your own purposes and learning needs so that they will be most useful for you.

A PROCESS FOR EFFECTIVE NOTETAKING

Earlier you read that effective listeners think about what they hear before they write anything. A listener can use the wait time, the time between a speaker's thought and actual speech, to think about and then to write down the important ideas, as shown here.

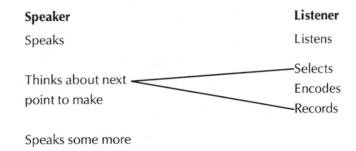

Speaker	Listener
Speaks	Listens
Thinks about next point to make	Selects / Encodes / Records
Speaks some more	

During wait time, you *select* from all the information that is spoken that which is most important. Then you *encode,* or translate, these important ideas into language that is more like your own. Finally, you *record* these ideas. This process of listening, selecting, encoding, and recording continues until the lecture ends.

IDENTIFYING USABLE NOTES

Imagine that you are preparing for a test in the introductory psychology course you are taking. You are studying your lecture notes from a session on memory. Two examples of notes from part of that lecture follow. Which set would you prefer to have available to you as you study?

Example 1:

Memory

Laboratory studies of memory show how much you know later as compared to how much you know right away. Really, memory study is study of forgetting.

In lab studies the subject is given task and then scientist measures how much learning occurred. Subject does activity to keep him/her from thinking about the new information. Later is tested again to see what of the new information is remembered.

Recall is reproduction of the learned material. Sometimes it is rote or verbatim, which means remembering it in the exact form. Recognition is recognizing something that was previously experienced, such as faces of friends. Relearning involves both recall and recognition. Scientist finds out how long it takes to learn the material as measured on a test. After an interval of time, the subject relearns it. (may test subject on it till he can pass the same test equally well on two occasions)

Ebbinghaus did first important studies on retention; used nonsense syllables. List of nonsense syllables had to be remembered in serial order. Found their was a rapid initial loss, followed by a gradual slower decline. (Memory Curve)

Why we forget? trace decay theory says knowledge we have learned just fades away, and the longer it remains unused, the greater we decay. interference theory—other learnings interfere with memory of a previous learning. Trance transformation theory—memory is active process; information stored is automatically transformed to make it more consistent with other knowledge we are remembering. Repression theory—believes that the things we remember and the things we forget are related to their value and importance to us. (Freud)

Adapted from Ruch, F. L., and P. G. Zimbardo. Brief version. *Psychology and Life.* 8th ed. Glenview, Ill.: Scott, Foresman, 1971.

Example 2:

Memory

Lab studies of Memory
- —show how much you know later as compared to how much you know right after learning.
- —mem. study is really a study of forgetting.

Lab procedures
(1) subject given task & scientist measures how much learning occurred.
(2) Subj. does activity—kept from thinking about new info.
(3) Subj. tested again later to see what new info is remembered.

Terms About Memory

Recall—
reproduction of the lrnd material.
Sometimes (rote) or (verbatim) (remembering it exactly)

Recognition—
recognizing something that was experienced before, i.e. faces of friends.

Relearning—
involves both recall and recognition.
see text
pg. 247
(1) Scientist finds out how long it takes to learn the material (may give a test)
(2) Later subj. relearns it. (may be tested till he can pass the same test equally well on two occasions)

STUDIES

Ebbinghaus
- —first imp. studies on retention
- —used list of nonsense syllables
- —syllables had to be remembered in (serial) order
- —Found rapid loss at beginning, followed by gradual slower decline.

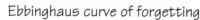
Ebbinghaus curve of forgetting

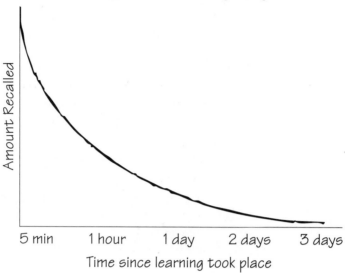

Source: Ebbinghaus, H. "Curve of Forgetting." 1908. Trans. and Ed. Max Meyer.
New York: Arno, 1973.

THEORIES of WHY WE FORGET

trace decay theory:
   what we lrnd just fades away,
   the longer it remains unused, the greater it decays.
interference theory:
   other lrngs interfere with mem. of previous lrng
trance transformation theory:
   mem is active process
? *information stored is automatically transformed to make it*
   more consistent with other knowledge we are remembering.
repression theory:
   things we remember and things we forget are related to their
   value and importance to us. (Freud)

Ibid.

▶ **Thinking About Your Reading and Writing**

ACTIVITY F. Your Notetaking Preferences

1. Which set of notes would you prefer? Why?

----

2. What differences do you see between the two examples?

_____

_____

_____

_____

_____

_____

_____

_____

_____

_____

NOTETAKING BASICS

If you had considered that the notes you chose were to be used to study for a test, you should have chosen the second example. Perhaps you recognized some of the following elements in this example, which are features of a good set of lecture notes.

1. The notes are dated. Dating the notes serves as a reference for you. You will be able to compare a set of lecture notes from a particular date with those of another student. Further, if your notes get out of sequence for some reason, it will be easy to restore order to them if they have been dated. Ideas from earlier lectures may have a bearing on those of lectures later in the semester.

2. The notes are organized so that the relationships between ideas are clear. This clarity results from the writer's systematic approach to notetaking. Main topics can readily be distinguished from minor ones because they have been placed apart from the details, and the margin of the page serves as the starting place for writing the main topics. Each new, important topic is written on a separate line. Details and subtopics are indented under the main ideas to which they relate. Major

details are distinguished from minor ones by indenting the minor details even further.

3. Important terms are quickly seen. A system of circling new terminology has been used. This will make it easy to go back to this notebook and to locate where new vocabulary has been introduced.

4. Only a few words are used to convey ideas. Because it is impossible, and also not a good idea, to write everything that is said word for word, effective notetakers learn to condense whole sentences into shorter phrases that convey the same meaning. This saves time and gives you an additional opportunity to reflect on the meaning. This is part of the process of encoding the material.

5. There is space for additional information. Even with the advantage of wait time, there is still the possibility that other related ideas or information will occur to you well after you have taken your original set of notes. In the second example, space has been left for such entries.

6. A personal shorthand system has been used for repeated and common words. The author of these notes recognizes that some words, like *subject* and *memory,* occur over and over again in this course. Having this system of abbreviations (for example, *subj.* and *mem.*) reduces writing time.

7. Areas of uncertainty are noted. By using a question mark to reflect areas needing further investigation, the author of these notes processes the ideas of the speaker during the lecture; the notetaker has asked himself, Am I understanding this? while the lecture is occurring. A question mark enables areas of uncertainty to be easily located later, and you will be able to seek assistance and clarification.

8. Diagrams have been carefully drawn. We cannot tell whether the student taking these notes drew the diagram without direction from the instructor to do so or whether it had been copied from the board or overhead. The important point, though, is that all parts are clearly labeled, and it will be a useful study aid during the semester.

9. References to pages in the textbook have been noted and are easily spotted. Again, we do not know whether this reference to the textbook was independently noted by the student or whether it had been pointed out by the instructor. But it is clear that the student will be able to refer to the text for further elaboration on this point. If the instructor made the reference and it had not been noted, the student would have lost out on this opportunity.

10. The notes are legible. All the information is easy to read. Some students who incorporate many of the basics of effective notetaking into their study skills repertoire still have a serious problem when they try to study from their notes because they can't read what they have written. This may result from writing too fast, which can occur if you try to write the lecture word for word. Carefully selecting what to write means that you will need to write less; this, in turn, means that you can take

the time to write legibly so that you can successfully use notes later for review. Bear in mind that excessive doodling can also make useless an otherwise good set of notes.

▶ Thinking About Your Reading and Writing

ACTIVITY G. Analyzing Your Notetaking Processes

1. Which notetaking basics do you already use?

----

2. Which basics might be hard for you to follow? Why?

NOTETAKING SYSTEMS

There are more ways than one to take good notes from lectures and textbooks. We describe two of the most popular notetaking systems in this section. You should examine each and then decide which system will work best for you, which will most satisfactorily help you achieve your own notetaking objectives. You will need to keep an open mind as you try your selected approach. You might start using one system but later decide that you need to try another approach because your first strategy is not working for you.

The Cornell Method

This notetaking method, developed by Walter Pauk (1974), is highly recommended by study skills experts. Although it is a little more structured than the notes in Example 2 that you reviewed earlier, it is popular with students because it is easy to use, and it encourages reflection about the material both during and after the lecture or initial reading. To use the Cornell method, you will need a full-size (8½-by-11-inch) notebook that has an extra-wide left margin (legal ruled or summary ruled). Such notebooks are available in bookstores, or you may rule the margins yourself. The Cornell method involves a two-phase process of notetaking. During the lecture or initial reading of the assignment, you write information in a right-hand (6-inch) column. Write each main idea on a separate line, and write supporting details beneath each of these. A set of notes written this way for a lecture in a business course is illustrated next.

Cornell method example (phase 1):

February 19, 1996

Careers in Marketing

Mktg. is a broad field; many opportunities
  Can be involved with product any time—from creation til after sale, incl. service and maintenance
  1983—demand for sales & mktg. execs. rchd 5 yr. high, esp in Southeast & Midwest
  Over ½ labor force in service is in some aspect of mktg.
  Career opp. in: selling, advertising, sales promotion, publ. rela, product mngmnt, mktg resrch, retailing, wholesaling, physical distrib, mktg mngmnt.
Selling has many opportunities
  more employees than any other mktg. occup
  some salespeople are own boss; most work for others
  most jobs routine—structured work schedule, regular pay
  ed. & trng vary
      for standardized goods & svcs—only h.s. dip.;
        e.g. Retail trade sales—interest cust. in product; demonstrate prod., prep sales slips, receive cash, give change and receipt—req. h.s. dip.
      for manufacturers salespeople—college degree req.
        e.g. sell to factories, banks, wholesalers, schools, hospitals, libraries
Advertising jobs very competitive; good starting salary
  Jobs are in advertising depts. of producers and intermediaries; ad agencies; w/ media firms.
  e.g. adv. mgr—directs program; decides allocation of $, type of ad and ad agcy to use.
      rsrch directors—survey cust buying habits; test sample ads.
      production mgr—arranges for printing ads (or film, t.v., radio)

Jobs in Public Relations
req. college deg in jrnlism, communications, or pub rela
helps orgs. build & maintain positive pub image; must
underst. pub concerns & communicate this info to mngmnt

Adapted from Megginson, L. C., L. R. Trueblood, and G. M. Ross. *Business*. Lexington: D. C. Heath, 1985. 420–423.

In the second phase of using the Cornell method, you review the information that is in the center of the page and then edit and summarize it. In editing, you may correct spelling, insert punctuation, delete or add words, and improve the organization of the notes, perhaps by numbering ideas. When you summarize, you want to make it easy to find the key topics that were discussed and to state the main ideas. To do this, you write on the left-side margin (the remaining one-third page) any key words, phrases, or questions that summarize the main ideas and pull together important facts from the right side of the page. These summary notes will serve as important cues when it is time for you to review for subsequent readings or lectures or to study for exams. As a part of your summary, you also write one or two sentences that state the main idea of the lecture. This summary is written at the bottom of your final page of notes. You create the space to write it by drawing an additional line at the bottom of the notebook page, 2 inches up from the edge. When you summarize ideas in this way, you are giving yourself an additional opportunity to review and reflect on the lecture and to organize it into meaningful units of information. The next example illustrates this second step.

Cornell method example (phase 2):

February 19, 1996

Careers in Marketing

Mktg. is a broad field; many opportunities

Can be involved with product any time—from creation til after sale, incl. service and maintenance

1983—demand for sales & mktg. execs. rchd 5 yr. high, esp in Southeast & Midwest

Over $\frac{1}{2}$ labor force in service is in some aspect of mktg.

Career opp. in: selling, advertising, sales promotion, publ. rela, product mngmnt, mktg resrch, retailing, wholesaling, physical distrib, mktg mngmnt.

Selling has many opportunities

more employees than any other mktg. occup

some salespeople are own boss; most work for others

Job Opportunities Where are they located? What types of jobs?

Opportunities in Selling

	most jobs routine—structured work schedule, regular pay
	ed. & trng vary
variety and requirements	for standardized goods & svcs—only h.s. dip.;
	e.g. Retail trade sales—interest cust. in product; demonstrate prod., prep sales slips, receive cash, give change and receipt—req. h.s. dip.
	for manufacturers salespeople—college degree req.
	e.g. sell to factories, banks, wholesalers, schools, hospitals, libraries
Advertising	Advertising jobs very competitive; good starting salary
	Jobs are in advertising depts. of producers and intermediaries; ad agencies; w/ media firms.
variety	e.g. adv. mgr—directs program; decides allocation of $, type of ad and ad agcy to use.
	rsrch directors—survey cust buying habits; test sample ads.
	production mgr—arranges for printing ads (or film, t.v., radio)
Public Relations requirements variety	Jobs in Public Relations
	req. college deg in jrnlism, communications, or pub rela
	helps orgs. build & maintain positive pub image; must underst. pub concerns & communicate this info to mngmnt

Summary: There are many job opportunities in marketing, including jobs in selling, advertising and public relations. The jobs have different education requirements and involve different types of responsibilities.

     Ibid.

The Outline Method

You may find that in some instances an outline format is more useful for notetaking from lectures and texts. This is particularly true when a lecturer or text is very well organized, provided you are comfortable with numbering each topic and detail as the lecture or reading proceeds. Outlines may be written using only topics, sentences, or paragraphs. However, outlines often use a combination of main idea sentences and subtopics supporting each main idea. The importance of each idea in relation to each other is shown on the outline through the use of either a Roman and Arabic number-and-letter system or a decimal numbering system. The first outline, which is based on a class lecture, illustrates the Roman numeral system. The decimal system is illustrated in the second outline.

Example outline A:

The Human Nervous System

I. Divisions
   A. Central Nervous System (CNS)
      1. Housed in skull and vertebral column
      2. Consists of brain and spinal cord
   B. Peripheral Nervous System (PNS)
      1. Distributed throughout the body
      2. Consists of afferent and efferent fibers and sense organs

II. Interactions
   A. The two systems interact constantly
   B. Both systems are necessary for voluntary actions and involuntary actions

III. Activities of Central Nervous System
   A. Reception
      1. From motor (efferent) divisions of PNS
      2. From sensory (afferent) divisions of PNS
   B. Integration
      1. Of information about internal and external environments
      2. Decides on course of action
   C. Action
      1. Distributes "instructions" to effector organs
      2. Effector organs may be glands, blood vessels, fingers and toes, etc.

Example outline B:

The Human Nervous System

1. Divisions
   1.1. Central Nervous System (CNS)
      1.1.1 Housed in skull and vertebral column
      1.1.2 Consists of brain and spinal cord
   1.2. Peripheral Nervous System (PNS)
      1.2.1 Distributed throughout the body
      1.2.2 Consists of afferent and efferent fibers and sense organs

2. Interactions
   2.1. The two systems interact constantly
   2.2. Both systems are necessary for voluntary actions and involuntary actions

3. Activities of Central Nervous System
   3.1. Reception
      3.1.1 From motor (efferent) divisions of PNS
      3.1.2 From sensory (afferent) divisions of PNS

3.2. Integration

    3.2.1   Of information about internal and external environments

    3.2.2   Decides on course of action

3.3. Action

    3.3.1   Distributes "instructions" to effector organs

    3.3.2   Effector organs may be glands, blood vessels, fingers and toes, etc.

▶ Thinking About Your Reading and Writing

ACTIVITY H. Selecting a Notetaking System

Of the several notetaking systems introduced in this section, which do you believe will be the best one for you? Why have you selected this approach?

◻ Working Together

Compare your responses to the questions in Activity H with those of a partner. How are your notetaking system needs similar? How are they different?

ACTIVITY I. Creating Notes from Lectures and Textbooks

Select a textbook chapter or a lecture to attend for notetaking practice. Take notes using the notetaking method you prefer. Then write a one-page analysis of how the method worked for you and what changes, if any, you think you should make in your approach.

USING YOUR NOTES EFFECTIVELY

Once you have a good set of notes, you will want to make the best possible use of them. We outline six strategies for effective use of notes in this section. As you read these strategies, see whether you have used any of them before. Also try to identify any suggestions that you would like to use from now on.

Edit Your Notes

Edit immediately after a lecture or after completing a reading assignment while the ideas are still fresh in your mind. Your goal for editing is to create a set of notes that you will still understand weeks, or even months, after you have heard the lecture or completed the reading. When editing, you should:

1. Be sure everything is legible.
2. Add any punctuation that is needed for clarity.
3. Check your abbreviations; write out the complete words for abbreviations that you do not frequently use.
4. Check the spelling of technical terms and proper names.
5. Check the accuracy of dates.
6. Be sure the hierarchy of ideas is clearly seen from your layout.

Cross-Reference Text Notes with Class Notes, and Vice Versa

Class and text notes should support each other; that is, one should add more information to the other. Textbook or other assigned readings often address the same subject as lectures. Note in your reading material the lecture dates that address the same subject, and write in your lecture notes the related text page numbers.

Check Your Notes for Accuracy

While you are editing your notes, you may find that you are unclear on some points or that information seems incomplete. In such cases:

1. Get clarification on the ideas and terminology about which you are uncertain. To do this, you can refer to the relevant portions of your text, compare your notes with others, discuss the material with your instructor, or refer to other materials on the same subject.
2. If you are describing a sequence of events, a procedure, or any series that you will need to remember in order, be certain you have included

all parts of the sequence. If there appear to be gaps in the sequence you have recorded in your notes, you will again need to check others' sources to make your notes complete.

Summarize Key Points

Do this as soon as you feel you have reviewed a "chunk" of related information. Write down your summaries. When you put ideas on paper, you can see whether you really are able to state a few sentences that will express the main points of the lecture or reading, or whether there are some points on which you are uncertain. Follow these steps to write an effective summary:

1. Consider the entire lecture you have heard or text material you have read. Be sure the meaning is clear to you. Review what you have underlined and highlighted or noted as being a major point.

2. If a thesis was stated that connected the main points of the text or lecture, write it as the first sentence of your summary.

3. Write a sentence that states each key point of the lecture or reading. These are really statements of main ideas. For an hour's lecture, there may be only three or four main points.

4. Identify the major supporting details for each point that the lecturer or author has included. Try to consolidate these major details into one or two sentences, and then add them to your summary, following each main idea. The result will be a paragraph of perhaps seven to ten sentences, written in your own words.

5. Return to the material you have summarized to compare it to your summary. Be certain you have not omitted key points or changed the essential meaning.

Practice Distributed Review

How much of what you heard in class last week do you still remember? What about what you heard three or four weeks ago? There is so much information coming into the sensory storage area of our brain that it is impossible for it to stay there for more than just a few seconds. During this time, we need to decide whether to retain the information and transmit it to our short-term memory or to discard it. Information that we transfer to short-term memory we will retain for only a few seconds—twenty or less—unless we rehearse it, deliberately, as we might do with a shopping list or telephone number. Information that we wish to keep in permanent storage for a long time, such as ideas from lectures and textbooks, must be reviewed regularly, or it will be difficult to retrieve. Research shows that without such periodic review, we quickly forget what we learned. Three days after learning something, we forget most of it if we make no effort to re-

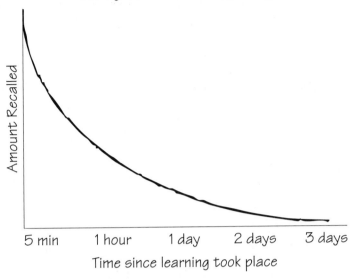

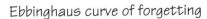

Ebbinghaus curve of forgetting

Amount Recalled

5 min   1 hour   1 day   2 days   3 days

Time since learning took place

Ebbinghaus Curve of Forgetting   Source: Ebbinghaus, H. "Curve of Forgetting."
1908. *Abriss der Psychologie.* Trans. and Ed. Max Meyer. New York: Arno, 1973.

member it. The curve of forgetting that appeared earlier in the memory lecture notes is shown again here. It illustrates the point that if you periodically review your notes, you will keep the information fresh in your mind and significantly reduce the amount of material you will need to relearn. It will be easier for you to retrieve the ideas for tests and class discussion or as prior knowledge to help you comprehend later material.

Formulate Questions from Your Notes

See how many different ways you can ask a question that will yield similar information. This will get you used to hearing requests for the information in different ways, and you will then be more likely to know when your instructor's question is calling for certain information. To create and work with your questions:

1. Use the headings you have written in the left column (Cornell method) or the topical headings of your outline.

2. Make as many questions from the headings as you can so that you will have the chance to include all of what you have studied in your responses.

3. Use question words such as *how* and *why.* Questions worded in this way require more thorough answers than those beginning with *what, who, when,* or *where.*

4. Be sure you can answer your questions. Refer to your notes for verification, and be honest with yourself. If you don't know the answer during your review, you certainly won't know it for an exam.

▶ **Thinking About Your Reading and Writing**

ACTIVITY J. Making Personal Decisions About Notetaking

Which of the suggestions for using your notes effectively are new ideas for you? Which of these new suggestions do you think you will try?

_____

_____

_____

_____

_____

_____

ACTIVITY K. Making Notes Usable

Choose a set of notes that you have written from a previous lecture or reading assignment. Make whatever revisions you believe are needed. Keep your original notes. On a separate sheet of paper, explain what you have done to make your notes more usable. Attach your original notes to the revised notes and your explanation.

Working Together

Review your revised notes with a partner. Can your partner suggest anything else to improve them?

PREPARING GRAPHICS FROM LECTURES AND TEXTS

One way to record information from lectures and textbooks that we have not yet discussed in this chapter is to make a graphic that shows the relationship between ideas. In Chapters 3 and 5, you worked with graphics that organized main ideas and details. In Chapter 8, you practiced creating and interpreting graphics that illustrated other types of relationships. You can create any of these graphics, such as time lines, circle charts, tables, flow charts, semantic maps, or Venn diagrams, to more visually express the ideas from lectures and texts. If you found the work with graphics in the previous chapters to be beneficial, you should consider using this strategy often.

ACTIVITY L. Creating a Graphic from Lecture or Text Notes

Select a set of notes you have taken from a lecture or reading assignment, and prepare a graphic to show the relationship between ideas or data. Choose the graphic format that best fits the data or information you have chosen to graphically illustrate. Be prepared to discuss why it is the best type of visual aid for the information.

UNDERLINING AND MARKING TEXTBOOKS

Did you experience "sticker shock" at the bookstore this semester when you purchased your textbooks? Most freshmen have not had to pay for textbooks in the past, and they are usually astonished at the prices. Once the shock is over, though, you can think about some of the advantages of owning the books, an advantage most students did not have in high school, where the books are typically owned by the school.

Owning your textbooks allows you to underline and make notations in them. If you use effective underlining and textbook notation strategies, you will be able to find important information and to review it more easily. Study the examples of textbook page notations that appear in the next three examples. All the examples have been taken from the same textbook page, but the notations were made by three different readers. See what differences you can find in how each reader has interacted with the text.

Example A:

The Supreme Court in Action

If your case should find its way to the Supreme Court—and of course the odds are that it will not—you will be able to participate in one of the more impressive, sometimes dramatic ceremonies of American public life. The Court is in session in its white marble building for thirty-six weeks out of each year, from early October until the end of June. The nine justices read briefs in their individual offices, hear oral arguments in the stately courtroom, and discuss their decisions with one another in a conference room where no outsider is ever allowed.

Most cases, as we have seen, come to the Court on a writ of certiorari. The lawyers for each side may then submit their *briefs*, documents that set forth the facts, summarize the lower-court decision, give the arguments for the side represented by the lawyer, and discuss the other cases that the Court has decided that bear on the issue. Then the lawyers are allowed to present their oral arguments in open court. They usually summarize the briefs or emphasize particular points in them, and are strictly limited in time—usually to no

[handwritten margin note: for decisions]

more than a half hour. (The lawyer speaks from a lectern that has two lights on it. When the white light goes on, the attorney has five minutes remaining; when the red flashes, he or she must stop—instantly.) The oral arguments give the justices a chance to question the lawyers, sometimes searchingly.

Since the federal government is a party—as either plaintiff or defendant—to about half the cases that the Supreme Court hears, the government's top trial lawyer, the solicitor general of the United States, appears frequently before the Court. The solicitor general is the third-ranking officer of the Department of Justice, right after the attorney general and deputy attorney general. The solicitor general decides what cases the government will appeal from lower courts and personally approves every case that the government presents to the Supreme Court. In recent years the solicitor general has often been selected from the ranks of distinguished law-school professors.

In addition to the arguments made by lawyers for the two sides in a case, written briefs and even oral arguments may also be offered by "a friend of the court," or *amicus curiae*. An amicus brief is from an interested party not directly involved in the suit. For example, when Allan Bakke complained that he had been the victim of "reverse discrimination" when he was denied admission to a University of California medical school, fifty-eight amicus briefs were filed supporting or opposing his position. Before such briefs can be filed, both parties must agree or the Court must grant permission. Though these briefs sometimes offer new arguments, they are really a kind of polite lobbying of the Court that declares what interest groups are on which side. The ACLU, the NAACP, the AFL-CIO, and the United States government itself have been among the leading sources of such briefs.

involved →

These briefs are not the only source of influence on the justices' views. Legal periodicals such as the *Harvard Law Review* and the *Yale Law Journal* are frequently consulted, and citations to them often appear in the Court's decisions. Thus the outside world of lawyers and law professors can help shape, or at least supply arguments for, the conclusions of the justices.

The justices retire every Friday to their conference room, where in complete secrecy they debate the cases that they have heard. The chief justice speaks first, followed by the other justices in order of seniority. After the arguments they vote, traditionally in reverse order of seniority: the newest justice votes first, the chief justice last. In this process an able chief justice can exercise considerable influence—in guiding or limiting debate, in setting forth the issues, and in handling sometimes temperamental personalities. In deciding a case, a majority of the justices must be in agreement: if there is a tie, the lower-court decision is left standing. (There can be a tie among nine justices if one is ill or disqualifies himself or herself because of prior involvement in the case.)

Though the vote is what counts, by tradition the Court usually issues a written opinion explaining its decision. Sometimes this opinion is brief and unsigned (called a *per curiam* opinion); sometimes it is quite long and signed by the justices agreeing with it. If the chief justice is in the majority, he will either write the opinion or assign the task to a justice who agrees with him. If he is in the minority, the senior justice on the winning side will decide who writes the Court's opinion. There are three kinds of opinions—*opinion of the Court* (reflecting the majority's view), *concurring* (an opinion by one or more justices who agree with the majority's conclusion but for different reasons that they wish to express), and *dissenting* (the opinion of the justices on

→

the losing side). Each justice has three or four law clerks (bright, recent graduates of the leading law schools) to help him or her review the many petitions that the Court receives, study cases, and write opinions.

Example B:

The Supreme Court in Action

If your case should find its way to the Supreme Court—and of course the odds are that it will not—you will be able to participate in one of the more impressive, sometimes dramatic ceremonies of American public life. The Court is in session in its white marble building for thirty-six weeks out of each year, from early October until the end of June. The nine justices read briefs in their individual offices, hear oral arguments in the stately courtroom, and discuss their decisions with one another in a conference room where no outsider is ever allowed.

Most cases, as we have seen, come to the Court on a writ of certiorari. The lawyers for each side may then submit their *briefs,* documents that set forth the facts, summarize the lower-court decision, give the arguments for the side represented by the lawyer, and discuss the other cases that the Court has decided that bear on the issue. Then the lawyers are allowed to present their oral arguments in open court. They usually summarize the briefs or emphasize particular points in them, and are strictly limited in time—usually to no more than a half hour. (The lawyer speaks from a lectern that has two lights on it. When the white light goes on, the attorney has five minutes remaining; when the red flashes, he or she must stop—instantly.) The oral arguments give the justices a chance to question the lawyers, sometimes searchingly.

Since the federal government is a party—as either plaintiff or defendant—to about half the cases that the Supreme Court hears, the government's top trial lawyer, the solicitor general of the United States, appears frequently before the Court. The solicitor general is the third-ranking officer of the Department of Justice, right after the attorney general and deputy attorney general. The solicitor general decides what cases the government will appeal from lower courts and personally approves every case that the government presents to the Supreme Court. In recent years the solicitor general has often been selected from the ranks of distinguished law-school professors.

In addition to the arguments made by lawyers for the two sides in a case, written briefs and even oral arguments may also be offered by "a friend of the court," or *amicus curiae.* An amicus brief is from an interested party not directly involved in the suit. For example, when Allan Bakke complained that he had been the victim of "reverse discrimination" when he was denied admission to a University of California medical school, fifty-eight amicus briefs were filed supporting or opposing his position. Before such briefs can be filed, both parties must agree or the Court must grant permission. Though these briefs sometimes offer new arguments, they are really a kind of polite lobbying of the Court that declares what interest groups are on which side. The ACLU, the NAACP, the AFL-CIO, and the United States government itself have been among the leading sources of such briefs.

These briefs are not the only source of influence on the justices' views. Legal periodicals such as the *Harvard Law Review* and the *Yale Law Journal* are frequently consulted, and citations to them often appear in the Court's decisions. Thus the outside world of lawyers and law professors can help shape, or at least supply arguments for, the conclusions of the justices.

The justices retire every Friday to their conference room, where in complete secrecy they debate the cases that they have heard. The chief justice speaks first, followed by the other justices in order of seniority. After the arguments they vote, traditionally in reverse order of seniority: the newest justice votes first, the chief justice last. In this process an able chief justice can exercise considerable influence—in guiding or limiting debate, in setting forth the issues, and in handling sometimes temperamental personalities. In deciding a case, a majority of the justices must be in agreement: if there is a tie, the lower-court decision is left standing. (There can be a tie among nine justices if one is ill or disqualifies himself or herself because of prior involvement in the case.)

Though the vote is what counts, by tradition the Court usually issues a written opinion explaining its decision. Sometimes this opinion is brief and unsigned (called a *per curiam* opinion); sometimes it is quite long and signed by the justices agreeing with it. If the chief justice is in the majority, he will either write the opinion or assign the task to a justice who agrees with him. If he is in the minority, the senior justice on the winning side will decide who writes the Court's opinion. There are three kinds of opinions—*opinion of the Court* (reflecting the majority's view), *concurring* (an opinion by one or more justices who agree with the majority's conclusion but for different reasons that they wish to express), and *dissenting* (the opinion of the justices on the losing side). Each justice has three or four law clerks (bright, recent graduates of the leading law schools) to help him or her review the many petitions that the Court receives, study cases, and write opinions.

Example C:

The Supreme Court in Action

If your case should find its way to the Supreme Court—and of course the odds are that it will not—you will be able to participate in one of the more impressive, sometimes dramatic ceremonies of American public life. The Court is in session in its white marble building for thirty-six weeks out of each year, from early October until the end of June. The nine justices read briefs in their individual offices, hear oral arguments in the stately courtroom, and discuss their decisions with one another in a conference room where no outsider is ever allowed.

1. Most cases, as we have seen, come to the Court on a writ of certiorari. The lawyers for each side may then submit their briefs, documents that set forth the facts, summarize the lower-court decision, give the arguments for the side represented by the lawyer, and discuss the other cases that the Court has decided that bear on the issue. Then the lawyers are allowed to present their
2. oral arguments in open court. They usually summarize the briefs or emphasize particular points in them, and are strictly limited in time—usually to no more than a half hour. (The lawyer speaks from a lectern that has two lights on it. When the white light goes on, the attorney has five minutes remaining; when the red flashes, he or she must stop—instantly.) The oral arguments give the justices a chance to question the lawyers, sometimes searchingly.

Since the federal government is a party—as either plaintiff or defendant—

to about half the cases that the Supreme Court hears, the government's top trial lawyer, the solicitor general of the United States, appears frequently before the Court. The solicitor general is the third-ranking officer of the Department of Justice, right after the attorney general and deputy attorney general. The solicitor general decides what cases the government will appeal from lower courts and personally approves every case that the government presents to the Supreme Court. In recent years the solicitor general has often been selected from the ranks of distinguished law-school professors.

[margin note: job of Sol. gen'l]

[margin note: 3.] In addition to the arguments made by lawyers for the two sides in a case, written briefs and even oral arguments may also be offered by "a friend of the court," or *amicus curiae.* An amicus brief is from an interested party not directly involved in the suit. For example, when Allan Bakke complained that he had been the victim of "reverse discrimination" when he was denied admission to a University of California medical school, fifty-eight amicus briefs were filed supporting or opposing his position. Before such briefs can be filed, both parties must agree or the Court must grant permission. Though these briefs sometimes offer new arguments, they are really a kind of polite lobbying of the Court that declares what interest groups are on which side. The ACLU, the NAACP, the AFL-CIO, and the United States government itself have been among the leading sources of such briefs.

[margin note: amicus curiae] These briefs are not the only source of influence on the justices' views. Legal periodicals such as the *Harvard Law Review* and the *Yale Law Journal* *[margin note: ← also]* are frequently consulted, and citations to them often appear in the Court's decisions. Thus the outside world of lawyers and law professors can help shape, or at least supply arguments for, the conclusions of the justices.

[margin note: 4.] The justices retire every Friday to their conference room, where in complete secrecy they debate the cases that they have heard. The chief justice speaks first, followed by the other justices in order of seniority. After the arguments they vote, traditionally in reverse order of seniority: the newest justice votes first, the chief justice last. In this process an able chief justice can exercise considerable influence—in guiding or limiting debate, in setting forth the issues, and in handling sometimes temperamental personalities. In deciding a case, a majority of the justices must be in agreement: if there is a tie, the lower-court decision is left standing. (There can be a tie among nine justices if one is ill or disqualifies himself or herself because of prior involvement in the case.)

[margin note: order of voting]

[margin note: 5.] Though the vote is what counts, by tradition the Court usually issues a written opinion explaining its decision. Sometimes this opinion is brief and unsigned (called a *per curiam* opinion); sometimes it is quite long and signed by the justices agreeing with it. If the chief justice is in the majority, he will either write the opinion or assign the task to a justice who agrees with him. If he is in the minority, the senior justice on the winning side will decide who writes the Court's opinion. There are three kinds of opinions—*opinion of the Court* (reflecting the majority's view), *concurring* (an opinion by one or more justices who agree with the majority's conclusion but for different reasons that they wish to express), and *dissenting* (the opinion of the justices on the losing side). Each justice has three or four law clerks (bright, recent graduates of the leading law schools) to help him or her review the many petitions that the Court receives, study cases, and write opinions.

[margin note: types of opinions ① ② ③]

Wilson, James Q. "The Supreme Court in Action." *American Government.* 5th ed. Lexington: D. C. Heath, 1992. 410–411.

ACTIVITY M. Evaluating Notations

Which of the three examples do you think has the most effective notations? Why?

You may have noticed some of the following about each example:

Example A: Very little has been marked. Only single words and short phrases have been underlined, and they have little relationship to one another. The meaning of marginal notes is unclear.

Example B: A great deal has been underlined. It is hard to distinguish between important ideas and details.

Example C: Symbols have been used. Technical terms have been circled. Main ideas have been underlined, and related details are numbered. This is the most effectively marked page. This page is useful for study purposes because the important ideas and technical vocabulary stand out from the rest. The reader will not have to reread the entire page to get the most from it.

There are a few guidelines to follow when you are deciding what to mark on textbook pages. These guidelines also apply to any other reading materials that you will later need to reread and study. These guidelines incorporate principles of good textbook reading and good notetaking from lectures and textbooks. At this point, they should sound very familiar to you:

1. Make predictions about chapter content before and while you read the chapter. You will then know, at the outset, the most important concepts to be discussed. You may want to review the process for predictions and previewing discussed in Chapters 2 through 5. As you preview, be sure that you analyze the introductory and concluding paragraphs, headings, and subheadings, as well as graphics and questions that may appear at the end of the chapter.

2. Read sections of information before you do any marking. It is surprising how many students think that if they have highlighted something they've read, they will remember it. The mere act of highlighting does not ensure memorization. Some students' textbooks are filled with highlighted page after highlighted page. It is clear that little reflection

actually went into deciding what to mark since all of it was considered important. The three-step process for highlighting or underlining is to:

Read with your marker or pen down.
Think which of the many ideas are the most important.
Mark the ideas you selected as important.

3. Develop a marking system. Students use a variety of these, but features of the most popular ones include:

Double underlining—for main ideas
Double vertical lines—for very long main ideas
Single underlining—for important details
Arrows—to show connections
Marginal notes—for personal comments on an idea (if these are very long, you may want to write them on an adhesive note and to attach this to your page)
Question marks—to indicate uncertainty
Brackets or circling—to note important terms
Numbers—to note a sequence or a listing of details related to a main idea

4. Review your notated pages regularly. Treat your marked textbook pages as you would your notes from lectures and texts. Review them periodically so that you can easily recall the material when you prepare for tests and class discussion.

ACTIVITY N. Underlining and Marking Textbooks

Select two or three pages of a reading assignment that interests you. Mark the material, following those guidelines described that you believe will be most helpful to you. On another sheet of paper, indicate which guidelines you followed.

Working Together

Review your notations with a partner. See whether your partner can quickly spot the important information on the page. Does your partner have any additional suggestions for making your notations?

CHAPTER SUMMARY

Based on your reading of this chapter, list at least five points that were made that you believe will help you with future academic assignments.

1.

2.

3.

4.

5.

Now that you have worked with the strategies necessary for active listening and notetaking, you can practice applying them to other academic situations. Choose (or your instructor may choose) a reading selection or a classroom listening experience that is typical in a college setting. Use this selection or lecture to practice:

- Using active and positive listening
- Creating a set of usable notes
- Creating a graphic from lecture or text notes
- Using your notes effectively
- Underlining and marking textbooks

Decide the practice strategies you will use. Apply them to your selection. Then in a few paragraphs, write a description of what you did and how the strategies you used worked for you.

Name of material used (or lecture heard): _____

Page numbers (or date of lecture): _____

Your description:

Chapter 10

Assessing Your
New Knowledge

*C*ongratulations! You have now practiced using all the major reading and study strategies necessary for meeting many of the literacy challenges you will face at college. It is time to reconsider how you feel about your ability to meet these challenges. You may recall that you completed the following survey when you started to use this textbook. Complete it again, and then you will have an opportunity to analyze your pre- and poststudy survey results.

Survey of Academic Self-Esteem

Directions: For each item, circle the number that you feel best describes you as you are now (1 = not true of me at all; 4 = very true of me).

1.	I can successfully prepare to take exams.	1	2	3	4
2.	I can figure out what will be asked on tests.	1	2	3	4
3.	I have successful strategies for taking notes on lectures and reading assignments.	1	2	3	4
4.	I know how to preview my textbooks.	1	2	3	4
5.	I know how to come prepared for class.	1	2	3	4
6.	I know how to mark and underline reading material for review purposes.	1	2	3	4
7.	I know how to make predictions when I read.	1	2	3	4
8.	I am able to answer questions in a college classroom.	1	2	3	4
9.	I am able to read a college textbook with understanding.	1	2	3	4
10.	I know when to slow down my reading rate for better comprehension.	1	2	3	4
11.	I know how to use context to get the meaning of unknown words in college-level material.	1	2	3	4
12.	I have good strategies for thinking critically about things I have read.	1	2	3	4
13.	I am able to figure out the main ideas of college-type reading materials (for example, sociology, psychology, science).	1	2	3	4
14.	I am able to set purposes for my reading.	1	2	3	4
15.	I can read and interpret maps, graphs, and charts.	1	2	3	4
16.	I know how to create summaries and visual aids to help me remember what I have read.	1	2	3	4
17.	I know how to distinguish between important and unimportant details when I read.	1	2	3	4
18.	I am able to participate successfully in a college classroom.	1	2	3	4
19.	I am able to ask a professor for help when I have a question.	1	2	3	4
20.	I believe I will be admitted to the major of my choice.	1	2	3	4
21.	I believe I have a lot of knowledge to share with others.	1	2	3	4
22.	I believe I will graduate from college.	1	2	3	4

23. I believe I will have a successful future.   1   2   3   4

Let's analyze the results of this poststudy survey. The following chart shows the category into which different items fall. Place your ratings on the chart. Then respond to the questions in Activity A.

SURVEY ANALYSIS

Category		Question Nos.							
Study Skills		1	2	3	4	6	14	16	
Your ratings:	___	___	___	___	___	___	___		
Reading Skills		7	9	10	11	12	13	15	17
Your ratings:	___	___	___	___	___	___	___	___	
Participating in College Classrooms		5	8	18	19	21			
Your ratings:	___	___	___	___	___				
Expecting a Successful Future		20	22	23					
Your ratings:	___	___	___						

ACTIVITY A. Assessing Your Academic Self-Esteem

1. Based on the information you've obtained from this survey, in which area(s) do you seem particularly strong?

   _____

   _____

   _____

   _____

   _____

2. Look at the responses you gave to these areas in Chapter 1. How have you changed?

   _____

   _____

   _____

   _____

   _____

3. In a few sentences, describe the academic self-esteem goals you feel you have achieved this term.

_____

_____

_____

_____

_____

_____

_____

_____

4. What are some of the areas of academic literacy you would like to continue to develop?

_____

_____

_____

You should now be able to recognize that you have gained a great deal of knowledge and self-esteem concerning your ability to read and study academic material. You should also realize that these changes would not have occurred if you had not taken responsibility for your learning and had not applied yourself seriously to the material in this text. This is true for any learning situation. It is up to you to decide you much you will get out of it.

Remember: You are in control.

Credits

Index